Should I Not Return

The most controversial tragedy in the
history of North American mountaineering!

Jeff Babcock

Since 1978

PO Box 221974 Anchorage, Alaska 99522-1974
books@publicationconsultants.com—www.publicationconsultants.com

ISBN 978-1-59433-270-8
eBook ISBN 978-1-59433-271-5
Library of Congress Catalog Card Number: 2012930733

A haunting story about the pioneer climbs on Denali,
Some of the men who died while doing them,
And one man who came back to tell their stories.
Should I Not Return is based upon true events.

Manufactured in the United States of America.

Dedication

This novel is dedicated to my Green Valley friend and climber, Frances Chamberlin Carter, an amazing woman and pioneer climber of Denali, and countless other mountains around the world, who as she entitled her wonderful presentation truly lived *A Life in the Mountains*.

Should I Not Return is also dedicated to the seven victims of the terrible 1967 tragedy, to their friends, their families, and to their courageous and humble leader Joe Wilcox.

Finally, my intent is to also pay homage to the countless men and women who have ever taken on the difficult challenge of climbing Denali or any of its neighboring peaks, or any of the other great mountains around the world, and lost.

Denali, that Great Grail Castle in the Clouds continues to thrill and kill with each passing year. As of the fall of 2011, 133 climbers have perished on Denali, ever since Allen Carpe and Theodore Koven became the first to die upon its icy slopes in 1932.

And, for Brooke, Gunnar, Laura and Leif; my children.

"We see things not as they are, but as we are."

John Milton, *Paradise Lost*

Archdeacon's Tower, a shark-finned
snow, ice, and rock pinnacle climbs
to 19,537 feet above sea level. It was
named after the Archdeacon Reverend
Hudson Stuck who was the leader of
the first team to successfully reach the
summit of Mount McKinley.

Photo: courtesy of Chuck Kime, Copyright 2008
Writphotec, Inc.,"

JAMES M. TABOR

AUTHOR OF *FOREVER ON THE MOUNTAIN*

Foreword

Should I Not Return's action takes place in Alaska, which calls itself The Last Frontier. Cavers and astronauts and oceanographers might dispute that claim. But Alaska is undeniably a realm of extremes—biggest, highest, coldest, deadliest. As such, it contains more challenging frontiers within its borders than any other state--and most other places--on earth. Ultimately, that is why we love, hate, and keep coming back to Alaska, despite fervent vows not to at end of our last grueling, tortuous, near-death-experience trips. *Ever*, damnit.

Though a non-Alaskan, John McPhee, wrote the greatest of all books about Alaska--*Coming Into the Country*. I do believe that only an Alaskan could have written a book like *Should I Not Return*. Jeff was not born there, true, but our actions define us and, judged by that standard, Jeff is as Alaskan as they come. Thus it is appropriate that he has given us a book about extreme frontiers and their crossings and set in Alaska.

Just as Alaska is not your typical state, neither is *Should I Not Return* your typical book. It is an autobiographical novel (or, as the author engagingly calls it, a nonfiction novel) about young, callow Henry Locke's coming of age in the crucible of North America's worst mountaineering disaster. Though fiction, it hews closely to the truth throughout. The deaths of seven good, young climbers during the 1967 Wilcox Mt. McKinley Expedition form the book's crucial event, true. But this core tragedy is wrapped within layers of drama—familial dysfunction, alcoholism, sibling rivalry, infidelity, to name a few—that raise this book far above the me-and-Joe-climbed-a-mountain genre.

I once wrote about Mt. McKinley that it was the kind of place from you cannot return unchanged. Some books are like that, too, and I'm pleased to say that *Should I Not Return* is one.

Good Things Take Time

Most of this happened when I was a young man and very naive. The parts about Alaska are pretty much true. I really was a member of a rescue team that searched for seven missing climbers on top of Mt. McKinley in the summer of 1967.

One man on our team nearly drowned while crossing the frigid waters of the McKinley River. A large grizzly charged two other men who were relaying gear up through the foothills to the base of mountain. The only woman on our team descended with the five survivors of the ill-fated group because she was coughing up blood. One of our climbers almost died from high altitude pulmonary edema near the summit. I was caught out in the open below Archdeacon's Tower[1] and had to crawl back to our high camp in a raging blizzard. These things happened during what is often described as one of the worst climbing disasters in North American Mountaineering. I have changed some of the names and some of the events.

Today more than one hundred people have died on Denali,[2] the Athabaskan name given the mountain before prospector William Dickey re-named it Mt. McKinley[3] after Presidential candidate William McKinley in 1897. As the years have gone by the names of more climbers[4] have been added to the list; before my brother and I first climbed *The High One*, only four men had perished on Denali.

---

1   Web Link photo: *Archdeacon's Tower*. Photo Credit: Chuck Kime, Writphotec, Inc. http://www.flickr.com/photos/30652603@N07/2884322280/

2   Hudson Stuck, *The Ascent of Denali (Mount McKinley)*, New York: Charles Scribner's Sons. February 1914. Page viii.

3   Web link: Mt. McKinley vs. Denali. http://photos.alaska.org/alaska-photos/Denali-National-Park-Photos/denali-flightseeing-map/mount-mckinley/

4   Web link: *Two McKinley Climbers Dead...* May 26, 2011. http://current.com/community/93249350_two-mckinley-climbers-dead-2-injured-in-denali-pass-fall.htm

My mother had a saying, which she used whenever something terrible happened to someone else, like what happened to those seven men we tried to rescue.

"There but for the grace of God, go you and I."[5]

Perhaps she is right about our climb up Mt. McKinley in the summer of 1967, although I do not know if I would credit God with keeping us alive. Yet, during our two month long journey, it did seem as though something beyond my understanding was patiently keeping watch over me, my brother—and the rest of our team.

Conflicting accounts have been written about why those seven young men died. Some of the details surrounding the tragedy are based in fact, while others offer embellishments of the truth; both approaches are aimed at developing an author's point of view, which he of course believes to be true.[6] Blame and vindication from accusation play heavily into the details of two earlier renditions, written by two survivors of the ill-fated expedition.[7] Most writers want to make their stories interesting and will sometimes stretch the truth so that it supports their own perceptions. The same will certainly be true for me.

My mother had another saying, which always made sense to me.

"We're only human." She would then often refer to the Biblical passage in Deuteronomy 29:4. "If only we had the eyes to see, and the ears to hear."

When it was all over and done with (the climb that is) I flew back to the east coast to Branford, Connecticut, where I lived in the Cherry Hill Apartments with my mother and my other brother Reggie, Jr. I remember my mother making one final comment about our tragic climb.

"I thank God that you and your brother didn't die up there like those other poor souls."

After that, she never mentioned the incident again.

Her reasoning rings true, yet the person I thank most of all for our team's survival is my older brother, the leader of our expedition, who was then 29 years old.

I do want to give credence, however, to my mother's belief in some form of divine intervention. As mentioned above, it did appear to me, on more than one occasion, there was indeed some mysterious force at work to our benefit, either ethereal or providential. Yet, this perception was mine, and mine alone. Even today, a chill runs up and down my spine when I think about what happened to me below Archdeacon's Tower, as I crawled on my hands and knees down to

---

5   John Bradford, *The Writings of John Bradford, Volumes 1 & 2.* Cambridge: Cambridge University Press, 1853.

6   James Tabor, *Forever on the Mountain,* New York: W.W Norton & Company, July 17, 2007.

7   Howard Snyder, *The Hall of the Mountain King,* New York: Charles Scribner's Sons, 1973. And Joe Wilcox, White Winds, Los Alamitos, California: Hwong Publishing Company ... 1981.

our snow cave shelters at 18,000 feet in the middle of a terrifying storm. I truly believed I was going to die, when all of a sudden something beyond explanation happened to me. My brother believes that my mind was playing tricks on me.

A few other things may be of interest. I have been trying to write this book now for more than forty years. My first attempt began in the fall of 1969, after I graduated from Nasson College in Springvale, Maine. I was still too young then to appreciate the enormity of my first real confrontation with death. I had just been hired as a sophomore high school English teacher at Fitch Senior High School in Groton, Connecticut. Frank Hammer, a teacher who taught down the hall from me took me under his wing. Frank had been in the teaching and writing business far longer than I, and after I shared with him my own interest in writing a book about my adventures in Alaska, he took a distinct interest in my story.

"You know Henry, I believe I can help you out with this. I've already had a couple of books published, and I tell you, your story has all the makings of a blockbuster. I would be happy to work on it with you, if you like. You provide me with the info and I'll start putting it together. What do you say?"

I said, "Sure."

I was still naive, even though I did feel somewhat special at the time. After all, I had climbed all the way to the top of North America! Climbing Denali in 1967 was still a major accomplishment. At the time only 208 people[8] in the world could lay claim to that achievement.

Three months later, however, the ecstasy and the agony of Frank's and my joint writing venture came to a slow fizzle, 'not with a bang, but a whimper.'[9] Ever since that experience, I have been highly suspect of any story that has the byline as told by attached to the author's name. I feel similarly about the anonymous ghost writer, who gets hired by a publishing firm, or someone with a lot of money to feed upon the public's craving for the likes of someone like Sarah Palin, the former governor of Alaska, who in her own right is a very charming person.

Our paths had crossed from time to time when I lived in Alaska, and I found her to be a very engaging, certainly attractive, and for the most part, a seemingly sincere person. Nevertheless, her blockbuster book *Going Rogue*[10] not only helped to perpetuate her mythical rise to stardom on the political scene, but it also helped to elevate her to the position of Tea Party goddess and to my astonishment, and

8   Bradford Washburn, *A Tourist Guide To Mount McKinley*, Anchorage, Alaska: Alaska Northwest Publishing Company, July 1974, p. 71.

9   T. S. Elliot, from *The Hollow Men*, Published / Written in 1925.

10   Sarah Palin (& Lynn Vincent), *Going Rogue*. Harper Collins. (Owned by Rupert Murdoch's *News Corporation*). November 17, 2009.

many others, as a potential Presidential candidate for 2012. My wife's brother, Tim, even gave her a copy of Sarah's book as a Christmas present in 2009.

As for my book, I was too young and too enamored with what had happened to me, and for the most part, I really did not have the foggiest idea what I wanted to say about my life-changing experience. In addition, Frank Hammer was not as good a writer as is Lynn Vincent,[11] the bestselling conservative American writer, journalist, and author or coauthor of ten books. In 2010, Vincent wrote with Todd Burpo, *Heaven is for Real: A Little Boy's Astounding Story of His Trip to Heaven and Back,*[12] the story of the four-year old son of a Nebraska pastor who during emergency surgery visits heaven.

I wonder if Sarah Palin knew what she wanted to say, as she and Ms. Vincent sat down to pen her authorized autobiography. Since then, numerous unauthorized books have been written about her. Palin's second book, *America by Heart: Reflections of Family, Faith, and Flag,*[13] has continued to help keep her in the public's eye.

I remember my children's mother had a saying. "Things take time. Great things happen all at once."[14]

I don't consider Sara Palin's rise to fame a great thing, although I am sure many would differ with me on this. Yet, the "things take time" part of this saying seems to ring true regarding Jenny's and my marriage, which began to fall apart somewhere between year seven and eight, if memory serves me right. I guess you could call it *The Seven Year Itch,*[15] like in that old Tom Ewell/Marilyn Monroe classic comedy back in the 50s, aside from the fact that our break-up was anything but humorous.

Governor Sarah Palin congratulates the author's daughter at her High School Graduation Ceremony at the Sports Arena in Wasilla, Alaska.

Photo: Jeff Babcock.

My very young first wife (thirteen years my junior) was itching to get out of her

---

11   Wikipedia web link: Lynn Vincent. http://en.wikipedia.org/wiki/Lynn_Vincent

12   Lynn Vincent (with Todd Burpo), *Heaven is for Real: A Little Boy's Astounding Story of His Trip to Heaven and Back.* Thomas Nelson; original edition (November 2, 2010).

13   Wikipedia link: *Going Rouge and America* by Heart.
     http://en.wikipedia.org/wiki/Sara_palin.

14   Web link: *In Search of the Real Deal.* http://coralcap.wordpress.com/2010/05/14/quote-for-thought-good-things-take-time/, Also from the movie, *Rat Race,* Paramount Pictures, directed by Robert Mulligan. 1960.

15   George Axelrod, *The Seven-Year Itch* (a three-act play). The film was co-written and directed by Billy Wilder. Released by 20th Century Fox. 1955.

commitment to me, which she did. Jenny did thankfully however remain true to our children. In truth, without going into the sordid details, the demise of our marriage, like so many others, happened for very good reasons; poor choices in which we were both active participants. Of course, to paraphrase my mother, "we were only human," each of us playing out the scripts from our respective pasts.

The urge to write did not come again until I was well into my mid-forties, somewhere in between suffering the pangs of a predictable divorce, becoming accustomed to the split-joint-custody of our son and daughter, and at the same time, embarking upon my first major mid-life crisis. My psychotherapist, not unlike Frank Hammer, offered a suggestion.

"Maybe you should try delving back into your mountain story again?"

"What do you mean? Do you want to help me write my book?"

"No, but now that you've got some free time on your hands, it might be of value for you to reflect upon that time in your life? Who knows, it might even be therapeutic," she smiled. "You know, a vay for you to *get in touch vith your feelings*, maybe even trigger some of your old scripts."

Vivian Mulchanov had a pleasant way about her, along with having a pretty good, though not necessarily subtle, sense of humor. As a Jungian[16] analyst, she became not only my mentor, but also my teacher. Journaling my dreams (and nightmares) became a daily ritual. I also learned to reconstruct the repressed aspects of my psyche using a child-like assortment of action figures, doll house furniture, and a plethora of other interesting objects, which I freely laid out upon the sand table in Vivi's office.

Using these standard Jungian techniques I began to look at a myriad of possibilities for viewing the world in ways I had never before imagined. At times it felt as though I was regaining the eyes to see, along with a new perspective on certain memories from my past. The New England puritanical code of ethics, under which I had supposedly been raised as a child was beginning to fall apart. The facade of self-righteous godliness, unchecked hypocrisy, and a judgmental attitude that saw more bad than good had clearly taken its toll on my sense of self-worth.

Of course, Dr. Mulchanov was right.

Reflecting upon my epic coming of age climbing journey to the top of North America turned into exactly what she had expected. After a few months of writing, I soon found myself plunging a very sharp ice axe right into the middle of my past, tearing to shreds my preconceived notions about home and family, and for the first time in my life, I began to take a serious look at what I had always believed to be my happy childhood.

---

16   Wikipedia web link: Carl Jung. http://en.wikipedia.org/wiki/Carl_Jung.

Now, I don't want you to think that this is going to be another one of those woe is poor little ole me stories. I loved both of my parents dearly, as did they their three sons, and much of our childhood was indeed, very happy. However, for the first time in my life, I started to look at my family's heritage from my parent's perspective. I began to understand some of the harsh conditions under which they had been raised, and the impact their past had obviously had upon them, upon me, as well as my two brothers, and it was not always a pretty picture.

"The truth is sometimes a hard pill to swallow,"[17] my mother, a virtual encyclopedia of common sense witticisms, would often remark.

Yet, after several months of intense introspection, I found once again that I simply had to give up the grueling task of writing about my mountain climbing adventure, which by now had turned into my autobiography, and one that was not written from anyone else's perspective, except mine. However, I felt like I was dangling from the end of a rope in the bottomless crevasse of my soul, barely hanging on to the worn out threads from my own past, let alone my parents. A voice inside me, probably something my father had once said, finally brought me to my senses.

"Okay son, it's time for you to pull yourself up by your boot straps. Get on with your life. Stop your bellyaching and just grow-up. You're not a little baby anymore, you know. You've got kids of your own now to look after. You've got to provide for them, just like I had to do for you and your brothers—and your mother."

I can remember how every once in awhile my father would surprise me by giving me a gentle hug—and then he would look at me with the eyes of a loving parent who understood exactly what I was going through. My father even came north to Alaska and stayed with me for a few months, after my divorce was finalized, and after I had driven my two children clear across the country to live with their mother and their new stepfather, Dr. Jeremiah Menachem back in Rhinebeck, New York.

I remember my mother would often scoff at the saying, "Cleanliness is next to Godliness,"[18] something which has probably been debated since the beginning of time. It was always a bone of contention between our mother and our father.

Poppa had always liked Jenny, mainly because she kept a neat and tidy home. Peg did not however fair as well since keeping things ship-shape has never been high on her list of priorities. Instead, Peg chose to spend untold hours with our father caring for and listening to him as the insidious turmoil of growing old crept into his being. She often became his only companion, in my absence, and

---

17 Web Link: A Hard Pill To Swallow. http://joelssermons.wordpress.com/2010/05/06/a-hard-pill-to-swallow-5210-acts-111-18-john-1331-35/.

18 Web link: Is cleanliness next to godliness? http://www.jasnh.com/pdf/Vol6-No2.pdf.

top The author pretending to be the 'Skipper' of his father's yacht down in Ft. Lauderdale, Florida in 1958.

Photo: Reggie Babcock, Jr.

right The author's father came north and spent time with him in his home in Wasilla shortly after his divorce.

Photo: Jeff Babcock.

would sit patiently with him to calm his frequent bouts of anxiety, until we found it necessary to move him into a care facility.

Keeping things ship-shape on the home front was of course a trait my mother rarely achieved, and as Vivi was quick to point out one day, "Ah… Now you have another opportunity to verk on an old family wound."

My father, as did Jenny's own mother, always hoped Jenny would have a change of heart and return to me. Her marriage to Jeremiah, however, the man she had left me for, put an abrupt end to that possibility.

"Life has never been easy, son, and that's just a fact of life. Let's face it; it's about time for you to get back out there onto the playing field and see what happens. You'll bounce back son. You'll see. You just can't give up. Believe me, things will start to come around for the better. You'll see. There's always a light at the end of the tunnel."

Not unlike my mother, my father was a truly wise, generous, and genuinely kind person; though not particularly good when it came to expressing his thoughts. Nor was he particularly faithful when it came to our mother. Yet, he always came through for each of his sons, "when the going got tough," and he certainly did that for me.

I did bounce back and after a few rough starts I finally got a grasp on what little sanity was still left inside my burned out brain. About a year or so later, when Peg came into my life, the blown-apart pieces of my heart were finally beginning to heal.

Peg and I were both full time teachers at Chugiak Elementary, located about twenty miles northeast of Anchorage, where we of course had met and fallen in love. At the same time, we were also trying to bring together our blended family of four children, a girl and a boy each from our previous failed first marriages.

Our first attempt to do this however occurred over Christmas break and nearly ended in disaster. Peg and I still get a chuckle out of that particular event, whenever one or the other of us reflects upon it. At the time, however, neither of us found the situation very funny.

"Do you remember how Laura kept us up all night in that motel at South of The Border?"[19] Peg smiled. "You we're going to give me and her a lesson in *Active Parenting*,[20] remember? You carried Laura out to our car in the parking lot and told her you were putting her in time-out, until she settled down."

Peg shook her head from side to side. "Little Laura just looked at you and laughed and started jumping up and down in the passenger seat, right beside you. Remember?"

"Yes, I also remember how desperately I needed to get some sleep."

"You do remember that I was ready to buy an airline ticket back to Alaska the next morning, so I could get Leif, Laura, and myself as far away from you as I could possibly get?"

"Yeah, but then Laura triggered the alarm on the car next to ours, which started blasting away, so I quickly scooped her up and brought her back inside our motel room, before everyone else came running outside to see what all the commotion was about."

It was my idea to take our newly blended family to Disney World in Orlando over Christmas break. Peg and I and her two children flew from Alaska to Albany, New York, picked up a rental car, a 1993 white Ford *Aerostar* at the airport, and then we drove down to Rhinebeck to gather up my two offspring for our road trip down the east coast to *The Magic Kingdom*.

Jeremiah held his and Jenny's new six-month old daughter Faith in his arms, as he and Jenny stood beside the van to bid us farewell. Jenny seemed a bit hesitant. Jeremiah smiled.

"Now listen if things don't work out, or start to get a little too antsy, don't hesitate to give us a call. I can easily fly down and pick up our two, no prob. Okay?" Jeremiah smiled again. "Nice to meet you Peg."

19   Website link: South of the Border, http://www.thesouthoftheborder.com/

20   Website link: http://www.activeparenting.com/APN_author, Michael H. Popkin, PhD.

If you're new to the blended-family mix, beware. Watch out for vacations. Afterward, my children were with Peg and me in Alaska during summer vacations, the designated time allotted us by Jenny's divorce attorney, a friend and associate of Jeremiah's back in Rhinebeck. As the years went by, Brooke and Gunnar would also come to visit with us on alternating Christmas Vacations. Long distance shared custody arrangements leave much to be desired, but that was the best we could come up with.

During one of my therapy sessions with Vivian Mulchanov, the light bulb inside my head began to burn brightly, causing me a severe migraine. Vivi saw very clearly what my brain was trying to get me to acknowledge.

"You do realize you've recreated your own childhood experience vith your own children. You do see that don't you?"

The years went by fast. Every so often I would attempt to get back to my book, which I then called *Divine Fate*, a somewhat sarcastic response to what I perceived back then as a distinct lack of divine intervention in my life on God's behalf.

Thousands of pages later, some discarded, others stashed in folders on the two external drives to my computer, I would continue to "sweat blood and tears,[21]" over my mountain book. I have even penned three different screenplay versions.

Along the way I feel I have grown from being a mediocre writer to slightly above average. I have also learned many interesting things about the history surrounding those brave men and women who tried to climb Denali—those who failed, those who succeeded, and the ones who never returned. Many of those climbers who were killed on Denali have since joined the ranks of the seven men from 1967 and the four before them, who Jim Tabor eludes to in his 2007 book;[22] whose spirits remain "forever on the mountain." The bodies of ten of those eleven climbers were never brought down from the mountain, but simply receded into Denali's glaciers forever.

As the years passed, I began to realize something far more important about this life-long obsession of mine to finish my book, something Vivi Mulchanov had probably known from the start. In writing my version of the '67 disaster, my climb up Denali had become something far greater than simply another rendition of the same tale; it had become something more along the lines of Melville's classic whaling adventure *Moby Dick*.[23] If only I were another Melville. In my mind Denali had become the monster of my dreams, and I had

---

21   Wikipedia web link: Blood, Sweat & Tears. 1967. http://en.wikipedia.org/wiki/Blood,_Sweat_%26_Tears.

22   James Tabor, *Forever on the Mountain*, New York: W.W Norton & Company, July 17, 2007.

23   Herman Melville, *Moby Dick*. New York: Harper & Brothers. First Edition, 1851.

become the everyman protagonist Ishmael, trying to pen the epic drama of his life.

Ten years after the '67 tragedy, I even led my own expedition, a 68-day traverse of Denali, which followed the routes of Belmore Browne,[24] Hudson Stuck,[25] and the Sourdoughs of 1910.[26] Our team even carried along a 14-foot spruce pole to place below the summit of the North Peak, as Charlie McGonagall had done.

Yet, we were in for an unexpected surprise. At the onset of our climb, our group, called *The Anderson Pass Expedition*, (named after another of the Sourdoughs, Pete Anderson) had the misfortune of becoming involved in a terrible train accident.

One of our two dog teams collided with the Alaska Railroad's daily run to Fairbanks along a three-mile stretch of track near the mouth of the SE fork of the Chulitna River, not far from the long abandoned *Colorado* log cabin depot alongside the tracks, the actual starting point of our climb.

Because of this mishap, it took us one month to relay our gear fifty miles up and over Anderson Pass to the base of the mountain at *McGonagall Pass* on the north side of The Alaska Range. Like the early pioneers our intent was to relay the bulk of our gear (about 2,500 pounds) using dog sled teams. After the train accident we were forced to make three separate relays using small orange pulk sleds minus the use of the dog teams, which Belmore Browne's team had used sixty-five years before us.

After successfully reaching the summit eight weeks later, our team then traversed down the *West Buttress* side of Denali, got caught in an horrific storm at 17,200 feet for five days, and then finally descended to the Kahiltna airstrip and flew off the mountain to Talkeetna on day 68.

My worst fears were realized on Denali during these two separate climbs and in the end, I did finally come face to face with the Grim Reaper himself. Writing about my experiences on Denali has not only helped me to discover many new things about myself; more importantly it has shown me that my journey to Alaska in the spring of 1967 was the actual pivotal point of my life. The rest of my adult life, my two marriages, the raising of my four children, and my career as a Special Education teacher all took place in Alaska, and this only occurred largely because of my involvement in a deadly climb up Denali in 1967.

In short, I spent the better parts of my life struggling to embrace those aspects

---

24   Belmore Browne, The Conquest of Mount McKinley, New York: Harper & Brothers. First Edition, 1913.

25   Hudson Stuck, *The Ascent of Denali (Mount McKinley)*, New York: Charles Scribner's Sons. First Edition, 1914.

26   Terris Moore, *Mount McKinley: The Pioneer Climbs*, New York; The Mountaineers Press. First Edition, 1967.

Lenticular 'cloud caps' begin to form over Denali's two Summits, the South Peak Dome and the more rugged looking North Peak.

Photo: Jeff Babcock

'The frozen canyon of the Chulitna River,' the very same route used both by the MCA team and Belmore Browne's team in 1912.

Photo: Merle LaVoy, image scanned from Belmore Browne's The Conquest of Mount McKinley, 1913, with copyright permission from Isabel Driscoll, Belmore Browne's granddaughter.

of myself I tried desperately to ignore from my past. As my mother so often proclaimed, "The truth is a hard pill to swallow."

The experiences I encountered during both of these climbs up Denali have been incorporated into my version of North America's worst mountaineering disaster. Along the way you may perhaps glean some threads of wisdom, which you may recognize within your own coming of age tale, which each must endure as a right of passage into adulthood. Therefore, like the authors before me, I have played with the truth of what actually happened. Everything I have written about did occur; but these events took place over a span of ten years, countless climbs, and during two separate expeditions on Denali.

One final piece to my story remains. Peg's and my life in Alaska took a dramatic turn in June of 2009. She and I retired from our teaching jobs in Alaska and moved from our home in Wasilla (yes, Sarah Palin country) to Green Valley, Arizona.

That very same year I suffered a heart attack and had to have three stents placed in arteries on the left side of my heart. Saying goodbye to The Last Frontier and retiring from a thirty some year career as an elementary special education teacher was like saying farewell to a good friend or lover; and it caused a wound in my heart that was not only psychological, but also physically real. Fortunately for me, Peg and our children were there at my side to help me make this painful transition.

We now reside in Green Valley with Peg's ninety-four year old father, a former Presbyterian minister from Oregon. I can hear my mother chuckling to herself, either up there in Heaven, or out there in that mysterious realm from where each of us came, and to where each of us is destined to return.

Peg and I now work part time at the local ACE Hardware store in Green Valley. One day I received a phone call from an older woman in town, whom I have since come to know and admire. In fact, Frances Chamberlin Carter (Freddie) used to meet up with Peg and me on a regular basis at one or the other of Green Valley's two doggie bark parks. Peg and I have two dogs: Jacques, a small Scotty, and Kavik, an older black and white collie mix, who has seen better days back in Alaska. Kavik has been with us for sixteen human years, which makes him 112 years old by dog standards. Freddie's dog is named Raggs, a small mixed-breed, who could easily have been a stand-in for the film star *Benji*.[27]

Over time Freddie and I have grown close, due in part to our shared interest in mountain climbing, but also because she is such an endearing woman. One day Freddie presented me with two treasured mementos, which were given to her by her father. I was astounded by her gifts.

After meeting with her the first time, I soon discovered that Freddie is the first

---

27   Wikipedia Web link: *Benji* (film). http://en.wikipedia.org/wiki/Benji_%28film%29.

Dr. Bradford Washburn and his wife, Barbara, stand on the summit of the South Peak of Denali on June 6, 1947.

Photo: Courtesy of Betsy Washburn Cabot and Decaneas Archive

woman[28] to ascend the High Mountain Points in all fifty states of the U.S. and she is the fifth person to ever accomplish this feat. She had read about my interest in setting up a video business in town from an article a reporter had written about me in the *Green Valley News*.[29] A paragraph detailing my own adventures in mountaineering caught Freddie's eye.

So Freddie and I got together and I helped her transfer her slides into a DVD photo presentation entitled *My Life in the Mountains,* a wonderful accumulation of the photos that she, her father, and her husband had taken over the course of their lives together.

Freddie believes she is the second woman to have reached the top of Denali, which she climbed in 1962, fifteen years after Bradford Washburn's wife Barbara became the first,[30] and five years before I set foot on top. The Park record, however, lists Anore Bucknell[31] as the second female to accomplish the feat. Freddie, who has a spunky, sometimes argumentative nature about her, disagrees and she sees the whole thing quite differently, and makes no bones about her opinion.

"You know Jeff, I don't think that woman made it to the top at all! I remember when that happened. I was talking to someone about the whole thing, and he said she sprained her ankle and only got up to the football field. Then she turned

28   Web link: *Highpointers of U.S. states.* Frances Carter Chamberlin. http://highpointers.org/48.shtml.

29   Web link: *The Green Valley News.* http://www.gvnews.com/

30   Website link: Barbara Washburn. http://www.mos.org/washburnclimb/barbara.php.

31   Bradford Washburn, *A Tourist Guide To Mount McKinley, Anchorage,* Alaska: Alaska Northwest Publishing Company, July 1974, p. 66.

around and she went back down. So I think I'm the second woman who got up there. I believe that woman told a fib and now she's got her name in the record book as being second, even though she never did it!"

Freddie is getting older, and like many old timers, our thoughts may appear to be sometimes disjointed, repetitive, and perhaps even mistaken. Maybe Freddie is correct in here estimation of the facts, and then again maybe she's not. My mother had another saying she used whenever two people expressed differing opinions about a given event.

"God only knows."

Ever since Peg and I moved down to the retirement community of Green Valley, our four children (who are now all grown) joke with me about turning into an old fart. Our youngest daughter, Laura now has her own child, a seven-month old baby girl named Alexia, Peg's and my first grandchild. She and her husband live in Marana, a small community just west of Tucson, and I have the delightful pleasure of baby-sitting Alexia for four hours in the mornings, while Laura is taking courses at the University of Arizona.

When Alexia is sitting beside me on the floor, I am amazed at how she looks at everything with such an inquisitive nature. As babies go, Alexia seems to be an exception to the rule. She is always smiling, rarely gets upset and she is perhaps the happiest baby I have ever known, her mother included. As I sit there and watch her intently, she reminds me so much of what my mother used to say, even after she turned into an old fart. "If only we had the eyes to see, and the ears to hear."

For me, Alexia is a clear example of "one of God's children," as my mother would have called her, had she lived to be as old as my father-in-law. Alexia of course sees things quite differently from the rest of us old timers, and I wonder how long it will take before the tunnel vision of her elders (myself included) begins to impact her clear vision of the world as she now sees it in all its glory.

On August 8, 2011, I am checking into St. Mary's hospital in Tucson, AZ for my second knee replacement, this time on my right knee, which is bone on bone. Most former climbers suffer a similar fate when it comes to bad knees and old age. I find myself hobbling around a bit slower these days and sometimes I really do think of myself as being an old fart. The operation will slow me down even further, for at least a month or two, I am told, but that should give me enough time to finish up this book. At least that is my plan.

Freddie has a few years on me though since she will celebrate her 87th birthday on August 19, 2011. Peg and I are planning a birthday dinner for her, and I hope to be up and somewhat mobile by then.

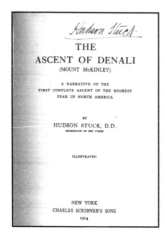

left The actual copy of Hudson Stuck's The Ascent of Denali (Mount McKinley), which bares author and leader of the first successful ascent of Denali, Hudson Stuck's signature at the top.

Photo: Jeff Babcock.

right The photo is a copy of the Belmore Browne painting given to the author by his friend Frances Chamberlin Carter.

Photo: the author, December 8, 2011.

In partial payment for the services I provided for Freddie, when I helped to put together her presentation, Freddie did an amazing thing for me; a gesture I have since come to believe has particular significance, regarding the completion of my book, which I now call *Should I Not Return*. Two years ago Freddie surprised me with this announcement.

"Now you know Jeff, you're a climber, and you are someone who I know will appreciate these two gifts, which my father gave to me so long ago. They were given to him by two of those early pioneers on Denali. Now, I've told you he knew all those old timers, and he was even supposed to go on that climb in 1932 with Theodore Koven and Allen Carpe." Freddie's voice took on a sad tone.

"Well, it's a good thing he didn't go. Those two were the first to die up there on Denali, you know. They both fell into one of those terrible crevasses on the Muldrow."

On the wall above my desk in the Green Valley residence of my father-in-law is a painting by Belmore Browne, the leader of the incredible 1912 expedition to climb

The author spending time with his grand daughter Alexia in Green Valley, AZ.

Photo: Kathy Hawthorne.

Denali, whose three-man team got to within a few hundred feet[32] of the South Peak Summit, only to be turned back by a fierce storm. The other astounding gift, which Freddie Carter gave to me, is an autographed copy of *The Ascent of Denali*,[33] signed by the Rev. Archdeacon Hudson Stuck himself, the man who led the first successful expedition to the top of the continent the following year in 1913.

For some reason beyond my comprehension, Freddie Carter and I were destined to meet. Here is a woman whose entire life was devoted to climbing mountains, not only in North America but also all over the world. Somehow our paths have miraculously crossed in of all places, Green Valley, Arizona.

The time has finally come for me to finish my mountain book. It has taken me a lifetime to do this, forty-five years to be exact, nearly the same year of my birth. If my book turns out to be a good thing, it will have been worth the wait.

"Good things take time. Great things happen all at once."

---

32 Web link: http://www.nps.gov/history/history/online_books/brochures/1941/dena/sec1.htm
Ascents of Mount McKinley. Denali Guidebook 1941.

33 Hudson Stuck, *The Ascent of Denali (Mount McKinley).* New York: Charles Scribner's Sons.
February 14, 1914.

"Listen ...."

*"True love is like the appearance of ghosts;
everyone talks about it but few*

have seen it."[34]

34 Francois VI, Du de La Rochefoucauld, *Reflections*; or *Sentences and Moral Maxims*.
    Published 1665.

CHAPTER 1

The Beginning of The End

Henry Locke received a down sleeping bag in the mail from his father, Captain Reginald F. Locke, on his nineteenth birthday. The bag has long since disappeared, but Henry still remembers it to this day mainly because of what happened to him during one of the saddest, yet most profound experiences of his life.

Henry was huddled inside the tan cotton bag with its sky blue nylon lining, trying to stay warm inside a hollowed out snow cave two feet under the ice, at about 18,000 feet on Mt. McKinley. A terrific storm had been blasting away over his head for about a day and a half, when Henry suddenly awoke and realized he had to go to the bathroom.

Henry grabbed hold of the zipper below his chin, jerked it in a downward motion too quickly, and sure enough it jammed tight into the cotton fabric of the bag and would not budge. His plastic pee bottle was already inside his sleeping bag, so he decided to relieve himself in the dark, so to speak.

His brother Johnny was snoring away soundly right next to him as Henry struggled to accomplish the urgent task at hand. He located the bottle, then quickly unscrewed the wide plastic top, dropped it like a hot potato inside his bag, and with equal finesse he unzipped his pants and made the necessary placement; soon Henry felt that tremendous sense of relief that is surpassed only by that other form of pleasure associated with the same bodily part.

When his bladder was empty and the bottle perhaps ¾ full, Henry groped inside the bag for the bottle's top, but for some reason he could not find it. Undeterred, Henry carefully set the bottle between his legs, and went to work on freeing the stuck zipper on his bag. By accident, Henry bumped into his brother.

"Henry? What the hell's going on," Johnny grumbled. "Go back to sleep. We aren't going anywhere until this storm blows over."

A fierce roar pounded away at the entrance to their cave just below their feet. Even though Johnny had wedged an ice block into place to prevent spindrift from filling their frozen tomb-like shelter, the monster outside howled unceasingly to be let in.

Henry breathed a sigh of relief as the zipper finally gave way. He blew warm air onto the tips of his frozen fingers and held them against the skin of his cheeks. Ever so carefully Henry crawled from his bag, with the fingers of his right hand carefully grasping the wide circumference of his plastic pee bottle. As Henry moved slowly toward the designated corner of the cave to empty his stash, Johnny rolled onto his side and this time he bumped hard into Henry's arm.

"Look, Henry. Quit farting around and go back to sleep."

It was too late. The contents of Henry's pee bottle spilled, thoroughly saturating the down filling and cloth fabric of the mid-section of Henry's bag. His brother sat up again.

"Shit. What's that smell?'

"It's not shit, Johnny. It's the other stuff."

CHAPTER 2

Sir Edmund Hillary and William McKinley

Captain Reggie Locke was at that moment skippering the 75-foot yacht called the *Franny B* toward the Isle of Bimini in the Bahamas. Bimini is the nearest island to the coastline of Florida, about fifty miles east of Miami Beach.

Henry's sleeping bag was a gift from the son of an old friend of Captain Reggie's boss, Mr. Alvin. E. Broughton. Broughton, a New York manufacturer and the owner of the *Franny B*, had named the pleasure cruising yacht after his third wife, Frances. Broughton's friend just happened to be the famous New Zealander and renowned mountaineer Sir Edmund Hillary.

Always one eager to rub shoulders with the rich or the famous, Al Broughton extended an invitation to Sir Edmund and his family to "come to the states" sometime in the future for a sailing trip to the Bahamas.

Over the years, Sir Edmund did take Al up on his invitation more than once, and on this occasion it was Sir Edmund's son, Peter, and a close friend who were among the guests traveling aboard the *Franny B* with Captain Reggie. Peter Hillary had presented Johnny and Henry's father with the sleeping bag when he landed at Miami International airport.

"Here Captain, dad and I thought one of your boys might have use for this goose down bag on their climb up Denali this upcoming summer."

Before taking off on their cruise the following morning, Captain Reggie had sent the package off to Henry who lived in Branford, Connecticut.

Yes, the sleeping bag was a gift Henry would put to good use when he embarked upon the mountain climbing adventure of his life, an assault of Mt. McKinley, North America's highest peak.

Henry beamed with pride and excitement as he sat there in his mother's living room tinkering with the assortment of climbing gear that lay before him. It

top A picture of the yacht Captain Reggie was 'Skipper' of down in Ft. Lauderdale, Florida named the *Franny B.*

Photo: Unknown.

bottom left George Herbert Leigh Mallory, renowned climber of Mt. Everest died 8-9 June 1924 at the age of thirty-seven on The North Face of the highest mountain in the world.

Photo: taken in 1916 is unknown. Wikimedia Commons.

bottom right Captain Reggie, Al Broughton, and members of his family are seen on the stern of the *Franny B.*

Photo: Unknown, courtesy of the author's family photo collection

was Spring break and Henry was home from his first year at New England College in Henniker, New Hampshire.

Rolled out on the rug in front of him was a half-inch thick cream-colored ensolite sleeping pad, upon which sat his new Auckland, New Zealand down sleeping bag. A hickory shafted ice axe lay beside his "bed," and below the sharp metal spike at the bottom of the axe's shaft was a pair of steel Grivel[38] crampons with leather straps. Henry's most recent purchase, one that his brother Reggie, Jr. had helped him buy was a brand new Kelty Pack and aluminum frame. A few piles of neatly folded clothing (several pair of nylon and wool socks, two pair of wool mitts, two pair of silk underwear, a sweater) and a Swiss Army knife[39] also lay amongst the other items, which included two wide-mouthed plastic water bottles and a two-quart Aladdin thermos.

Henry's mother Katherine, however, was not as enthusiastic about her youngest son's proposed journey. She sat in a chair

Sir Edmund Hillary became the first man to set foot on top of Mt. Everest on May 29, 1953 along with sherpa Tensing Norgay.

In 1999, however, an expedition searching for the remains of George Mallory,[35] the renowned early British pioneer climber of the Himalaya, did indeed discover his body, raising some speculation as to whether or not he or his partner Andrew Irvine[36] actually made it to the top of Mt. Everest in 1924, twenty-nine years before Hillary and Norgay's successful ascent. The pair's last known sighting was only a few hundred meters from the summit; yet afterward they disappeared, and no evidence surfaced until 55 years later, which helped to shed some light on the mystery.

In 1979, Chinese climber Wang Hongbao recounted to Ryoten Hasegawa, the leader of a Japanese Alpine Club reconnaissance expedition on Mt. Everest, that four years previously, in 1975, he (Wang) had seen the body of an "English dead" at 8100m (26,574 ft.). However, before more information could be obtained, Wang was killed in an avalanche the following day.

The details surrounding Mallory and Irvine's demise have been thoroughly scrutinized, yet as of the spring of 2011, no evidence had been discovered to verify one way or another, whether either of the two ever made it to the top in 1924.[37]

35   Wikipedia link: *George Mallory*. http://en.wikipedia.org/wiki/George_Mallory.

36   Wikipedia link: *Andrew Irvine*. http://en.wikipedia.org/wiki/Andrew_Irvine_%28mountaineer%29.

37   Website link: You Tube video: http://www.youtube.com/watch?v=0nBH6NeyFpw.

38   Website link: Grivel Crampons. http://www.grivel.com/products/ice/crampons/

39   Wikipedia link: Swiss Army knife. http://en.wikipedia.org/wiki/Swiss_Army_knife.

The upper slopes of North America's highest mountain, 20,320-foot Mt. McKinley, often called Denali, the Athabaskan name given to it meaning 'The High One.'

Photo: Jeff Babcock.

Members of the 1910 Sourdough Expedition were *(left to right):* Charlie McGonagall, Pete Anderson, Tom Lloyd *(seated),* and Billy Taylor.

Photo: Unknown, Website source: http://www. nps.gov/history/history/online_books/dena/hrst. htm#illustrations, Courtesy Historical Photograph Collection, University of Alaska Archives, Fairbanks

So large is this mountain that it is comprised of two separate peaks, the North and South. The upper portion of its lofty heights is separated on the north side by the ice-crusted, wind-blown surfaces of the Harper Glacier, which span two miles in between the two peaks.

Denali Pass, the point, at which the two peaks merge, provide climbers ascending the mountain from the north side with an access to traverse the mountain down the West Buttress side, which today is the most popular route used for climbing Denali.

In 1910 the famous Sourdough

Expedition[40] placed two hearty Alaskans on the summit of the lower of the two pinnacles, the North Peak, which from the Kantishna foothills and Fairbanks, appeared the higher reaching an elevation of 19,470 feet. The South Peak of Denali, however, was the higher summit, which was first successfully climbed by Archdeacon Hudson Stuck's team three years later on June 7, 1913, and proved the continent's highest landmark at 20,320 feet. Yet, most people knew of the famous mountain as Mt. McKinley, named after our country's 25th President, William McKinley.

across from Henry smoking a cigarette. Her drink of choice, Old Grand-Dad Whiskey on the rocks, sat on the table beside her. An expression of sadness, yet smoldering determination exuded from her eyes. Thoughts raced across her mind, as the smoke from her cigarette encircled her head like a building storm.

Within less than a month her youngest son would be flying off to Alaska, often called *The Last Frontier*, to climb a massive mountain of snow and ice, which the indigenous Athabaskans called *Denali*.

Katherine interrupted her son's tinkering with what she referred to as his "grown-up boy toys."

"You know Henry, I've got something I've been itching to tell you, and you may not be all that happy with what I'm about to say. McKinley," Katherine took a drag on her cigarette. "And I don't mean your G. D. Mountain, but President William McKinley was the fourth president to be killed, or I should say assassinated by some crazy nut, a few years before I was born, back right around the turn of the century. Most folks only remember Lincoln, and now of course Kennedy. However, William McKinley was assassinated, too. Did you know that?"

Distracted, Henry simply looked at his mother and shook his head.

"In fact, I still remember my mother and father talking about it, when I was just a little girl."

Katherine raised her drink to her lips and took another swig.

"Believe it or not, my parents were in the reception line at the Temple of Music at the Pan-American Exposition in Buffalo, NY in 1901, where it happened, and they actually saw McKinley get shot. Now, if you ask me that was no coincidence. In fact, I think it was an omen telling me, that something terrible is going to happen to you and your brother, if you two go through with this crazy fool-hearty idea to climb Mt. McKinley."

Katherine took another drag on her cigarette, and then downed a final swig from her glass of bourbon and ice, which she now slammed hard upon the walnut-top coffee table in front of her.

"Of course Johnny's old enough now to make up his own mind all by himself. After all, he's almost thirty--and God only knows why he's still trying to prove himself by going off on all these crazy mountain climbing expeditions."

"Well, at least he's gotten out and seen the world." Henry countered. "Not everyone gets to go off and explore some of the places he's been too. Mom, you should be proud of what he's accomplished, instead of always trying to tear him down or make light of some of the things he's done."

"Oh sure. He's escaped the drudgery of living around here, all right. However, right now I'm more worried about you Henry, than I am about Johnny. There's a

This Photo shows five of the participants of Hudson Stuck's 1913 Expedition: Tatum, Esaias, Karstens, Johnny and Walter, at the Clearwater Camp.

Photo: Hudson Stuck. The Ascent of Denali (Mount McKinley) New York, Charles Scribner's Sons, 1914.

Clipping of a wash drawing by T. Dart Walker depicting the assassination of President William McKinley by Leon Czolgosz at Pan-American Exposition reception on September 6, 1901

Photo: This image is in the public domain because its copyright has expired.

The author's older brother is shown in the fall of 1966. At the age of 29 he was chosen to lead the Mountaineering Club of Alaska (MCA) expedition to the top of Denali in the summer of 1967.

Photo: The author's sister-in-law, courtesy of the author's family photo collection.

good chance he may very well get you into some terrible predicament that you won't be able to get yourself out of."

"He's not going to let anything happen to me."

"If you ask me Johnny should be thinking about settling down and taking care of his wife and four children, instead of traipsing off all over the world. First down there in South America with the Peace Corps, and now he's got all of them up there in Alaska—and he's still got that damn climbing bug eating away at him. Mark my words Henry one of these days he's going to get himself killed, and where are Bonnie and those beautiful kids going to be, then? Answer me that?"

"Johnny's not going get himself killed, and neither am I. He knows what he's doing and he's not going to let anything happen to either of us."

Henry dropped to his knees and started to roll up his new sleeping bag. "We're both going to do just fine climbing to the top of Mt. McKinley."

A stillness came over the room. The only sound to be heard was a spattering of conversation coming from Katherine's old Sylvania black and white console television set, on the far side of the living room. Henry noticed an episode of *Star Trek* was playing at low volume.

Katherine sat quietly in her chair without saying a word, and merely stared off into the kitchen as if Henry wasn't even in the room. She seemed consumed by what was going on inside her head.

Thoughts began to race across Henry's mind too, a behavior that was easily triggered whenever his mother started drinking. He remembered reading an article a few months earlier about a recent accident on the mountain in *Time Magazine*,[40] telling of a French climber, Jacques Batkin who died in a crevasse fall. Batkin became the fourth climber to perish on the mountain during Denali's first winter ascent. The accident was a grizzly reminder of what could happen, even to a seasoned climber.

Batkin had fallen sixty feet into a crevasse and landed on an ice block at the bottom. At the time, he was unroped and ferrying equipment up the Kahiltna glacier from the team's base camp at 7,250 feet. Henry could feel a lump forming at the back of his throat.

Lingering thoughts of death had already put a damper on Henry's enthusiasm, yet he still had a strong desire to go. He sometimes felt that climbing Denali might be the most exciting and adventurous thing he would ever do.

To date there had been less than fifty successful attempts on the mountain, yet the idea of climbing such a massive peak was also quite intimidating. From the

---

40 Time Magazine website link: *Mountain Climbing: the Challenge of Winter.* http://www.time. com/time/magazine/article/0,9171,836814,00.html March 17, 1967.

article he read in *Time,* coupled with his mother's premonition of doom, Henry knew that such an endeavor could also be deadly.

"I think you just worry too much, mom. That's all there is to it. Poppa feels the same way." Henry glared at his mother. "So does Johnny and Skipper, too."

Reggie, Jr. had acquired the nickname Skipper from his own father's chosen occupation. Captain Reggie had served four years in the U. S. Coast Guard during WW II and had been sailing yachts up and down the east coast ever since.

For as long as Henry could remember, the concept of a stay-at-home dad had never even entered his mind—he assumed most everyone's father either worked or lived away from home. Only his childhood friend down the street, Margie Fryer, had a father who was employed at the Branford post office and came home every night. As far as Henry was concerned, Margie's father was the exception to the rule.

When Henry's first grade teacher, Mrs. Smith, asked him why his father never visited school, Henry didn't give it a second thought when he said, "Oh. My Poppa's the Captain of a boat and sails around the world. He comes back and sees us at Christmas time to give us presents with Santa's; Poppa comes to see us in the summer, too."

The first time that Henry and Skipper were given a glimpse of what a two parent family felt like was during a five-year stint they had beginning in 1957. Katherine and Captain Reggie moved the family down to Florida, in an attempt to revitalize their failing marriage, and at the same time, to make a conscious effort to deal with Katherine's drinking problem, a behavior she had acquired, along with most of her brothers and sisters, from their alcoholic father, Pop Spaulding.

After Katherine, Henry, and Skipper had moved down to Ft. Lauderdale, Florida, Captain Reggie and Henry became actively involved with Westminister Presbyterian Church's Boy Scout Troop 131. Henry and his father attended weekly meetings each Wednesday night along with a hand-full of the other dads and some thirty or so scouts, who met at the little Quonset hut behind the church.

Scoutmaster Zeke Landis and Captain Reggie became good friends and helped the boys plan monthly camping trips into the Everglades, and bi-yearly jamborees down on the city park strip. Henry even earned his Eagle Scout badge and became a member of the Order of the Arrow, two honors for which Henry's father beamed with pride.

However, Captain Reggie's eldest son Johnny always seemed to make it into the conversations Henry had with his father—and from Henry's point-of-view, he always seemed to end up on the short end of the stick when it came to any kind of praise from his father, while being compared to his older brother Johnny.

"I'm proud of you, my boy. You remind me so much of your brother Johnny, when he took over the scout meetings back there in Brockett's Point."

Two years later, Henry became Troop 131's senior patrol leader.

"Nice going son, nice going. You're turnin' out just like your older brother Johnny."

Katherine downed the final drops of bourbon, crushed her cigarette into an ashtray, then got up and staggered across the living room toward the kitchen.

"You leave your father and ..." Katherine stumbled and nearly fell down. "Your brothers out of this. Your father started calling me an ole worry wart long before you were even born, and now he's got all three of you boys saying the same thing about me."

"Well, you do get worked up a lot about things, mom."

"But I swear to God Henry, it's different with this McKinley thing. It really is. I've got a terrible feeling about this climb. And I don't know what to do about it."

Katherine turned and looked at Henry with hurt eyes. "You see your brother as some sort of a god, don't you? You worship the ground he walks on. But let me tell you a little secret, Henry. Johnny's just as fallible as the rest of us."

Katherine looked down at the empty glass in her hand. She laughed. "In fact, he's a lot like me and your father, too. Just like us, Johnny's going to have to face up to his own little demons one of these days, whether he likes it or not. You're going to find that out too for yourself, when you get older."

Katherine paused for a second or two. A deep sadness came into her eyes.

"Let me tell you something. The truth is a hard pill to swallow. You may think I'm crazy, but I can feel this one deep down in my bones. Something terrible is going to happen on this climb, and I just pray to God that you two aren't part of it."

"Mom, nothing's going to happen to us."

"Well, you're not getting my blessing on this one. I may not have any say over what your older brother does with his life anymore, but as long as you're living under my roof, you're going to play by my rules, and I want you staying put right here where you belong. Do you hear me?"

Katherine had always been overprotective with her youngest son. When Henry was first born, she believed in her heart she was giving birth to a lovely baby daughter. After birthing two boys, the thought of caring for a baby girl was a joy Katherine looked forward to ever so much; she could hardly bare it.

When little Henry popped out of her womb, Katherine became so depressed she literally would have nothing to do with Henry for well more than a week. At that point, she finally came to her senses, accepted the reality of birthing yet another son, and began to nurture and care for Henry accordingly, even though her initial desire had been forsaken by destiny.

top left The author's mother and father with their first-born son. Captain Reggie had enrolled in the Coast Guard in Groton, Connecticut and was preparing to go over seas to fight in the Pacific during WW II.

Photo: Unknown, courtesy of the author's family photo collection

top right (left to right) is the author, his mother, and his older brother Reggie, Jr. otherwise known as 'Skipper.' This photo was taken during the five years the family spent together in Ft. Lauderdale, Florida.

Photo: The author's father, courtesy of the author's family photo collection.

bottom left The author is being honored at the Eagle Scout Ceremony for Troop 131 in Ft. Lauderdale, Florida. Scoutmaster Zeke Landis is seen in back wearing an Indian headdress.

Photo: The author's father, courtesy of the author's family photo collection

bottom right The author is seen here at about six months old sitting on the beach at Lamphier's Cove at Brockett's Point, Connecticut, a nearby suburb of Branford, the author's hometown.

Photo: The author's mother, courtesy of the author's family photo collection

Yet, Katherine remained guilt-ridden for the rest of her life for having neglected Henry during those first crucial days, when a mother's love is known to be so important.

Henry's mother was right about one thing however, and she did feel somewhat vindicated from her feelings of guilt in her attempt to deter her sons, particularly Henry from climbing Denali. The death of President William McKinley[41] turned out to be exactly what she said it was from the beginning. It truly was a bad omen.

Katherine was now a grey haired middle-aged woman whose worn features never-the-less still showed some of her natural beauty, along with a steady gaze and occasional smile, which had once turned many a young man's head in her youth.

This evening the worrywart emerged from the kitchen with yet another Old Grand Dad on the rocks, in her hand. As she made her way down the hall toward her bedroom Katherine glared at her youngest son.

"Mark my words, you're staying put right here—where you belong. You're going to get a job and earn some money this summer for college, instead of traipsing off to Alaska to get yourself killed on some G. D. mountain. The death of William McKinley is a story that's stuck with me ever since I was a little girl, and now I finally know why it's made such an impression on me after all these years."

She stopped and turned toward Henry.

"That's all I have to say about it. Do you hear me?"

The last photograph of the late President William McKinley taken as he was ascending the steps of the Temple of Music, September 6, 1901.

Photo: E. Benjamin Andrews, Public domain copyright.

This is an image of the author's mother taken in front of the family's Brockett's Point home, in Branford, Connecticut in the early 1950s.

Photo: The author's older brother, courtesy of the author's family photo collection.

---

41   Wikipedia link: *The Assassination of William McKinley*. http://en.wikipedia.org/wiki/William_McKinley_assassination.

William McKinley, 25th President of the United States, who favored the gold standard over silver, was chosen by prospector William Dickey to have North America's highest mountain named after.

Photo: Unknown, Public domain copyright.

The 25th president of the U. S. died from gangrene poisoning *eight days* after Leon Frank Czolgosz had shot him, on September 6, 1901 at the Pan American Exposition in Buffalo, New York. Katherine's parents had been there at the exposition when it happened, during their honeymoon.

"Oh my .... The President's been shot!"

When Louella and John Spaulding returned to New Haven, a week later, and sat at the breakfast table a few days afterward, they were devastated to read in the newspaper that the President had died. Like everyone else in the country they too believed President McKinley had survived the assassination attempt—he did not.

Twice Czolgosz had shot McKinley at point blank. The first bullet grazed McKinley's left shoulder, but the second went through his stomach, pancreas, and kidney, and then became lodged in the muscles of his back. Doctors extracted the first bullet but decided to leave the second one alone, since they feared they might do more damage if they tried to remove it. They were also reluctant to use the newly developed X-ray machine that was on display at the fair, since again they were uncertain as to what side effects it might have upon the President.

It was true that McKinley's doctors believed he would recover, and he convalesced for more than a week in Buffalo at the home of the exposition's director, John Milburn. Yet, there were other reasons why the doctors remained cautious about attempting to remove the second bullet.

The operating room at the exposition's emergency hospital did not have any electric lighting, even though the exteriors of many of the buildings at the extravagant exposition were covered with thousands of light bulbs. The surgeons were unable to operate by candlelight because of the danger created by the flammable ether used to keep the president unconscious, so doctors were forced to use pans instead to reflect sunlight onto the operating table while they treated McKinley's wounds.

On the morning of September 12th, the president felt strong enough to receive his first food orally since the shooting: toast, an egg, and a small cup of coffee. However, by afternoon he began to experience discomfort and his condition rapidly worsened. McKinley began to go into shock, and at 2:15 am on September 14, 1901, William McKinley died.

Henry gave in as his head slowly bobbed up and down in a sad retreat.

Henry sat there on the couch gazing down upon all the climbing gear he had laid out on the floor in front of him. By now his mother had gone to bed. The house was silent except for William Shatner's voice coming from the television. Henry looked toward the set and felt something odd.

Like the shock that hastened William McKinley's demise, a feeling of deep sadness came over Henry, disheartened by his mother's adamant refusal to give him the go-ahead on his plans to climb Mt. McKinley. Yet, beneath this sense of despair there was another feeling more terrifying that crept into his being like the pitch darkness of the early morning hours just before dawn.

A chill ran up and down Henry's spine as he sat there in what he would come to call his very own Witching Hour.[42] Henry rose quietly from the couch and walked to the old black and white Sylvania. With the forefinger on his right hand Henry pushed the button that sometimes stuck the first time it was pressed.

Henry heard a slight click, but the set remained on. Henry looked at the screen and noticed Captain Kirk of the *Starship Enterprise* talking into his wrist radio transmitter, while standing on what appeared to be a barren white mountainous terrain on some lonely planet. Captain Kirk could easily have been standing on the top of Mt. McKinley, Henry thought to himself.

"Beam me up Scotty—and make it fast. This storm is getting worse."

Henry pushed the off button again and this time the screen faded into a fuzzy whiteness, a man made blizzard of snow and ice. Henry imagined the dying roar of the wind as the staticky sound on the television faded into silence.

Again a sense of terror melted over Henry's body. Captain Kirk had surely felt the same way, Henry imagined. Henry could almost taste the lingering sense of fear as it slowly vibrated throughout his body and crept into his heart. The house became perfectly quiet, a stillness that Henry would never forget, and it was a feeling that would re-visit him on the icy slopes of Mt. McKinley.

---

42 Wikipedia link: *Witching Hour.* http://en.wikipedia.org/wiki/Witching_hour.

CHAPTER 3

North to Alaska

K atherine tried her best to dissuade Henry from joining his older brother the following month in Alaska, but Henry held strong, or so he thought. She remained silent during most of their drive from New Haven, across Route 15 / the Wilbur Cross Parkway, and then down the Merritt Parkway all the way into New York City.

Captain Reggie was behind the wheel while Henry sat in the front passenger seat. Henry's mother chose to sit in the back seat as they made their way into the city. His father stood there beside him at the ticket counter in John F. Kennedy International Airport[43] as Henry checked in. Reggie Locke was there to offer his support and to bid his son farewell.

"Well, son. God bless you, and know that I'll be thinking about you and your brother these next few months, even though I'll be down in Florida. Don't you worry, everything's going to work out just fine."

Henry's father looked back over his shoulder.

"And don't you get all worked up about the way your mother's reacted to this whole thing. She's just an ole worry-wart. You know that. Always has been, always will be. Then again, don't forget your mother still loves you boys very much, and she'll be keeping you in her prayers, too. You can bet on that, believe me."

Originally the John F. Kennedy International Airport had been named Idlewild, for the area where the Idlewild golf course had been located from 1927 to 1935. However, one month after the assassination of John F. Kennedy, the airport was renamed in his honor on December 24, 1963.

Henry looked over his father's shoulder and saw his mother standing in front of a large window, smoking a cigarette, and staring off into the drizzling rain outside.

---

43 Wikipedia link. *John F. Kennedy International Airport.* http://en.wikipedia.org/wiki/Jfk_airport.

She turned and saw Henry looking her way.

Henry raised his hand to wave goodbye, but Katherine did not acknowledge her son's gesture. Instead, she turned away, and once again looked out the window into the gray skies outside the terminal. Above her darkened silhouette Henry noticed the smoke from her cigarette slowly rise to the high ceilings over their heads.

"Goodbye dad. I love you."

"Take care son, I love you, too." Captain Reggie leaned forward and gave his son a gentle and somewhat stilted embrace. "Take care, my boy. You take care. I'll be seeing you sometime around the end of July."

Henry's flight across the country to Seattle was the first time he had ever ridden in an airplane. Henry grasped the seat handles tightly with both hands as Pan American's flight 212 to Seattle climbed quickly up into the skies over New York City. Pan Am had led the industry since 1958 when it decided to go all jet over the traditionally used turbo-prop engines. Henry's huge jet propelled plane seemed to blast off like a rocket ship headed for outer space. As Henry felt the wheels beneath his plane snap hard into place in their wheel compartments, he knew it was really happening—he was on his way not to the moon, but to Alaska—*The Last Frontier* of these United States.

Even when Henry flew across the country that day from New York, he found it difficult to believe that he was going to this distant, wild and dangerous place up above the western end of Canada, where his brother and his family now lived. As his connecting flight lifted off the runway in Seattle, it seemed to Henry as though he was flying to a foreign country almost as though, like Captain Kirk of the *Starship Enterprise*, he was on his way to some other galaxy light years away.

This time it was a McDonnell Douglas DC-10, one of American Airlines' jet-propelled aircraft that was transporting Henry the final 1,400 miles on the final leg of his journey across the open skies of North America. Awestruck, Henry gazed down from the small window at his right to the great expanses of wilderness that lie below.

A few hours had gone by when he glanced out the window again and noticed through the billowing clouds below, something he had never seen before; on the perimeter of the land below him, Henry spotted the icy snout of a large glacier dropping down to the water's edge—the edge of the Pacific Ocean. Further inland Henry saw an endless array of snow covered mountain peaks.

"Yes," Henry thought to himself. "I am definitely on my way to Alaska."

Time passed slowly and soon Henry dozed off into a deep sleep. A few hours later the airplane began to bump, thump, and shudder as a turbulence of strong winds rocked the plane back and forth. Henry woke up and noticed an elderly woman, apparently a Native American, perhaps Athabaskan, or possibly Eskimo, directly across the aisle from him, whom he remembered seeing when he first boarded the plane.

"Ladies and gentlemen. This is your captain speaking. As you can tell, we have run into a bit of turbulence. Therefore, I'm going to try and get us up above this rough patch of weather and see if we can find some smoother skies a little higher up. Our cruising altitude at this time is slightly above 20,000 feet, right around the elevation of Alaska's Mt. McKinley, which is still another 250 miles north of us. Please be sure to fasten you seat belts tightly, hang in there, and bare with me while I try to find us a smoother flying altitude up above in the so-called jet stream. Thank you for your patience and your cooperation."

The old Native woman appeared calm yet her expression conveyed an almost hypnotic effect upon Henry, even though the two seats in between them sat empty. She blinked her eyes a few times as she looked straight toward Henry without saying a word, almost as if she were looking right through him into the sky and clouds outside the plane. Henry averted his gaze and wondered if she was going to speak.

"What brings you up here? You just like the rest … comin' for fame and fortune?"

Henry was surprised by the old woman's desire to initiate a conversation; most native people he felt were quiet, less prone to the loud and showy talk, which many *Cheechakos* [44] sometimes demonstrated.

"Uh. I'm sorry. Were you talking to me?"

"Yah. I'm talking to you." The old woman spoke curtly.

"No, my… uh. My brother lives up here, in Anchorage … with his family." Henry smiled with a glint of enthusiasm in his eye. "He's asked me to join him on a climb up Mt. McKinley."

The old woman laughed and scoffed at Henry's innocent sense of bravado. "Another one of them climbers, huh? Yah know … You're not the first person to climb our mountain."

"Uh, I know that."

In truth, Henry had checked out a few books about Mt. McKinley from his college library. One of them was by the Rev. Hudson Stuck, the clergyman who had led the first successful climb up Denali in 1913.

"You do, huh? Well, you young pups comes up here every year … think you're discoverin' our mountain for the first time, all on your own, right? Think you're the first ones to conquer Denali."

"No, I don't feel that way."

---

44 Web link: *Dictionary.com*. Cheechakos, http://dictionary.reference.com/browse/cheechakos.

Henry knew there were lots of other people who had already been to the top, more than a couple of hundred he remembered reading in a *Time Magazine* article; there had also been a few women. Prior to 1967, only 208 climbers had successfully reached the South summit of Denali and only three had ever died in their attempt to do so. Then during the winter expedition of 1967 the French climber Jacque Baktin became the fourth.

"Year in, and year out … you kids from the lower forty-eight comes up here, lookin' for adventure … think you're gonna conquer the world."

"Uh … Sorry." Henry was at a loss for words. He was clearly taken back by the old woman's assertive nature. She looked Henry straight in the eye.

"Walter Harper was the first man to set foot on the top of Denali.[45] That was back in 1913. He was also an Alaska Native. Not like one of you white kids from outside."

The old woman paused, for a few seconds—as if she were reflecting upon her past. Again her eyes looked through and beyond Henry, as she spoke.

"I used to take care of Walter's dogs, when I was just a little girl. He was from my village, up on the Yukon River. He and my dad were good friends."

A deep sadness came into the old woman's face.

"One day, he went away with his new bride … and he never come back."

"What happened?"

"My dad said he got himself kilt. My dad kept his dogs, and I took good care of them, but I never saw Walter again. He was gone."

"That's awful. Do you know what happened to him?"

"Him and his new bride drowned in a boating accident down near Juneau. It happened just a few years after he climbed to the top of Denali."[46]

The old woman's eyes were beginning to water.

"Now, dare was a man. Yes, sir. Dare was a real man. Not like one of you pups, I sees … comin' up here every summer."

"Well, uh… I, uh…"

"Probably gonna get yourself kilt, too … up on our mountain. Denali takes one or two, yah know … every now and then."

She turned toward Henry, and looked him straight in the eye, this time, with hardly any expression in her face. She seemed quietly upset.

"I think it's only fair, if you ask me."

The old native woman was done. As she sunk back, the small elderly woman nearly disappeared into her seat. Her pursed lips and solemn stare into the seat in

---

45   Wikipedia Link: Walter Harper. http://en.wikipedia.org/wiki/index.html?curid=6704727.

46   Wikipedia link: The wreck of the Princess Sophia at Vanderbilt Reef. http://en.wikipedia.org/wiki/SS_Princess_Sophia.

left Walter Harper was the first man to set foot on the summit of Denali. (Mt. McKinley) He was with the expedition of Archdeacon Hudson Stuck.

Photo: Unknown, Public domain copyright

right Princess Sophia (steamship) ca 1912. On October 25, 1918, the Sophia sank with the loss of all aboard after grounding on Vanderbilt Reef in Lynn Canal near Juneau, Alaska. Walter Harper and his new bride were among the 343 people who were lost.

Photo: Unknown, Public domain copyright.

front of her was all that Henry could see. There was a deadly stillness in the cabin except for the drone of the plane's twin engines.

A bell went ding and the overhead fasten your seat belt sign above the aisle lit up. The Captain's voice once again came over the intercom. "Good morning, Ladies and gentlemen. Well, we're about to begin our descent into Anchorage, where we will be setting down in just about eight minutes. I'd like to be the first to welcome you to Anchorage, Alaska, what many folks up here call the drop-off point to *The Last Frontier.*"

Henry leaned over and looked down from the window. A small cluster of lights could be seen ahead, which opened below to the broad vista of Cook Inlet.

Henry's heart beat faster, as his plane flew over the slush-filled waters along Turnagain Arm as it slowly banked toward the triangular shaped peninsula, where Captain Cook and the HMS *Resolution* had once dropped anchor.

The McDonnell Douglas DC-10 landed at the comparatively small Anchorage airport, on its single lane, barely lit runway. Today, Anchorage International Airport is a bustling, modern expanse of huge buildings with numerous runways and a continuous flow of airplanes landing and taking off every few minutes, comparable to many urban facilities worldwide. The slightest resemblance to anything that existed there in the summer of 1967 is gone. The image of a

left The death of Captain James Cook, 14 February 1779. The native is carrying a feather helmet and cloak that are in the Vienna museum. Zoffany borrowed them for the painting. Oil on canvas, c. 1795.

Artist: Johann Zoffany, 1733-1818, Public domain copyright

right The HMS *Resolution* (1771-1782), James Cook's ship, watercolour by midshipman Henry Roberts.

Artist: Henry Roberts, Public domain copyright.

Cook Inlet was named after the renowned British explorer Captain James Cook[48], who first sailed into the frigid waters below in 1778, just two years after the Colonists declared their independence from King George of England.

After failing to discover the Northwest Passage the following year, Captain Cook turned around again, as he had done in Turnagain Arm, over which the plane now flew just south of Anchorage. When he returned to Hawaii, he and his crew vacationed there for about a month.

Then an unimaginable thing occurred.

When some of his men got into an unfortunate scuffle with some native Hawaiians on February 14 at Kealakekua Bay, Captain James Cook was brutally stabbed to death. It has even been postulated that some of the flesh was cut from his bones and roasted for human consumption, a practice reserved for the chiefs and highest elders of the Hawaiian society at the time.

Despite this sad turn of events, the Hawaiian people thought very highly of Captain James Cook, and his statue now stands in Waimea, Kauai commemorating his first contact with the Hawaiian Islands at the town's harbor in January 1778.[49]

---

47   Wikipedia link: James Cook. http://en.wikipedia.org/wiki/James_Cook.

48   Wikipedia web link: http://en.wikipedia.org/wiki/James_Cook,
      Third voyage (1776-79) and death.

relatively small building with its miniscule waiting area for passengers waiting to depart or to arrive is now nothing more than a memory.

One of Henry's favorite songs from the sixties was performed at Woodstock, NY on the now famous 15-acre plot of land called Yasgur's farm,[49] during a concert that Henry and some of his friends would attend along with some 500,000 concert goers two years later.

Crosby, Stills, Nash and Young sang the song—and every time Henry hears it, he is reminded of his journey to Alaska in the summer of 1967 when he flew into the small city that bordered the edge of North America's Last Frontier, a place and time for Henry that now lives only within the confines of his mind.

In a way, Henry felt like Captain James Cook sailing into a new and unexplored territory. At the time, he wondered what lay ahead for him and his brother on the icy slopes of Mt. McKinley. Henry hoped that they would not experience a fate comparable to that of Captain James Cook, the possibility of 'being kilt' as the old Alaska Native woman aboard his McDonnell Douglas DC-10 had predicted.

When Crosby, Stills, Nash, and Young reach that fateful phrase, in perhaps one of their most popular songs, *Teach Your Children Well*,[50] Henry says that his body tingles with a rush of feeling and usually his eyes begin to water for yes it is sadly, so true. "For the past, is just a goodbye."

---

49   Wikipedia web link: Max Yasgur. http://en.wikipedia.org/wiki/Max_Yasgur.

50   *Teach Your Children*, by Crosby, Stills, Nash & Young, Album: Déjà Vu Released: 1970. Wikipedia Web link: http://en.wikipedia.org/wiki/Teach_Your_Children.

CHAPTER 4

Time Will Tell

Henry stepped onto the stair case unit that had been rolled into place at the door. A panoramic view of Chugach Mountains rose before him as a backdrop to the city at his left and spread across the horizon all the way down to Turnagain Arm to his right. The rising sun was cresting the summit of Ptarmigan Peak[51] as a warm radiance of color melted into the tundra valley across *Powerline Pass.*[52]

As Henry made his way down the steps, he heard someone utter a deep sigh of relief. He turned and saw the old Native woman standing at the top of the platform. The pinkish glow on her smiling face had transformed her stern demeanor into an embodiment of kindness and wisdom.

Henry remembered seeing that expression in his own grandmother's eyes, Grammy Spaulding, as she stood at the head of their oak dining room table with the Thanksgiving Day turkey in her hands, still hot from just having been taken out of the oven. Of course, this iconic moment became

A view of the Chugach Mountains showing Powerline Pass, Ptarmigan Peak is seen on the right. This view is similar to the one the author saw as he stepped down the staircase after landing in Anchorage in 1967.

Photo: the author's photo collection.

---

51   Wikipedia link: *Ptarmigan Peak.* http://en.wikipedia.org/wiki/Ptarmigan_Peak_%28Alaska%29.

52   Web Link: *Powerline Pass.* http://www.alaskahikesearch.com/Hikes/PowerlinePass.htm.

Standing in front of their East Haven, Connecticut home *(left to right)* are the author's grandparents and his mother.

Photo: Unknown, Courtesy of the author's family.

Rockwell, who often viewed those moments in life with those eyes that see the inherent goodness of humankind, summed up his own form of idealism when he said,
"I paint life as I would like it to be."

Capturing those moments of pure innocence and beauty was Rockwell's way of dealing with the silent unrest and sadness that lay beneath the facade of the American ideal, along with his own insecurity of being pigeonholed as a lowly illustrator. Coupled with a serious midlife depression, which landed him in the hands of psychoanalyst Erik Erikson, it is easy to see that Rockwell's personal life was anything but a bed of roses.

His later work, however, like *The Problem We All Live With*, depicting Ruby Bridges accompanied to her New Orleans school by four U.S. marshals, gives a clear example of the other side of the coin, which he portrayed so vividly depicting the inherent ugliness we also share.[55]

immortalized in Norman Rockwell's famous painting, entitled *Freedom from Want*.[53]

Henry remembered looking around the table and seeing the smiles on everyone else's faces, especially on Aunt Sophie's and Aunt Hazel's, Katherine's two younger sisters. Pop Spaulding was still in good spirits, although he was obviously a bit tipsy, as he bowed his head in reverence and delivered a somewhat sardonic version of grace.

"Our dear heavenly father. We thank you humbly for this food, and for all the blessings you have bestowed upon this family." Pop reached for his glass of wine and took a drink—a gesture on his part, which turned smiles into frowns, Henry recalled.

"May you continue to watch over this family, and help each us to better understand the mystery of your ways, and the miracles of your love."

Grandpa Spaulding then did something, which was very puzzling to Henry at the time. Pop smiled and looked directly at his two youngest daughters, Henry's Aunt Sophie and Aunt Hazel, and he raised his glass of wine, as if he were making a toast directly to each of them.

"In Jesus' name. We thank you. Amen."

---

53   Wikipedia link: Freedom from Want. http://en.wikipedia.org/wiki/Freedom_from_Want_%28painting%29.

54   Web link: *Norman Rockwell*, http://artchive.com/artchive/R/rockwell.html.

John Spaulding's moodiness and judgmental condescension had not yet clicked in to put a damper on the proceedings. Henry remembered looking into the joyful expression on his own mother's face—her eyes glowed with warmth, like the old native woman's. Yet, her expression too quickly turned into a frown when Katherine saw her own father gloating over her two younger sisters with what appeared to be a menacing intent.

Henry's painful memory suddenly vanished, when he spotted his brother waving to him from a window in the small terminal. Once inside the building, Johnny and Henry greeted each other with tears forming in the corners of their eyes. Johnny picked Henry up into the air with one of his famous bear hugs, just like he used to do back on the beaches of Brockett's Point and Lamphier's Cove. For Henry, it felt like he was coming home again. The two brothers collected Henry's bags from the tiny conveyor belt at the back wall; then they crossed the street into a small parking lot in front of the terminal.

As Henry hopped into Johnny's 1965 VW bus, he noticed the flower and peace symbol decals on the side door.

"The kids helped decorate the outside over Christmas. Bonnie and I have both about had it with our involvement in Viet Nam. I never thought I'd say it, but I think I'm turning into one of those liberal pacifists. The corporate greed and the US domination of all these third world countries is enough to make anyone sick to their stomach."

"What are you talking about?"

"Henry, you wouldn't believe some of the things I saw down in South America, and it's all being done under the guise of hoodwinking the American public into thinking our main purpose for being there is to spread democracy. I swear I could write a book about the greed and corruption I saw down in South America with The Peace Corps. Sure, we're doing a lot of good, but the main reason we're down there is to protect our own interests and capitalize on whatever profits can be made."

Henry looked at his brother with a puzzled expression.

"The same thing's true for Viet Nam. If you ask me, we need to get out of there, and let those folks figure out their own problems, without us butting in and taking charge."

Henry was surprised by his brother's sudden outburst. As the VW pulled away from the terminal, and headed toward town, Henry turned his attention to the vivid colors and beautiful landscape on the outskirts of Anchorage. The road bordered the broad waters of Cook Inlet and there was not a cloud in the sky. On the horizon some 150 miles to the north Henry spotted three snow-covered peaks, which rose above the massive wall of snow, rock, and ice appropriately named The Alaska Range.

top Seated in the family Volkswagon Bus
are the author's sister-in-law with her three
daughters.

Photo: The author's older brother, Spring of 1967.

top right An aerial view of downtown Anchorage
and the south addition area, with port and fuel
tanks in right background.

_Photo: Ward W. Wells, Aug. 28, 1967, Courtesy of the
Anchorage Museum at Rasmuson Center._

right The author's sister-in-law, taken during her
college years in the late 1950s.

Photo: Courtesy of the author's family.

It seemed to Henry as though the civilized world had had little impact upon this rugged terrain. The city of Anchorage came into view and seemed little more than a cavalry outpost on the edge of a yet to be explored wilderness.

The VW's engine made a loud grinding noise, as Johnny shifted into a higher gear. Soon they were barreling down an open stretch of highway, which led back into town. The gears groaned again.

"Uh, whoops. I think. Well, I hope I can get another year out of the old girl, if the gears don't go." Johnny patted the top of the bus's hard white metal dashboard to the right of the steering wheel.

Henry noticed a picture of Bonnie and their four children, scotch-taped beside the speedometer dial. Johnny saw Henry looking at the photo. Henry smiled at Johnny, but for some reason, Johnny's eyes averted Henry's gaze. It seemed to Henry as though Johnny was trying to hide something.

"So, are Bonnie and the kids pretty happy with their new home here in Alaska?" Henry inquired.

"Oh, they're all fine. They're doing …" he shrugged. "They're okay."

Johnny looked straight ahead and nodded his head up and down, without saying a word. Henry felt strange. Johnny's god-like image seemed slightly tarnished from what he remembered. Where was that sense of confidence Henry had always admired in his brother? Something was different.

Johnny slammed on the breaks and the Volkswagen came to an abrupt stop.

"Look at that. You don't see too many of those back in Branford, I'll bet."

A huge moose, and two calves slowly crossed the road right in front of Johnny's VW.

"Whoa, Johnny! That's amazing. Look at the size of that mother. That's really something. This place really is the Last Frontier, isn't it?"

Johnny smiled, "That's what they say."

The VW finally pulled into the backyard driveway of Johnny and Bonnie's Fairview home, splashing through a large mud puddle as it pulled up alongside the garage.

Bonnie had apparently been waiting up for them to arrive. Henry noticed her smiling face, as she stepped out from a small screened in back porch. Henry noticed that Bonnie walked slowly down the back steps, yet before Henry had a chance to open the door, she was standing beside him.

"Well, at last. You've finally arrived! I'm so glad you're here, Henry. You must be exhausted?"

Henry, like his mother Katherine, and even his father, had never been an overly affectionate person. The occasional stilted hug like the one he performed with Johnny at the airport was his usual greeting. Henry was also good when it came to mustering up a firm handshake. Captain Reggie had always encouraged his boys to demonstrate their strength in this manner.

"Remember boys. Always look a person right in the eye when you first meet them, and when you shake their hand make sure its a good firm grasp. No one likes to shake hands with the tail end of a dead fish," he would often joke.

Once, in Florida, when he was about twelve, Henry went around with a catfish he had caught right off the dock next to the *Franny B*. Henry kept running from one family member to another trying to get them to shake hands with the tail end of his fish. He laughed when he handed the tail to his boyhood friend David Bumstead.

"Now remember, Dave. A good strong handshake and looking a person straight in the eye shows that person he's meeting someone like John Wayne or maybe even Superman."

However, when it came to smacking someone on the lips, particularly some-one as pretty as Bonnie, Henry had always found himself a little weak in the knees, and such an encounter could even trigger his heart to skip a beat.

Without warning, Bonnie threw Henry for a loop after he stepped down from the VW, when she suddenly wrapped her arms around him tightly. Henry felt the warmth and softness of Bonnie's breasts, as they pressed up against his chest, and then suddenly she planted a firm moist kiss right on top of Henry's lips.

Henry could feel his heart flutter. When Bonnie finally released him, Henry stumbled backward a few steps, and got his feet wet in the mud. Johnny glanced at Henry and then gave Bonnie a questioning look.

"You must be famished? Can I get you something to eat, or how about a nice cold drink?"

"No. No, that's okay. Thanks Bonnie, I already ate something on the plane. I'm tired for the most part, more interested in sleep than anything else. You know, I guess that jet lag thing has finally caught up with me."

"How about a nightcap? Before you go to bed?"

"A nightcap? Henry's mind flashed to his mother.

"No, that's okay Bonnie. I think I'm just going to hit the hay. I'm pretty much beat."

Henry averted his eyes from Bonnie's gaze, as he turned his attention to the physical appearance of Johnny and Bonnie's home. Back in Connecticut, in his mind's eye, Henry had always envisioned Johnny and his family living on the outskirts of town in a rustic log cabin, like the ones he and Skipper had built with their toy Lincoln logs, or maybe even like the one the Cartright family had supposedly lived in on the television series *Bonanza*.

As Henry stood there trying to re-adjust his perception to the harsh reality of the small ramshackle wooden-planked single floor house in front of him, he could not help wondering what had happened to his idealized vision.

Most of the time this summer Henry would be in a tent on the snow-covered slopes of Denali. Still, Henry felt disheartened, as his brother's idealized life in Alaska did not meet up to his expectations. The morning sun continued to shed more light on Henry's surroundings, as it rose higher above the magnificent Chugach Mountains.

Johnny and Bonnie's dilapidated house reminded Henry of some of the places his Aunt Sophie and Aunt Hazel had lived in over the years.

"What's the matter?" Johnny inquired.

"Oh, nothing. I just thought things would be a little different. That's all."

"Well, we've got a bed made up for you in the garage." Bonnie interjected. "Johnny, show Henry where he's going to sleep."

Johnny helped his brother move his gear not into the main house, but instead into the garage. There was literally no room in their small home for Henry to sleep, so Johnny, whose carpenter skills left much to be desired, had built a small plywood bunk in the garage on which Henry was to bed down.

Johnny threw Henry's Kelty Pack frame onto the floor of the garage, which lay cluttered with an accumulation of boxes, climbing gear, a push lawnmower, and even an old Schwinn bicycle. Together Henry and Johnny went back outside into the yard.

"Get some rest. You're gonna need it. Tomorrow we've got a practice climb lined up on a glacier just outside of town."

Bonnie stood on the steps of the porch and waved.

"Good night, Henry. It's great to have you here."

Johnny nodded toward Henry, then jogged up the steps past Bonnie, as he went into the house. Bonnie smiled and waved again. Then she too turned and went inside.

Henry took off his pants and lay down on the green army surplus bag his brother had laid out for him on top of the bunk; a half-inch thick ensolite pad served as the bed's mattress, which proved less than soft. Henry removed his own pad from his Kelty and laid it on top of the other one. He tried to sleep but he was still too wired, so he sat up, pulled on his jeans again and decided to go for a short walk.

Gambell Street was a block from their house, the main road that had been partitioned off back in the forties to separate downtown Anchorage from what most folks then viewed as the other side of the tracks; a hodgepodge community of ramshackle homes similar to Johnny and Bonnie's called Fairview. Only a small portion of the Chugach Mountains could be viewed from this location, hence the name.

Henry followed Gambell for a couple of miles, which led him to a bluff that overlooked Ship Creek, the original 1914 town site of Anchorage's famous Tent City.[55] Henry had seen old photos of this last of the frontier towns in one of the books he had checked out from his college library.

On the horizon roughly 120 miles to the north, Henry could see the Crown Jewel of the Alaska Range, *Denali*, otherwise called Mt. McKinley, bathed in a pinkish glow from the rising sun. As it towered above the city of Anchorage like some distant castle in a children's storybook tale of long ago, the mountain seemed so immense, almost larger than life. Henry's thoughts were again racing across his youthful mind.

---

55   Website link: A Brief History of Anchorage. http://www.anchorage.net/485/ctm.

'City of Tent Homes,'
Anchorage, Alaska.

Photo: Hettel, Carpenter
Collection, Copyright: No known
restrictions on publication.
Library of Congress Prints
and Photographs Div.
Washington D. C.

The sprawling campsite of more than one hundred large white, canvas wall tents had presented the Alaska Engineering Commission with a major sanitation problem, and it reminded Henry of a scene from Charlie Chaplan's 1925 silent film classic, *The Gold Rush*. To resolve this health hazard in 1915, its board of trustees decided to move the city up onto the overlooking bluff.

On July 18 Andrew B. Christensen, Anchorage's land office chief closed the sale on 655 lots when he auctioned off the new 350-acre town site. A removal order cleared residents from Ship Creek flats, and brought in a total of just under $150,000 in revenue for the Commission. Construction of the new Alaska Railroad was by then in full gear and so too was the building of the new town site of Anchorage.

"How in the world are we going to be able to reach the summit of this magnificent *Castle in the Clouds?*" From Henry's perspective, this dream for which he had risked everything seemed quite impossible, well out his grasp. Was his mother right? Would this whole thing turn into a terrible nightmare?

Henry gazed across Cook Inlet, toward the Susitna River basin, the route that the infamous charlatan Dr. Frederick Cook[56] had first used during his two attempts to reach Denali's lofty heights back in 1903 and again, in 1906. Would Johnny and Henry be confronted with a similar dilemma? Would they have to turn back, like Dr. Cook, without reaching the top? Would this massive buttress of ice and snow prove to be too much for them to overcome?

Henry thought about what his father had said to him long ago, his pat expression for answering the never-ending questions of a toddler's mind. Just as his Poppa was getting ready to board a plane at Idlewild Airport, in New York City, to fly back to Miami, little Henry ran and grabbed hold of one of his father's legs and wouldn't let go. Henry looked up into his father's eyes, as tears ran down his face.

---

56 Bradford Washburn, Peter Cherici, *The Dishonorable Dr. Cook: Debunking the Notorious McKinley Hoax* (illustrated), Mountaineers Books, Seattle, (September 2001).

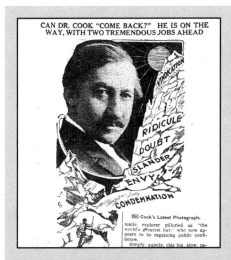

"Can Dr. Cook 'Come Back?'"

Courtesy of the Chicago, Illinois Newspaper Archives,
'The day book, September 08, 1913, Image 24.

Rather than admit defeat, Dr. Cook chose to spend the rest of his life embroiled in one of exploration's most outrageous frauds, one that is still contested. A website[57] exists even today, which continues to provide viewers with evidence that the good doctor had gone down in history as one of exploration's greatest martyrs.

In the fall of 1906, Dr. Cook made the astounding claim that he and another man had finally succeeded in reaching the top of Mt. McKinley in less than a week! Cook even had photographic proof, a picture of blacksmith Ed Barrill standing on what he claimed to be the top of North America. Yet history would prove Cook to be a fraud.

"Daddy? When do I get to go to Your-ami?"

His Poppa reached down and rustled the hair on the top of his head with his left hand. "Time will tell, Little Henry. Time, will tell."

Tears were beginning to form in Captain Reggie's eyes, too, as Katherine knelt down beside their youngest son.

"Come on, Henry. Your father has to get on the plane. He has to go. It's his job, you know that." Henry's mother picked Henry up into her arms, as he continued to cry.

Henry stood there on the bluff, gazing across the inlet toward his adversary. He shrugged his shoulders and tried to quell the turmoil that raged inside his head, but it was too much. Henry turned away from this magnificent vista and slowly made his way back down Gambell toward Johnny and Bonnie's home and the shelter of his small room in their garage.

---

57   The Frederick A. Cook Society, http://www.cookpolar.org/dishonorable.htm.

top right Captain Reggie, the author's father, as a young man aboard the *Franny B*.

Photo: Unknown, Courtesy of the author's family.

left Frederick A. Cook's picture of Ed Barrill atop a peak claimed to be the summit of Mt. McKinley, but actually almost twenty miles away.

Photo: Frederick Cook, Public domain copyright.

bottom right Aerial view of Mulcahy ball park in Anchorage, Alaska , looking east with Gambell and Ingra Streets running across center of photo. Aug. 28, 1967.

Photo: Ward W. Wells, Courtesy of the Anchorage Museum at Rasmuson Center

CHAPTER 5

Pitchler's Perch

It was after 3 am before Henry finally dozed off on the make shift bunk Johnny had built for him out in the garage. He slept straight through the morning and into early afternoon.

A young boy, Johnny's and Bonnie's eldest child was tickling Henry's feet with what appeared to be an Eagle's feather. Henry had remained awake just long enough to remove his shoes and socks, but then crashed from utter fatigue, without even crawling into his sleeping bag. Two other children, an older girl and her younger sister, were smiling and giggling, barely able to contain their laughter. "Wake up Uncle Henry. It's time to get up," the boy was first to speak.

"You slept through breakfast," the older girl spoke next. "Mommy's saved you some of our Sloppy Joes from lunch. Daddy's putting his stuff together and he told us to come in and wake you up."

"Yeah," said the youngest girl. "He said you had to get a move on?" she looked puzzled. "What's a move-on Uncle Henry?"

After lunch Johnny and Henry started pulling climbing gear from the garage, along with Henry's full Kelty pack and frame, which they loaded into the back of Johnny's VW in preparation for Henry's first glacier adventure.

It was late afternoon before they finally pulled out of the driveway and headed north for Eklutna Lake, where they were to meet up with the Mountaineering Club of Alaska (MCA) team at the end of Eklutna Valley. Henry was very excited, but also a bit nervous. This would be his first encounter with the other members of Johnny's team and the last thing he wanted to do was to disappoint any of them.

Seated in the front yard of their 9th Avenue home in Anchorage are the children of Bonnie and Johnny.

Photo: the author's sister-in-law, Courtesy of the author's family.

Moving north out of the city they traveled along a two-lane highway, which bordered Ship Creek. Henry even noticed the small bluff upon which he had stood twelve hours earlier, as the VW veered right. Henry gazed off toward the massive Alaska Range, which was now hidden behind a sea of clouds.

Traveling further up into the Matanuska Valley, the small communities of Eagle River and Chugiak gave evidence of the gradual encroachment of the civilized world below the foothills of the Chugach Mountains. On the north side of the road Henry saw a sign, which read Eklutna Village. About fifty yards ahead he saw a very strange sight, what appeared to be a row of furniture; a couch, a few sofas, and a couple of tables were lined up along the side of the road. Henry saw two elderly Native men sitting quietly on the couch. They smiled and waved at Johnny and Henry as they sped by.

Johnny's VW bus veered south into the mountains and began a slow climb up a gravel road that zigzagged its way up toward the edge of the Chugach Mountains,[58] the 5.4 million acre United States National Forest in South Central Alaska surrounding Prince William Sound, the eastern Kenai Peninsula, and the delta of the Copper River. It's the second largest forest in the U.S. National Forest system, and northernmost. It was originally designated in 1907 by Theodore Roosevelt. Approximately one-third of the area of the forest is rocks and ice.

Johnny and Henry finally crested the endless series of steep switchbacks, and slowly moved up into a wide and lush mountain valley. The strain on the VW's engine, and the occasional grinding of its gears subsided. From high overhead the

---

58   Wikipedia link. *Chugach National Forest*. http://en.wikipedia.org/wiki/ Chugach National Forest.

Eklutna Lake with Bold Peak on the horizon at the left of the photo. This is the view the author saw as he and his brother drove toward Eklutna Glacier

Photo:
Jeff Babcock.

Another shot alongside Eklutna Lake, this one showing the glacier below (at center of photo) with 'Peril Peak' looming above. Two men at back of the Ford Bronco are former climbing students of the author.

Photo:
Jeff Babcock.

Another shot along the twelve-mile road into the trailhead to Eklutna glacier, showing again Peril Peak looming in the distance.

Photo:
Jeff Babcock.

nine-mile expanse of Eklutna Lake came into view with rolling hills and mountains on either side of this immense and picturesque valley, a favorite camping and hiking area. As Johnny maneuvered the bus along a backwoods road on the north side of the lake, he pointed over the dash.

"You see that narrow canyon at the end of the valley?"

"Yeah, is that where we're headed?"

"You got it."

At the end of the lake, several tall mountains formed a blockade to the snow covered ice fields beyond.

As the bus came around a curve Henry spotted the icy snout of Eklutna Glacier off in the distance, nestled between two towering canyon walls like a sleeping dragon. He marveled at the beautiful countryside. Looming above Eklutna Glacier was a treacherous looking mountain that reminded Henry of an Alaska version of the Matterhorn.

"You see that mountain above the glacier?"

"Yeah, looks pretty hairy!"

"It is. It's called Peril Peak. One of the climbers on our team, Grace Jensen Hoeman, and her husband Vin, climbed it with me this past summer. We pushed a new route up the NW couloir." Henry smiled, once again impressed with another one of his brother's accomplishments.

Johnny's VW finally came to the end of the road, where two other vehicles were parked between two large boulders. To the left of the cars the silt-ridden, gushing rapids of the Eklutna River flowed down from the glacier, which was still another mile up the valley. Two climbers were midway across the nearly waist deep water. One of the men made it to the other side and waved at Johnny and Henry, then continued to make his way up the valley.

After getting out of the car, Johnny yelled over the continuous roar of gushing waters to the second man who had just reached the other side.

"Gene! Is everyone else up ahead?"

Gene Soft, a tall, gangly bearded man with a receding hairline and bald spot on top of his head, called back to Johnny from the middle of the river. He motioned with his right hand and appeared to chuckle to himself. Gene was always one for cracking a joke, "I think Hans is dropping a load in the woods. We all had a late lunch at Gwennie's this afternoon. By the time we got here, Hans jumped out of the car and made a quick dash for the woods." Gene smiled. "Too much Bratwurst, if you ask me."

Johnny smiled and then he and Henry loaded up their heavy packs and started to cross the frigid cold, gushing waters of the Eklutna River. As Henry stumbled slowly into the water, his feet began to freeze.

"Man, this water is cold!"

By the time Henry got half way across, the throbbing aching feeling in his feet was deadly. Henry wanted to move faster, but the water was waist deep, and it was all he could do just to keep his balance. Johnny followed close behind backing Henry up just in case he began to topple over.

They at last reached the other side, took off their socks and boots and wrung their socks out. Then they put them back on and continued on their way.

"Your feet will warm up in a bit. You'll see."

"Seems like a lot of extra work to me."

"Listen, we've got a whole mile wide stretch of glacial streams like this one to get across, when we hit The McKinley River. Then it's a fifteen-mile trek to the base of Denali with two other river crossings, before we even start climbing."

"How do we keep our feet from freezing?"

"That'll be the least of our worries. First we'll be departing from a little whistle-stop along the railroad tracks, which is roughly fifty miles from the base of the mountain. Then we'll make our way up the West Fork of the Chulitna River Basin, up, over and through Anderson Pass to the north side of the mountain, and then across the tundra to Wonder Lake. So, you better get used to making river crossings."

"Yeah, but it's so damn cold! Seems as though it'll be next to impossible to keep our feet from falling off?"

Johnny smiled, "You'll see. Where there's a will, there's a way."

By now, six climbers were slowly making their way up between the steep, narrowing walls and the jumble of scree and rock boulders that paralleled the river. As Johnny and Henry headed up the valley toward the snout of the sleeping dragon, Henry heard a rather caustic voice coming from behind him.

The ranting cadence of short staccato-like utterances reminded Henry of the dialect of a Nazi commandant from one of those WWII concentration camp movies he had seen on TV. Unfortunately for Henry, this proverbial thorn in his side would not stop; Hans Gruber would soon become the impetus for a gradual gnawing away of Henry's delicate sense of self worth as a climber, and this was only the beginning.

"Move it, or lose it!"

Henry was staggering under the weight of his seventy-pound pack. At the house it had only weighed around sixty pounds, but back at the car Johnny threw on a heavy climbing rope and then he added a bag of climbing hardware, "for good measure," he said.

Hans, a short, stocky, older looking climber in his mid forties quickly scooted by Henry.

Hikers (former climbing students of the author) make their way toward the icy snout of Eklutna Glacier.

Photo: Jeff Babcock.

"Toot, toot. Out-of-dah-way. Vee ain't got all day you know. We've got to get up to dah A-frame before it gets dark."

Hans had finished his dump in the woods and was now "fit for bear" carrying a huge load, which looked to Henry even bigger than his own.

Henry gazed in awe at the towering rock walls on both sides of the narrow canyon, as he watched Hans get smaller and smaller as he quickly charged up the boulder field ahead.

Finally, after another hour or so Johnny's team had reached the snout of the glacier, and now everyone was seated on rocks before the massive glacial moraine putting on their crampons. Henry was the last to arrive as he collapsed next to where Johnny was sitting.

"Make sure you put your crampons on good and tight. You don't want them fallin' off, half way up the glacier."

"I know, Johnny. I know. I've done this a few times before, you know, up on Mt. Washington in Tuckerman's Ravine. I'm not a beginner, you know."

"Hah. Vee'll see about dat."

Hans was seated on the other side of Johnny, and to Henry's chagrin, he blurted out another of his intimidating remarks, something that took Henry totally by surprise.

"I don't know, Johnny. Maybe vee should put Henry on a sled and drag him up the glacier. Vhut do you think?"

Johnny ignored Hans's comment and turned his attention to a rather tall dark haired Native looking man. "We're ready, Dan. Why don't you lead off? Henry and I will hook into your rope."

Daniel Sheath, the lean and very strong looking Alaska Native half— Eskimo member of the Johnny's MCA team was already standing on the ice tying into one end of a climbing rope. Although Daniel was soft spoken, he was Johnny's most dependable team member.

As Henry became better acquainted with this gentle Native man, he reminded Henry of the black panther character Bagheera, who had befriended Mowgli, the young hero of the Walt Disney film version of Rudyard Kipling's *The Jungle Book*, which Henry had just seen back east at the Branford movie theatre before flying off to Alaska.

"Sure enough, Johnny, sounds good to me."

Hans dissented. "No, Johnny. No. Let Henry go up the glacier vith Barney and me. I vant to see vhut kinda shape he's in." Johnny glanced toward his younger brother.

"You okay with that Henry?"

"Sure, Johnny." Henry replied, even though his reasoning was telling him exactly the opposite. "No problem. I'll go with Hans and Barney."

Hans walked over and stood beside Henry with a tangled coil of rope in his hand. "Okay, little boy. You hook in right behind me."

Hans dropped a tangled pile of rope at Henry's feet, just as he finished buckling the final strap on his left crampon.

"Come on, Henry. Vee ain't got all day. Let's go! Find dah middle of dah rope!"

Henry got up quickly and struggled to untangle the rope. Daniel moved out further onto the ice-encrusted moraine of the glacier, as his crampons dug sharply into the ice with a crunching sound. Johnny and Gene fed the rope out accordingly, while they waited to follow in Daniel's footsteps.

Without warning, Hans charged out across the ice, and deliberately passed by Gene, Johnny, and Daniel. As the rope between Hans and Henry tightened, Henry felt a hard tug at his waist, which nearly pulled him over.

"Come on Henry. Vee ain't got all day. Let's go. Let's go."

Hans began to literally pull Henry up the ice behind him. Barney Pleat, Hans's close friend and ally, who was shaped somewhat like a large bowling pin with a huge round stomach that tapered off at the shoulders, was behind Henry and he too, struggled to keep up with Hans's sudden dash up the glacier.

"For Chris sake, Hans! What's the rush?"

"I vant to see vhut kinda shape dis kid's in!"

As Barney went by Johnny and Daniel, he muttered something under his breath.

"I shouldah got on your guy's rope."

As the teams spread out across the top of the dragon's icy snout, a steady wind blew hard into Henry's face, pushing his unfastened parka hood down upon his neck. The cold wind cut into Henry's exposed face and ears like a knife. Hans was still charging up the ice about thirty feet ahead of Henry.

"Hans! Can we stop for a sec? I need to refasten my hood."

Hans looked back, shook his head in disgust.

"For Chris sake, Henry, you're slower den molasses going up hill in a snow storm." Hans proceeded to drag Henry up the glacier.

The hearty band of climbers traversed and zigzagged over a small icefall, as the team weaved its way around several gaping crevasses. Then they crossed the glacier to the opposite side, where a glistening waterfall plummeted down from the rock cliffs above.

Continuing for about another hour, the MCA group finally stopped at the base of a steep five hundred foot high snow slope, to break for a late afternoon snack. Johnny looked at Henry and then pointed upward.

"There's an A-frame hut up beyond the top of that slope. That's where we're headed. We'll base out of there for practice on the glacier tomorrow."

Johnny opened the top of his backpack and passed a small sack.

"Here, try one of these. Bonnie made them this morning, while you were still snoozing away out in the garage. Taste almost as good as mom's. See what you think."

Henry reached into the stuff sack and pulled out a plastic bag full of Chocolate Chip cookies.

"Hans been treating you okay?" Henry took a bite of one of Bonnie's cookies.

"Oh yeah. We're okay, I think." Henry smiled.

"He's a tad on the ornery side, though. Reminds me a little of Poppa. Remember how he used to put us on the spot, whenever he asked one of us to help him dock the *Franny B*. Sometimes Poppa made me feel like a such an idiot yelling and screaming at me, running back and forth on the boat, trying to get me to do the right thing."

"Yeah, I remember." Johnny smiled.

"I usually panicked and ended up throwing the rope in the water, instead of to the guy who was waiting for me to toss it to him on the dock."

Henry bit into one of Bonnie's chocolate chip cookies. "Hey, these taste a lot like mom's."

"They should. Kathy gave Bonnie the recipe, last time we were back east."

Johnny and Daniel now took turns with the exhausting process of kicking steps up the steep snow slope. Each step required several kicks to penetrate the hard crust of surface snow and sometimes ice. The two men also used their axes, to clean out each step.

After about an hour of exhausting work for the two men in the lead, Johnny finally crested the top of the slope. The rest of the MCA team was stretched out in rope teams below with cold feet, and by then everyone was eager to get up on top and hike to the A-frame to warm up. Within a short time the MCA team had moved off the steep and dangerous slope. In the distance, Henry saw the wooden A-frame hut Johnny had mentioned earlier come into view.

Peril Peak, the threatening looking Matterhorn look-alike he had seen from the lake, loomed to the right on the far side of Eklutna Glacier. Once on top Hans, Barney, and Henry crossed to the A-frame, which was anchored to the rocks with thick wire cables. Johnny was waiting outside to greet them.

"Well, Hans? How'd Henry do? Is he in pretty good shape?"

"Not dat bad for an easterner." Hans scoffed. "But, I vant to see how he does tomorrow on dah glacier. I still have my doubts."

The team retired for the night, and as Henry lay in his sleeping bag listening to the wind push gently against the plywood walls of the A-frame, he wondered about the next day, and whether or not he would be able to hold his own against these strong climbers, whose competence he feared was far greater than his own.

In the morning, the team all got up at the crack of dawn, cooked a hot breakfast of oatmeal, dried fruit, and one package each of hot chocolate and a Lipton tea bag. The climbers filled their water bottles and thermoses, loaded up their day-packs and then spent the better part of the morning down on Eklutna Glacier.

The climbers practiced rappelling[59] into and then falling into various crevasses below the looming rock slopes of Peril Peak. Team members took turns being pulled from the depths of seemingly bottomless pits in the ice, practicing the re-nowned Z-pulley[60] method for getting an injured climber out of a crevasse. During their lunch break, Johnny suggested a change in the routine for the afternoon.

"Okay, we're going to work this afternoon on self arresting[61] up on the steep slope we climbed yesterday, below the A-frame. Everyone okay with that?"

Hans spoke up. What appeared at first to be a joke, turned deadly serious.

"Yah, Johnny. Now you're talking. We all vant to make sure Henry's not going to pull any of us off dah gad damn mountain once vee get on Denali."

---

59   Wikipedia link: *Abseiling (rappelling)*, http://en.wikipedia.org/wiki/Abseiling.

60   Website link: *Z-pulley System*. http://www.highpeaksclimbing.com/Training/ZPulley.htm.

61   You Tube link: *How to ice axe self arrest*. http://www.youtube.com/watch?v=LM3xLshmNnk.

The A-frame structure at Pitchler's Perch is shown in this photo, which is located above the Eklutna Glacier on the Eklutna to Girdwood Traverse. Former climbing students of the author are seated in the foreground.

Photo: Jeff Babcock.

Members of the Mountaineering Club of Alaska Team practice on Eklutna glacier's crevasses below the A-frame at Pitchler's Perch.

Photo: Gayle Nienhueser

The author is shown above using the ascending devices called jumars in order to climb out of a deep crevasse.

Photo: Gayle Nienhueser.

Henry tried to ignore Han's blatant remark, and looked to his brother for support.

Johnny once again chose to say nothing. There was an awkward silence among the members of the team. Henry decided to change the subject as he gazed across Eklutna glacier toward the lethal looking Peril Peak.

"You guys climbed that? Must ah been some climb!"

Johnny smiled, as he stood and began coiling in one of the climbing ropes.

"It was." Johnny smiled. "This is a quite place, isn't it? Pitchler's Perch—one of my favorite places to come to whenever I want to get away from the rest of the rat race world back in the lowlands. It's close enough to Anchorage, yet you feel like you're in the middle of the Alaska Range."

The broad vista of Eklutna Glacier, Peril Peak, and the surrounding mountains offered a startling beauty. Eklutna Lake could be seen far below in the distance curving around the valley.

"It's incredible. It's a climber's paradise. And we're not even on McKinley." Henry gazed back toward Peril Peak.

"Peril Peak sort of reminds me of some ancient Egyptian pyramid. You know, like the one they showed in that old Boris Karloff movie, *The Mummy's Tomb*.

Johnny smiled. "I remember those horror movies used to scare the pants off you and Skip."

"Yeah, but I was just a little fart back then." Henry smiled. "It takes a lot more to scare me these days, a lot more than you creeping out of our toy closet in a skeleton mask with a white sheet draped over your shoulders."

"Well, be prepared little brother, I guarantee we're going to see some scary things on Denali. You can count of that, for sure."

"Yeah, I guess so—that old Native woman I met on the plane said we might even be meeting up with the Grim Reaper himself."

Johnny smiled, as he and Henry slowly made their way back up to the A-frame.

"Well, let's hope not. I'd just as soon avoid meeting up with that guy, if we can possibly help it." They reached the A-frame and joined the others who were already setting up belay anchors[62] and getting ready to plunge over the steep slope.

Hans was standing beside the snow picket he had just finished pounding deep into the hard packed snow.

"Here you go, Johnny boy. Let's see if Henry is any better at stopping himself with an ice axe than he was this morning with getting out of a crevasse."

Johnny frowned at Hans as he took hold of his coil of rope. Then he handed Henry one end.

---

62   Wikipedia link: *Anchor (climbing)*. http://en.wikipedia.org/wiki/Anchor_%28climbing%29.

"Here Henry, tie in and remember, head over heels down the slope. Do at least three somersaults before using your axe. Okay? Henry tied the rope into his sit harness.[63]

"Got it, on belay?"

"Belay on." Johnny looked at the large, loose pile of rope at his feet, and smiled. "So to speak."

Henry slowly trotted down the steep slope and rolled head over heels three times down the steep hard packed snow slope in his attempt to simulate an actual fall.

Hans was standing nearby, and once again was quick to place judgment on Henry's performance.

"Hah! Dis should be interestin'!" The pile of rope zipped down the slope behind Henry, as he picked up speed, tumbling head over heels. Henry tried several times, without success, to stop himself with the pick— the curved pointed end of his ice axe, which was also used for chopping out steps in hard ice.

Hans looked at the others and shook his head. "Yah! Hah! I told yah." He threw his hands up in the air. "Nobody ever listens to me."

Henry continued to pick up speed as he plummeted down the slope. After what seemed an eternity, the weight of his body snapped tight when he came to the end of the rope.

"Ah … whoof!" The air in Henry's lungs and stomach seemed to blast outward from his mouth. Henry gasped deeply as he tried to regain his composure, after he had fallen the full 150-foot length of the rope.

Johnny looked down from the top of the slope.

"Don't worry, Henry. You'll get the hang of it."

The adrenalin was still pumping through Henry's entire body, as he gazed upwards with some dizziness toward the others. Henry felt a wave of embarrassment come over him, not only for himself, but also for his brother Johnny.

"Climb back up, and we'll try it again."

Henry slowly plodded his way back up the steep snow slope. As he punch-holed new footsteps in the sixty degree slope, he overheard another snide remark from Hans who stood looking down from about twenty feet above.

"You just vait, Barney, I'll bet someone is gonna get himself into big trouble because of Little Henry's lack of experience. You mark my vords!"

As Henry reached the top, Johnny noticed a trickle of blood running down Henry's left cheek.

---

63   Wikipedia link: *Climbing harness*. http://en.wikipedia.org/wiki/Climbing_harness.

"Looks like you scraped yourself on the way down." Johnny took hold of Henry's jaw for a closer look. He turned to Daniel.

"Dan. Could you run up to the A-frame and grab the first aid kit?"

"Sure enough Johnny, will do."

Henry reached up and felt the small open wound on his cheek, as a reddish trickle of blood stained the snow beneath Henry's feet.

"Do you think I'll need any stitches?"

"No. Here, take this bandana and press it hard against your cheek. If it's still bothering you tomorrow, Bonnie will take care of it."

"What? Aren't you going to be around?"

"No, I've got some business I need to take care of up in Fairbanks."

By now Johnny had pulled in the rope and had layered it once again into a pile at his feet, from bottom to top, so it would once again run free. Daniel had returned with the first aid kit and finished bandaging up Henry's cheek accordingly.

"The kids are always getting cuts and scrapes." Johnny smiled. "You'll fit right in with them.

Hans again muttered an aside to Barney, but just loud enough for the others to hear.

"Hah! You can say dat again, Johnny boy."

Johnny decided once again to ignore Hans' comment.

"Anyway, we've still got time for another few hours of practice, before we have to pull out, so let's get at it."

Hans and Barney began to saunter back toward the A-frame. "Vell, Johnny boy, before me and Barney go at it again vee need to take a little break."

"What do mean, a break? We just started."

"Look Johnny." Hans exploded. "Don't start telling me vhut to do! You wouldn't listen to me before. Everyone knew it vuz a mistake for you to invite your little brudder along. I was the only one who brought it up." Hans looked at everyone else. "Dah rest of us have been climbing togedder for a whole year, and den poof, little Henry arrives on the scene vhut? two veeks before we're going to take off for dah mountain. Don't you start telling me vhut to do now!"

There was an awkward silence, while everyone watched Hans and Barney turn their backs on Johnny and continue toward the A-frame. Everyone expected Johnny to intervene. However, he did not.

"Come on everyone, let's get with it. We've still got some practice to do. Not everyone is as skilled as Hans and Barney, so we still need to work at it."

Henry saw Hans stop and turn around. He smiled at Johnny, but then turned his attention toward Henry. Their eyes met, but rather than continue the

Peril Peak in the Eklutna Glacier Valley.

Photo: Chugachpics.tripod.com/ flight11.jpg

argument, Hans glared at Henry with a look of disgust in his eyes. Then he blurted out, so everyone could hear.

"Come on Henry. Don't be such a big baby. You've got to learn dis stuff. Dis ain't dah pussy footing' around you've gotten used to back on dah east coast, you know? Dis is Alaska!"

After this final outburst from Hans, Henry stood there on top of the 500-foot snow slope, speechless. Henry felt as if he were standing there stark naked in front of everyone, and try as he might he could not think of anything to say.

Out of instinct or the sheer desperate need to escape this impossible predicament, Henry began to slowly trot down the steep slope, and then he rolled once, twice, and then once more, as Johnny had instructed him to do. The safety rope zipped down behind Henry, as he plunged down the slope into a total state of oblivion.

CHAPTER 6

Love Hurts

In the summer of 1967, Johnny and Bonnie Locke's residence was near the corner of 9th Avenue and Ingra Street, one block east of Gambell. It was nighttime, two days after Johnny and Henry's Eklutna Glacier trip. Through an outside window, Henry came into view sitting in an old sofa chair with three of Johnny and Bonnie's four children, two girls and a boy snuggled close around their Uncle Henry. He was reading them a bedtime story, Margery William's children's classic *The Velveteen Rabbit*. [64] Henry had a small bandage on his left cheek.

"Does it hurt? Asked the Rabbit. 'Sometimes,' said the Skin Horse, for he was always truthful. When you are Real you don't mind being hurt." Henry showed the children an illustration from the book, a picture showing the Skin Horse standing proud and tattered in the boy's bedroom with the Rabbit perched upon a stack of books, listening to him talk.

"Does it happen all at once, like being wound up," he asked, "or bit by bit?" The children were fascinated with the story. "It doesn't happen all at once," said the Skin Horse. "You become. It takes a long time. That's why it doesn't happen often to people who break easily, or have sharp edges, or who have to be carefully kept."

The youngest girl snuggled close to her

The Skin Horse Tells His Story.

The Skin Horse Tells His Story.

Illustrator: William Nicholson, from the children's classic 'The Velveteen Rabbit' by Margery Williams, Doubleday & Company, Inc. Garden City, NY, Public domain copyright.

---

64   Margery Williams. *The Velveteen Rabbit*. Finely bound by The Chelsea Bindery, New York: George H. Doran Company, 1922.

very own Velveteen Rabbit, which she held in her arms. Her stuffed rabbit was nearly identical to the one Henry had played with as a child, back in Brockett's Point. Bonnie entered the room, and quietly stood and watched from the doorway.

"Generally, by the time you are Real, most of your hair has been loved off, and your eyes drop out and you get loose in the joints and very shabby. But these things don't matter at all, because once you are Real you can't be ugly, except to people who don't understand." Henry noticed Bonnie's warm smile. Then, she raised her eyebrows, and held up the palm of her right hand.

"Okay, children. Time for bed."

They did not want Henry to stop. "No, please mommy. Please. Let us stay up a little longer. Please!" Their mother would not give in—Bonnie insisted upon the children going to bed. It seemed to Henry as though she had something else on her mind. The youngest girl held up her stuffed bunny as if she were showing it to Henry for the first time.

"This is my bunny, Uncle Henry. I talk to him, all the time. And he talks back to me." The little girl's brown eyes shown brightly , as the rabbit's in the story had done, after the boy had finally told him he was Real.

"Oh, really? What does he tell you?"

The girl paused for a few seconds with a puzzled expression on her face. "He says he's happy."

"That's good. I think we all want to be happy. Don't you?"

The toddler looked at her mother with a somewhat puzzled expression on her face, her sad puppy dog look. "Yeah, I kess so."

Bonnie noticed her daughter's puzzled look. "Well, we'll have to finish up this story another night? Okay? It's time for you kids to go to sleep."

"Say good night to Uncle Henry." The children gave their uncle hugs and even kisses, which took Henry by surprise. Then they scrambled off to their beds. Henry got up and left for the living room while Bonnie remained to tuck in her children.

As Henry sat down on the couch he saw that the television had been left on in their small living room. Bonnie surprised Henry as she entered the room from the kitchen.

Another episode of *Star Trek* was playing at low volume on the screen. Henry thought of that night with Katherine, over Spring break, when she had argued so vehemently with him about coming up to Alaska. Henry noticed one more similarity to that night with his mother. Bonnie held a small glass in her hand; a brownish liquid with ice.

Instead of sitting in a chair across from Henry, Bonnie came and sat down beside Henry on the couch. This whole scene suddenly took on a very strange almost déjà vu quality.

"Can I get you something to drink?"

"No. I'm fine. I'm fine. Thanks." The two sat together side by side for a few brief seconds. Bonnie finally broke the awkward silence.

"Hey, thanks for helping me put down the kids."

"Oh, my pleasure. *The Velveteen Rabbit* has always been one of my favorites. Kathy, you know mom, used to read it to us when we were kids. Mom had one of the original copies of the book when it was first published, back in the early twenties I think. Grammy Spaulding used to read it to them when they were all kids. Mom even got me my own bunny; looked almost the same as your little one's rabbit I think we still have it, too. Back in Connecticut, you know, in a box of stuff mom's hung on to."

As Bonnie slid closer to Henry, he noticed the smell of alcohol on her breath. Henry looked at the drink in her right hand, which he had at first thought was iced tea. "Is that bourbon?"

Bonnie raised her eyebrows and smiled. Then she gave Henry a sly look.

"You sure I can't get you something to drink? A beer, wine, or some of this." Bonnie nodded toward the drink in her hand. "You know Henry, there's nothing wrong with a little drinkie poo, every now and then." Then Bonnie thought of Katherine. "As long as you don't overdo it."

"No, thanks. I'm okay." Henry began to feel slightly uncomfortable. This sudden confrontation reminded Henry of the morning Bonnie first greeted him with that sudden embrace and kiss on his mouth. Yet, Henry faltered as he looked into Bonnie's eyes, and he tried to ignore his feelings of attraction, which stirred inside him and were beginning to cloud his judgment.

"So, does Johnny have to travel up to Fairbanks very often?

"No, but they've got him going all over the state, though." Bonnie moved closer, reached toward Henry's face, and then she very carefully removed the tape and gauze pad from his cheek.

"Ouch!" Henry winced and jerked his head to one side.

"Oh, don't be such a big baby."

Bonnie continued to fuss over Henry's wound, as if she were dealing with one of her children. Henry's heart began to flutter.

"He's usually gone a couple of weekends a month. Sometimes, during the week, too. Here, let me put on a new bandage."

Bonnie got up, went down the hall to the bathroom, and shortly returned with a new gauze pad, tape, and a small bottle of iodine. Bonnie again sat beside Henry, even closer this time. Henry felt her thigh push gently against his.

"Hold still." She put a few drops of iodine on the still open wound on Henry's cheek. Two butterfly Band-Aids held the wound closed, but the drops seeped into the sore and hurt. Again Henry winced in pain.

"Ow ... oooh! Ouch!"

"Oh, you're such a big baby. Here, put your finger on the gauze pad." Bonnie taped the dressing in place then she did something else, which made Henry's heart skip a beat. She held her fingers close to his cheek, and then she looked deep into her brother-in-law's eyes.

Henry and Bonnie stared at each other for a few seconds, without speaking. Then, Henry once again began to falter.

"Well, you know. It's ... uh, it's getting late. I guess ... uh, I uh ... I should be going to bed."

Bonnie was not going to give in.

"Oh, come on, stay up a while longer. It's still early. You know sometimes, I ... I get lonely around here. I get tired of just talking with the kids all day long.

"Yeah, I get lonely sometimes, too." Bonnie leaned in toward Henry and then slowly reached her hands up to his shoulders. Bonnie started to gently massage Henry's neck and shoulders.

"Well, you know. There's something we could probably do about that."

Bonnie dropped her gaze toward Henry's chest. Henry took in a deep breath, as he struggled to make sense out of what Bonnie was suggesting they do next. He could feel himself beginning to panic. Thoughts of crazy Aunt Sophie and his Aunt Hazel for some reason, flashed before his eyes.

"Hey, you're really tight aren't you? Here, let me help you relax. Turn around. I'll give you a back rub." Henry slowly turned away from Bonnie, as she continued to massage his shoulders.

Bonnie's touch melted the tension in Henry's neck and shoulders. "Oh, wow ... that ... that really feels good."

However, then Bonnie stepped across a boundary, which even Henry had not imagined. As she moved in closer to Henry, Bonnie's arms slithered slowly around his waist in a gentle embrace. She had stopped massaging his back and now, she simply held him close. Henry could feel the warmth of Bonnie's breasts against his back, as her chest rose and fell with each breath. They sat there on the couch in silence.

Henry glanced toward the kitchen, and he was suddenly jerked wide-awake by what he saw. Johnny stood there in the alcove, his eyes piercing into Henry's like two red-hot daggers.

"Huh. Wait a minute, Bonnie. Hold on, I don't know what's going on here," Henry took in several deep breaths.

"This isn't right." He paused and struggled to regain his composure, or what little of it was still intact. Henry looked again toward the alcove. Johnny was gone. He had only imagined that his brother was standing there.

"I'm gonna go to bed, Bonnie." Henry rose from the couch and quickly moved toward the kitchen, knocking over a chair as he headed for the back porch. Henry caught a glimpse of Bonnie, reaching for her drink on the table. She too, rose to her feet.

"You're right, Henry. I didn't mean to..."

Bonnie's voice stopped him cold. Henry turned, and faced her once again.

"I don't know Bonnie. What's this all about? Are you suggesting we ... I mean my ..., you and Johnny are married! You've got four kids. You two are supposed to be happy? In love with each other, right? What's going on? I really don't understand any of this."

Rather than confront the obvious, Henry's fight or flight mechanism kicked in. Moving quickly through the kitchen, out the back door, and then nearly stumbling down the porch steps, Henry headed for the garage. As he crossed the yard, he heard the porch door swing open behind him, and then bang shut. It was Bonnie, following close on Henry's heels.

"Henry. Just wait a minute. Please. Wait up." Bonnie started down the steps, but in the fading light of dusk, she tripped and fell to the ground. This time she was the one who winced in pain, as she hit the ground.

Turning quickly, Henry saw Bonnie sprawled in the mud about ten feet from where he stood. Quickly, he ran back to her.

"Jeez, Bonnie. What happened? Are you all right?"

Embarrassed, Bonnie slowly sat up and began to massage the muscles on her left leg. She took off the mud-drenched slipper on her left foot. Henry knelt beside her.

"Oh, I'm all right. It's just this damn leg of mine." Henry looked down and noticed that Bonnie's left leg was not only shorter than the other, but it was also much thinner.

"When did that happen?"

"Oh ... when I was just a baby. I was one of those unfortunate kids who came down with Polio before they came out with the vaccine. My leg's never been the same, ever since." She looked up at Henry and laughed. "You mean you've never noticed my limp? I guess I hide it pretty well, at least until I try to go down a few steps too fast."

"Johnny never told me about that."

"Well, there's probably a lot of things he's never told you about." Bonnie smiled, but then a note of seriousness came into her voice. "Do you know what your biggest problem is, Henry?"

A puzzled expression came over Henry's face.

"You haven't grown up yet, have you? You're still a little boy, and you're still seeing the world through rose-colored glasses." By now, Bonnie had regained her composure.

Henry simply gazed into Bonnie's crystal clear dark brown eyes; he was awe-struck by her natural beauty, which was now accentuated by the strange diffused day light of the full moon and setting sun, as it slowly dropped below the horizon to the west.

"Yeah, I think mom feels the same way about me. She says stuff like that all the time. You know, she never did give me her permission to come up here to Alaska."

Henry looked up at the moon. "She remembers hearing about President McKinley's assassination from her mother. Her mother and Pop Spaulding were actually there when it happened in Buffalo, NY. Anyway, she's got this crazy idea in her head that something terrible is going to happen to Johnny and me on McKinley. I think she's just way too … what? Over protective, I guess?"

"Maybe so, but you know Henry your mother loves you dearly. She just doesn't want anything to happen to you. That's all. Or to Johnny either, for that matter."

Henry was beginning to feel a lot calmer now. His heart had slowed to its regular beat. "Well, if you're okay, I think I'm gonna go to bed now, Bonnie. Are you sure you're all right?"

"Of course, I'll be okay." Henry helped Bonnie to her feet, but her bad leg gave in once again and she collapsed into Henry's arms.

"Ouch. Oh, my …. I think I might have sprained it."

"Here, let me help you." Bonnie put her left arm around Henry's neck, as Henry slid his right arm around Bonnie's waist.

"Take me to your room, Henry." Bonnie looked into Henry's eyes. "I don't think I can make it back up these steps." Henry hesitated for a second, then the two of them hobbled toward the garage and went inside.

It was that night when the light bulb first began to glimmer inside Henry's mind. He never forgot that mid-night encounter with his sister-in-law; it had been Henry's wake-up call. Yet it would take Henry the rest of his life before he realized what he had experienced with Bonnie was also the key to the *Pandora's Box* [65] of his own family's skeleton in the closet.

Later that night in the backyard, Bonnie opened the garage door and moved slowly across the backyard toward the house, still walking with a slight limp. Carefully, she made her way up the porch steps, then turned and looked toward the garage with a sad almost puppy dog look in her eyes.

Once inside the house, Bonnie went into the kitchen and fixed herself another drink before going to bed. Above the stove was an old black and white photo showing her two older children holding baby kittens and smiling happily. Below them was her toddler, holding her stuffed Velveteen bunny, but the small girl did not have a happy expression upon her face.

---

65   Wikipedia link: *Pandora's box*, http://en.wikipedia.org/wiki/Pandora's_box.

She had that same sad puppy dog look in her eyes that her mother's expression had shown only a few moments earlier. Like in the story of The Velveteen Rabbit, perhaps the little girl sensed something about her mother and her father that made her sad, the same way that the *Velveteen Rabbit* became sad when he found out that the gardener was coming to take him out behind the hen house, "to be burned with all of the other rubbish," which the doctor believed was contaminated with disease.

As he lay there behind the henhouse the little rabbit "thought of those long sunlit hours in the garden ... how happy they were ... and a great sadness came over him. He seemed to see them all pass before him, each more beautiful than the other, the fairy huts in the flower-bed, the quiet evenings in the wood when he lay in the bracken and the little ants ran over his paws; the wonderful day when he first knew that he was Real. He thought of the Skin Horse, so wise and gentle, and all that he had told him. Of what use was it to be loved and lose one's beauty and become Real ... if it all ended like this? And a tear, a real tear, trickled down his little shabby velvet nose and fell to the ground."[66]

As tears came into her own, Bonnie stared into her toddler's eyes for several seconds. She sighed, and then Bonnie took a slow sip from her drink. She turned and walked down the hallway, and once again entered her bedroom alone.

Henry lay on his plywood bed out in the garage and stared at the ceiling. He remembered as a child his own mother going to bed alone, in Connecticut nearly every night, at least whenever Captain Reggie was away.

Many years later after Henry and his second wife Claire had left Alaska and moved to Arizona, Henry too would lie awake in bed. He would look up at the ceiling and sometimes he would remember how his mother so often went to bed alone, much of the time, even when they lived in Florida, and finally, again after she and Captain Reggie had moved to Alaska, for their final years together.

Had his parents loved one another, or were they simply playing out the scripts from their own respective pasts. It was a sad thought, and one that would haunt Henry for the better part of his life.

---

66   Margery Williams, *The Velveteen Rabbit*. Finely bound by The Chelsea Bindery, New York: George H. Doran Company, 1922.

The author's nieces and nephew.

Photo: Jeff Babcock.

CHAPTER 7

Nightmare

Henry lay in his bunk with his eyes wide open, like little Portia's in the black and white photo above the stove. Sorrow, sadness and confusion filled his mind. Henry stared at the ceiling over his head, slowly breathing in and out trying desperately to fill his lungs with air. It seemed to him as though he was going to pass out from a lack of oxygen. A myriad of thoughts raced across his brain. What had happened to the ideal life he thought his older brother was living? Why did Bonnie seem so unhappy with her life here in Alaska? Were things that bad between her and Johnny? What about their children?

Henry glanced at the window across the room, toward the light of the full moon, which he could see in the strange early morning hours of this land of the midnight sun; a ghostlike ball of light, which cast strange shadows across the wall beside his bed. The wind outside blew a small branch against the window's pane ... Tap, tap, tap. Thoughts raced across Henry's mind like scattered debris flowing beneath the rapids of Eklutna River. Soon the branch's gentle tapping, like a metronome, lulled Henry, into a deep ... sleep.

The wind continued its gentle drone now in darkness. Henry heard a familiar sound, crampon points crunching into an icy slope. Then, in his dream he saw what appeared to be a rope team of two climbers slowly ascending the ice-crusted slopes of what he imagined to be the South Summit of Denali. The two climbers were now climbing along side a very dangerous cornice[67] about fifty yards from the summit. Henry recognized the two climbers; he saw they were Johnny and himself. Johnny was in the lead, as he plodded along the ice, kicking in each step with his cramponed boots.

---

67   Wikipedia link: *Snow Cornice.* http://en.wikipedia.org/wiki/Cornice_%28climbing%29.

One of Johnny's crampons, however, had suddenly balled up with snow and ice, as if a croquet ball was wedged under his right foot. Johnny tripped and fell hard. The large corniced slab of snow and ice, upon which he was standing broke loose beneath his feet. Johnny slid, at first, then he began to tumble down the steep slope head over heels, as Henry remembered doing during their practice climb below the A-frame on Eklutna Glacier.

A sudden YANK, pulled Henry off the ridge too, and together, both men plunged down a frozen gully, smashing into jagged rocks along the way. Finally, Johnny and Henry shot out over the edge of a cliff and plunged through the air into a seemingly bottomless void.

Henry was jolted awake, upright in his bed, gasping for air, awakened by the terrible nightmare of dying on Denali. Beads of sweat glistened across Henry's face as the early morning light shone through the garage window. Henry leaped from his bunk and then stumbled to the window, still gasping for air. As he looked up into a partially clouded sky, a light drizzle of rain began to spatter against the four panes in the window, one of which was cracked.

"Oh my!" Henry was still breathing in and out, desperately trying to catch his breath. "Oh my!"

CHAPTER 8

Despair At The Depot

Below the city of Anchorage, a train was chugging along the coastline of Cook Inlet just below a bluff, which seemed to have broken off or perhaps slid down into the inlet below.

Across the train's two blue and yellow painted engines were the words The Alaska Railroad. The engines were trailed by two blue and yellow passenger cars followed by a long string of flatbed and box cars carrying the produce and freight that had been shipped north to Seward from the lower forty-eight. The sky was partially overcast, as a light rain fell over the city. Some of the destruction from Alaska's 1964 earthquake[68] was still apparent in sections along the bluff, as the train slowly made its way toward the main depot at Ship Creek.

Johnny's VW bus traveled down a steep two-lane road below Fourth Avenue, the city street that slid … along with its string of bars and strip joints … down into Ship Creek, three years earlier. Johnny pulled into a parking lot in front of the Alaska Railroad depot.

Henry was seated in the back of the bus along with his pack, a large duffle bag, and some other miscellaneous gear they would be taking with them on their climb. Bonnie was seated in the front passenger seat; through the rear view mirror, Henry caught a glimpse of the unhappy expression on her face.

"Johnny. Let's make this fast. I'd like to get home before the kids wake up."

"Don't worry, our son's already up. He was watching cartoons in the living room, when I went out the door. I told him to keep an eye out for the baby. Told him we'd be back shortly."

Johnny opened the car door and stepped outside.

---

68   Wikipedia link: 1964 *Alaska Earthquake.* http://en.wiki[edia.org/wiki/
      1964_Alaska earthquake.

Damage to Fourth Avenue, in Anchorage Alaska, caused by the Good Friday Earthquake of 1964.

Photo: U. S. Geological Survey, Wikimedia Commons, a freely licensed media file repository.

Anchorage, Alaska railroad depot at Ship Creek.

Photo: Reywas92, Copyright granted by GNU Free Documentation License

"Still, I want to get back soon. Okay?"

"Okay, okay, for Chris sake. This won't take that long. Keep your pants on."

Johnny was impatient and he was preoccupied with getting their gear moved to the train depot, and with bidding farewell to his younger brother. Henry and three other members of the MCA team were leaving a few days before the rest of their team, which included Henry, but not his older brother Johnny.

Daniel Sheath, the Alaska Native climber on Johnny's team was waiting in the cab of his truck along with his younger sixteen-year-old sister, who, like Johnny's eldest daughter, was also named Rachel. Hans and Barney stood beside Daniel's trailer, which was filled with gear. Rachel's job was to return Daniel's truck and trailer safely to their home near Earthquake Park, the site where huge tracts of land slid into Cook Inlet, destroying 75 homes three years earlier.

As Henry got out of the Volkswagen, he turned and smiled at Hans and Barney and then gave them a half-hearted wave. Hans merely sneered back in Henry's direction, while Barney leaned into Hans and whispered something into his ear. They both began to laugh out loud.

Daniel and Rachel got out of their vehicle. Daniel shouldered his huge pack, and then he and Rachel made their way to greet Johnny and Henry.

left Aerial view of cleanup in Turnagain area, Anchorage, Alaska, after March 27, 1964 earthquake.

Photo: Photographer's # 349E, Cook Inlet Historical Society, US Army Corps of Engineers. Courtesy of the Anchorage Museum, Rasmuson Collection.

right Alaska Railroad Locomotive pulls into Anchorage depot.

Photo: jkbrooks85, Copyright license under the Creative Commons Attribution 2.0Generic license.

This time Hans whispered something to Barney, gave Henry another smirk, and then he shook his head back and forth. Then, he and Barney turned and both men began to unload Daniel's trailer. Johnny spoke first, as Daniel and Rachel approached the VW.

"Morning Daniel. Hi Rachel."

Daniel gave Johnny and Henry a warm, and enthusiastic smile. "Hey, Johnny." Daniel nodded toward Henry. "Morning Henry. You all set for our big departure?"

"As ready as I'll ever be, I guess."

"Well, I wanted to introduce you to my younger sister, Rachel."

Rachel shook hands with Henry. "Hello, Henry. It's so nice to meet you. Daniel tells us you're going to be a good man to have along on the climb."

"Well, I hope that's true." Henry glanced toward Hans and Barney. "I don't think everybody feels the same way."

Henry was still excited, even though Hans and Barney had already put a damper on things.

"Aww… You're gonna do fine Henry." Daniel remained optimistic.

"You bet. I'm gun ho!" Henry thought how his father would have said something like that … had he been there.

"Well, let's get a move on." Johnny was impatient, due in part to Bonnie's desire to get back to their children.

Johnny and Henry began to unload the VW, while Bonnie remained seated in the front passenger seat with a worried expression still on her face. Johnny slid open the side door on the van, reached inside, and began to shoulder Henry's heavy pack. Daniel and Rachel continued walking toward the depot. Rachel carried her brother's fully loaded daypack and his axe.

"Here. I'll take this. You grab some of the other stuff." Johnny grunted, as he lifted Henry's heavy pack, and then he turned to Bonnie.

"I don't see why you came, if you're going to be in such a hurry to get back to the house."

"Well, I just wanted to see Henry off. After all, you two are going to be gone for nearly the next two months."

Johnny shook his head, and then he took off for the train depot. As Henry reached in to get more gear from the back of the VW, Bonnie turned around and looked him in the eye.

"Henry. I just wanted to say ... uh ... be careful up there." Bonnie's voice was a bit shaky. Neither Bonnie nor Henry had said anything to each other since their encounter two nights before.

"If anything ever happened to you, or to Johnny," she laughed, nervously, "I don't think Katherine would ever forgive me."

Hans and Barney were walking past the VW with heavy loads. Henry noticed Hans make an aside to Barney, as they went by.

"Who dah hell is Katherine?"

Henry again tried to ignore Hans' comment. He looked at Bonnie.

"She wouldn't blame you. If she got mad at anyone, it would probably be Poppa. He's the one who finally said I was going, 'come hell or high water.'" Henry noticed the train pulling into the station.

"I should have made Johnny give up this whole damn thing last fall when he first got the idea in his head."

Henry looked toward the depot and saw Johnny enter the terminal doorway, just as the blue and yellow Alaska Railroad cars rolled to a slow stop, on the other side of the building.

Bonnie looked Henry in the eye, "Listen. You have a good safe trip. Okay? Don't either of you do anything foolhardy."

"We won't."

By now, Hans and Barney were headed back from the terminal. Instead of going inside, as Johnny had done, they had simply dropped their loads outside the depot door. Henry could see Hans was getting ready to say something as he approached.

"Don't Vorry, Bonnie. Vee von't let any ting happen to your baby brudder."

Bonnie smiled at Hans, and then she looked at Henry, with an after thought.

"Come here." Henry moved closer to the passenger window, and then Bonnie reached out and gently removed the tape and gauze pad from Henry's cheek. "There, that's better. You're as good as new. I'll bet you won't even have a scar."

Bonnie looked toward Hans and Barney, who stood directly behind Henry, on either side. "And remember, the last thing these guys need, is some little kid tagging along.

Hans and Barney began to chuckle, and then Hans nodded and said. "You can say dat again Bonnie!"

Bonnie acknowledged Hans's comment with a smile, and then, to Henry's chagrin, she said, "So prove to them all, you're a real man, and not some little east coast wimp. Okay?"

Before Henry could reply, Bonnie leaned forward and kissed Henry on the cheek right over his wound. Hans and Josh broke into hysterics.

Johnny was now headed back toward the VW, and he noticed Bonnie's kiss. Johnny remembered his wife's overly affectionate welcome from the night Henry had first arrived, as a tinge of jealousy caught him off guard.

Meanwhile, Henry stumbled back from the car door, now totally embarrassed by Bonnie's seemingly innocent, yet affectionate gesture. Hans and Barney looked at each other, and could barely contain their laughter.

"There! I've kissed away your boo-boo. Just like the kids. You're all better, now." Bonnie looked at Hans and Barney, then back at Henry.

"So, act your age. Okay?"

Henry was not only totally embarrassed, but speechless.

Hans rose to the occasion, and interjected another of his snide remarks. "Dis is your last chance, Henry. Maybe you'd better get out vile dare is still time." Hans looked at Barney. "I tink maybe you'd better stay home 'with Bonnie and dah kids?"

Hans and Barney laughed uproariously. Henry's cheeks turned a crimson shade of red, as Bonnie too joined in the joke, oblivious to Henry's total chagrin.

Johnny however felt that the laughter and the joke were at his expense. Very quickly the situation had become blown way out of proportion. This incident and the misunderstanding surrounding it would plant the seeds that would later spark a major confrontation between Johnny and Henry when the men got high on the mountain.

Hans and Barney were headed back toward the train, with another load and by the time they passed Johnny their laughter was beginning to subside.

Bonnie was still very much concerned about the climb and not unlike Katherine she was still very worried. "You two come back down safely, all right? The kids and I will keep you in our prayers."

"Thanks, Bonnie."

"You take care of Johnny, too. Okay?"

"Yeah, sure." Henry noticed that worried expression begin to creep back into Bonnie's eyes.

Then a strange thing happened. Henry looked up and he saw Johnny approaching the VW with a distinct look of anger on his face, the very same look he imagined seeing in Johnny's eyes the night Bonnie had made a pass toward Henry while they were sitting on the couch.

"What the hell's going on?"

Bonnie smiled, at first but then quickly saw the underlying intent in Johnny's question. The green-eyed dragon had again been awoken from its sleep, and it was evident that both Johnny and Bonnie had played this game before.

'Oh ... nothing." Bonnie's response was nonchalant, at first, but Johnny continued to glare at his wife.

Then, she countered. "Really! Nothing's been going on."

Henry was startled by Johnny's sudden burst of anger, which only added to his confusion and misunderstanding. Johnny turned his questioning gaze upon Henry.

"What about you? What's so funny?"

"Oh ... uh, nothing? What do you mean? Bonnie ... uh, she just wanted to say goodbye."

Henry found himself becoming embarrassed again, and this time he didn't have a clue why his brother was going into attack mode. Johnny was clearly upset as he continued to lock eyes with Henry. The awkward silence between them seemed to last forever before Johnny finally spoke.

"Come on then! Let's get the rest of the gear to the train."

Henry shouldered a large duffle sack, and then hastily shuffled his way toward the depot. Johnny was close on his heels, as he carried two thirty-pound five-gallon aluminum food containers, one in each arm.

Daniel was just exiting the depot door, as Johnny and Henry approached. Johnny was hesitant, still puzzled over Bonnie and Henry's seemingly affectionate behavior, but he re-directed his attention toward Daniel. Johnny set the two food containers down on the ground, next to Hans and Barney's cache.

"So, you guys will go up on the train this morning, then get off at Colorado later this afternoon. Okay?"

"Colorado? What's Colorado?" Henry too, wanted to forget his anxiety, so he tried to become part of this new discussion between Daniel and Johnny. Johnny, however, was still annoyed with Henry, and not just his question.

"It's the little whistle-stop along the tracks, where you guys will be getting off." Johnny turned his attention back to Daniel.

"The four of you will get off there, and tomorrow you'll start putting in the route for the dog teams up the West Fork of the Chulitna. The rest of us will catch up to you in two, maybe three days, at the most."

By now Daniel had sensed the tension between Johnny and Henry. "Yeah, those dog sleds are sure gonna make your trip a lot quicker than ours." Daniel smiled.

"Grace finishes up at the hospital tomorrow night, so she, Gene and I will start following your trail with the dog teams on Saturday. Vin was able to get that pro musher from Galena. So, my guess is we should be in good shape getting all our stuff to the mountain, hopefully by the end of next week. Got any questions, Dan?"

"Nope. Sounds good to me, Johnny." Daniel looked at Henry and winked. "I'll even keep an eye on ole Henry, here too. Just in case Hans gets outta hand."

Johnny finally cracked a smile, as Daniel made his way back to the trailer to retrieve more gear.

Henry looked at his brother. "Thanks for getting me in on this, Johnny. I know you were sticking out your neck when you asked me to come along." Henry hoped that the tension between he and his brother was beginning to subside.

"Yeah, right." Johnny, however, was still upset. He suddenly grabbed Henry around the waist and picked him up in what Henry thought was going to be another one of his friendly bear hugs, as he had done when he greeted Henry at the airport. However, this bear hug had all the tenderness of a Japanese Sumo wrestler.

"Well, let's hope you don't let any of us down." It seemed to Henry as though Johnny was trying to squeeze the life out of him, as he held Henry up in the air for far too long. A nasty seriousness came into Johnny's voice.

"Do you know what I mean, little brother?"

"Johnny. What're yah doing? I can hardly breathe."

Just then, Hans and Barney came through the depot door on their way back to the trailer. Johnny tossed Henry to the ground as if he was a sack of climbing gear. Henry stumbled backwards, lost his balance, and fell hard onto the icy sidewalk.

Hans and Barney stopped dead in their tracks. They both began to smile and chuckle to themselves, as they saw Henry sprawled out on the ground in front of them. Johnny noticed them, too as he quickly reached down with his right hand to pull Henry back up.

"Sorry, little brother. Uh … Sometimes, I flip back into one my old wrestling moves … uh, from college."

Hans intervened, as if to protect Henry from Johnny.

"Whoa. Easy boys. Let's take it easy. Ve're not even on dah mountain, yet. And you two are already getting into a scuffle?"

Hans frowned facetiously and looked at Johnny. "Dat's not good, Johnny boy. You're going to get little Henry all upset."

Johnny glared at Hans. "Cut the crap, Hans!"

Daniel was returning from the trailer and could tell that all was not well. "Hey. What's going on?"

Johnny looked at Daniel. "Oh, nothing. Nothing." It was Johnny's turn to be totally embarrassed. "Just keep an eye on this guy, okay?"

"Will do, Johnny, will do?" Daniel looked at Hans. "Henry's gonna do just fine."

This time, Johnny was speechless. Johnny again cast another suspicious glare toward Henry, and then he looked at Hans, who still had a smile on his face. After a second or two, he just turned away and headed back toward his VW.

Daniel helped Henry to his feet, as they both exchanged puzzled looks. Both men looked toward Johnny as he walked back toward the VW. Bonnie had watched the scuffle and sat in her seat staring at Henry with a look of concern. A very desolate expression had come back into her eyes, and she reminded Henry of Katherine. Before climbing into the driver's seat, Johnny called out from the car.

"See you guys on Saturday."

Daniel and Henry waved goodbye. Henry saw Hans lean forward and whisper something into Barney's ear, as the two men stood next to Johnny's VW. Once again the two men broke into laughter.

As Johnny drove up the hill toward the early morning lights on 4th Avenue, he and Bonnie appeared to be arguing. The VW turned left, and headed down the road toward Gambell Street. Ahead of them, Henry noticed a dark and ominous looking cloud bank beginning to form over the Chugach Mountains.

CHAPTER 9

A Drinking Town with a Climbing Problem

Daniel and Henry shortly found themselves boarding the Alaska Railroad along with Hans and Barney, as the four men began the first leg of their two-month long journey, an expedition headed inevitably for the upper slopes of Denali with its final destination the summit of North America's highest mountain, 20,320 foot Mt. McKinley.

The train slowly pulled away from the Anchorage depot, and from a bird's eye view, the sky opened up showing the city of Anchorage below as it looked in the summer of 1967. Ship Creek opened its mouth and yawned into the icy waters of Cook Inlet, as off in the distance a small tidal bore[69] (a powerful wave that is caused by the tide) slowly approached the city. The waters of nearby Turnagain Arm has the largest tidal range in United States … at about 30 feet (9.1 m), though there are many other larger tidal ranges globally such as the Bay of Fundy and Ungava at 55.7 feet (17m), and Bristol Channel at 49.2 feet (15m).

As their train moved slowly up into the Matanuska Valley, low-lying rain clouds blocked the view of the nearby Chugach Mountains, and of course, the Alaska Range was nowhere to be seen.

Henry became restless after they got underway, so he decided to move about the train to see if he could come up with a better view of what Mother Nature had to offer. Also, like the airplanes that had brought him north, this was Henry's first official ride on a real train, other than the amusement park rides he and Skipper had traveled upon down in Florida when they were children.

Rain-splotched windows blurred the passing landscapes, so Henry soon found himself standing upon a small platform between two passenger cars staring off into the cloud-ridden landscapes. The train slowly clicked along the tracks beside

---

69   Web link: Alaska.org, http://alaska.org/bore-tides.jsp.

left Aerial view of Anchorage taken in the 1940s looking west to Knik Arm from Merrill Field. Ship Creek is at the far right in the photograph.

Photo: Courtesy of the Anchorage Museum, Rasmuson Collection.

right View of area from space. The Knik Arm Bridge would cross from the city of Anchorage to Point MacKenzie, Alaska, the area to the NW of the city.

Source: http://www.terraprints.com Terra Prints, Inc. Copyright license under the Creative Attribution-Share Alike 2.5 Generic license.

the northern branch of Cook Inlet, called Knik Arm.

As Henry stood there, gazing out into the gloom, Daniel suddenly appeared from behind.

"Well, we're finally on our way. Weather sure doesn't look too hot, though. Yah know the odds are against most folks ever getting a glimpse of the mountain. They say the top's only clear about thirty per cent of the time."

"I wondered why I hadn't seen it, since the night I flew into Anchorage."

Today, one of the major issues of heated debate in Anchorage concerns the building of a bridge[71] across Knik Arm. The bridge would expand the commuter belt for Alaska's largest city by cutting an hour or more, from journeys from the southern part of the Matanuska/Susitna Valley. Cost estimates for the bridge vary wildly; more conservative estimates put the cost as high as $1.5 billion.

The Knik Arm Bridge is also known as one of Alaska's infamous Bridges to Nowhere. But, in 1967 there was little need for such expansion, since the valley's population at the time was around ten thousand, as compared today to a figure nearly ten times that size.

---

70   Wikipedia link: *Knik Arm Bridge*, http://en.wikipedia.org/wiki/Knik_Arm_Bridge.

top left Eklutna Village Cemetery.

Photo: Land Design North, copyright image licensed through Public Domain.

top right Eklutna Spirit Houses, Eklutna, Alaska.

Photo: Visitor 7, taken on 30 June 2007, Wikimedia Commons license under the Creative Commons Attribution-Share Alike 3.0 Unported license

'middle The party returns to Cook's "summit" in July. Merle LaVoy photographs Professor Parker. This picture should be compared with the one on page 227 of Dr. Cook's book, To the Top of Our Continent.'

Photo: Merle LaVoy, scanned with copyright permission from Isabel Driscoll, Belmore Browne's granddaughter.

bottom left View of Alaska Engineering commission Railway train, Wasilla, Alaska. Railroad station is at left and Herning's Place is at right.

Photo: AEC # G1012. Oct. 11, 1918. Courtesy of the Anchorage Museum, Rasmuson Collection.

bottom right View down Main Street, Wasilla, Alaska, looking south across the Alaska Railroad tracks to the road to Knik. Businesses shown include Knik Trading Company and Wasilla Hotel.

Photo: Cook Inlet Historical Society, 1931. Courtesy of the Anchorage Museum at Rasmuson Center, Anchorage.

It was true, Henry had seen no evidence of the Alaska Range, let alone Denali for more than ten days. He was beginning to think the whole thing might have been a figment of his imagination, a dream that he had not yet awoken from.

"Yeah. Most tourists come up here just to see Denali. Yah know what happens. Most of 'em end up going home with a picture post card." Daniel smiled, and then he went back inside the passenger car where Hans and Barney were still stretched out on their seats, taking a snooze.

Henry crossed to the opposite side of the train, and noticed up ahead the road leading up to Eklutna Valley, the area into which Johnny and he … and, of course Daniel and the others had ventured ten days earlier … to practice climbing skills on the glacier below Pitchler's Perch.

As the train rounded the bend up ahead, Henry saw a strange sight—the Russian Orthodox cemetery of Eklutna Village[71] (Mile 26.5 on the Parks Highway), which dated back to 1650, and is the area's oldest continuously inhabited Athabaskan Indian settlement. It reminded Henry of The Haunted Graveyard miniature golf course at the Savin Rock Amusement Park, back in East Haven, Connecticut, which his Poppa had taken them to as kids.

The train slowed down a bit; Henry assumed so passengers could get a look at and take photos of St. Nicholas Church, the oldest standing building in greater Anchorage. As the trained slowly clicked over the rails, Henry noticed a heavy set middle aged man snapping pictures of the colorful Spirit Houses built over the graves of the deceased, a custom that came from the melding of the two cultures, when Russian Orthodox missionaries came to Eklutna in the early 1800s.

Henry felt a cold chill run up and down his spine, as he imagined the ghostly spirits of the buried dead hovering over the graveyard. It was as if these ancient souls were still here, watching over the now small Native Athabaskan population still living in Eklutna Village, a once proud people who were nearly wiped out by the Caucasian influences of the 1918 influenza virus[72] and the onset of alcoholism.

Ten years later, in 1977, Henry would become a grade school teacher at nearby Chugiak Elementary School, and a handful of his young special education students would be some of the children from Eklutna village.

The Alaska Railroad's daily run to Fairbanks rounded the bend veering north and crossed a railroad bridge, which spanned Knik River. Then the train began backtracking its route, just as Captain Cook had done in Turnagain Arm. Now, Henry looked across the mud flats of Knik Arm at low tide toward Eagle

---

71   Wikipedia link: *Eklutna*, http://en.wikipedia.org/wiki/Eklutna.

72   Wikipedia link: *1918 flu pandemic, Mortality*. http://en.wikipedia.org/wiki/Eklutna.

Wasilla came into existence in 1917 with the construction of the Alaska Railroad. The history of Wasilla[74] began with the history of Knik,[75] the first boomtown in the Mat-Su Valley, which by 1915 boasted a population of 500. Knik served the early fur trappers and miners working the gold fields at Cache Creek and Willow Creek, and it was one of the stops along the way for the Iditarod Trail.

In 1912, early pioneer climbers, Belmore Browne[76] and Hershel Parker traveled through Knik toward their historic climb up Denali, which brought Browne to within 150 yards of the South Peak Summit! They were robbed of certain victory by gale force winds of up to 100mph that prevented them from reaching the top, one of mountaineering's most unfortunate failed summit bids.

Both Browne and Parker, members of Dr. Frederick Cook's earlier 1906 expedition had also been very interested in exposing Dr. Cook's fraudulent claim. In 1910, they disproved Cook's hoax by following a map given to them by Ed Barrill, Cook's companion during the suspect climb, and the man who stood on top in Cook's Summit photo. Brown and Parker actually found the site of Cook's 'Fake Peak,'[77] and re-shot their own photo of the 8,000 foot high summit, located thirteen bee-line miles from the true South Peak of Denali, an elevation of 20,320 feet, two-thirds higher than Cook's claimed rock outcropping.

Brad Washburn, Mt. McKinley's foremost expert, returned to the sight of Cook's early explorations[78] on many different occasions from 1955-1995,

trying his best to disprove prolonged attempts to the contrary, by Frederick Cook's daughter who then resided in Talkeetna, Alaska. Helene Cook Vetter, in 1956 had picked up the torch on her father's behalf (along with other family relations), and was joined in her vendetta to exonerate her dear father's reputation.

In 1957 she formed the Dr. Frederick A. Cook Society, with the purpose of winning "official recognition for the scientific and geographic accomplishments" of her father. In 1977, Helene Vetter died, passing the leadership of her father's cause to her daughter, Janet Vetter.

Janet Vetter and the Cook Society scored a major public relations victory in 1983, when they were able to finance a CBS made for TV film entitled *Cook and Peary: The Race to the Pole.*[79] It starred actor Richard Chamberlain, who had recently completed James Clavell's popular 1980 television miniseries, *Shogun*. Still trying to ride his recent wave of popularity, Chamberlain perhaps made an ill-fated career choice (not unlike Dr. Cook) when he decided to portray the misunderstood explorer who, according to scientific proof was not only the first man to reach the summit of Denali, but also the conqueror of the North Pole.

Cook's fraudulent claim to the pole is now established fact, as is Rear Admiral Robert Peary's claim to having reached the vicinity within five miles of its actual location, on April 6, 1909. The controversy over both alleged victories rages on, even today as evidenced by anyone who is willing to log on to *The Dr. Frederick*

Cook Society's internet website,[80] an organization that continues to regularly update its data base with current information, providing evidence in support of Dr. Cook's supposed achievements more than one hundred years ago.

In the case of Dr. Frederick Cook, the past seemed perhaps not to be a goodbye, from not only Henry's perspective, but also from that of The Dr. Frederick Cook Society.

Yet with of the construction of the Alaska Railroad and the laying of the very ties and trestles over which Henry now traveled, the boomtown of Knik had became a ghost town in only a few short years.

The current town-site of Wasilla was established at the intersection of the Knik-Willow mining trail now called Wasilla/Fishhook Road, and the newly constructed Alaska Railroad. Little did Henry know that twelve years later, his first wife Jenny and he would build a house there, in Wasilla, the place that would become the hometown in which Henry, Jenny, and later Claire would raise their four children.

River,   and then he could see the outskirts of Anchorage come into view on the far side. The proposed Knik Arm Bridge would have certainly shortened their trip, but in 1967 the thought had never even entered anyone's mind.

Thirty minutes later Henry's train slowed down again, and he noticed ahead another historical sight, the pioneer, almost rustic looking town of Wasilla.

Ten miles or so beyond Wasilla, Henry's train headed north into the Susitna River Valley basin, and after another forty-five minutes it slowed to one of its two actual whistle-stops along the way. An hour and a half had gone by, since they had passed through Wasilla, when Henry noticed a sign alongside the tracks, which read Talkeetna.

In less than a minute, the large steel wheels from the train's engine, and those on the long string of cars that rolled behind it, came to a gradual stop. As Daniel and Henry stepped down from the train, the conductor stood below to greet them.

"Well, gentlemen. Welcome to the quaint little drinking village, with a climbing problem. We'll be taking about a half hour break here, in Talkeetna."

Daniel was anxious to stretch his legs. "Let's walk down to the Roadhouse and have a cup of tea. What do you say, Henry?"

"Sounds good to me," Henry smiled. "Let's go for it."

---

73   Wikipedia link: Wasilla, Alaska. http://en.wikipedia.org/wiki/Wasilla,_Alaska.

74   Web link: The Frederick A. Cook Society, http://www.cookpolar.org/.

75   Wikipedia link: Bradford Washburn. http://en.wikipedia.org/wiki/Bradford_Washburn.

76   Website link: Belmore Browne. http://www.belmorebrowne.com/biography.html.

As they walked alongside the tracks, they came upon a group of German climbers who were unloading their gear from one of the boxcars. These men spoke in what Henry always thought of as a gruff foreign tongue; its clipped accent and intimidating tone reminded him of Hans. As they passed by these climbers, Daniel told Henry more about this pioneer village, which from all appearances had not changed much since it was established, in 1922.

"Most folks climb Denali from here." Daniel looked up into the sky.

Henry heard a loud buzzing sound and looked up to see a small plane, a Piper Cub flying over their heads.

"No kidding? Aren't we still a long way from the mountain?" Henry had remembered reading something about climbers flying onto the mountain, but he really didn't know all that much about it. Daniel pointed to the plane that was now banking at the far end of town, and preparing to land on a dirt runway.

"The Talkeetna mountain pilots fly climbers up onto the mountain and land 'em at about seven thousand feet on the Kahiltna Glacier.

As Henry and Daniel came to the downtown section of Talkeetna, Henry noticed an old wooden Welcome to Talkeetna'[77] sign posted directly at the head of the town's then dirt covered Main Street. From what Henry saw, it wouldn't have surprised him at all to see John Wayne, or more likely, Belmore Browne suddenly appear before his eyes, as he strolled across the dirt road from Nagley's General Store to his room at the Fairview Inn.

Brad Washburn pioneered the route back in 1951. It's called the West Buttress approach. It's the fastest and easiest way to get to the top. It can be done in two to three weeks, if the weather holds. Some hot shots have even done it in less time than that.

Dr. Bradford Washburn[81] was Mt. McKinley's chief historian, photographer, cartographer, and one of the few remaining pioneer climbers of this famous mountain.

Besides being a renowned explorer, he established and became the Director of the Boston Museum of Science from 1939-1980, and from 1985 until his death, Washburn served as its Honorary Director, a lifetime appointment. He was also a close friend of Belmore Browne,[82] who died in 1954. Sadly, Brad Washburn passed away from cancer at the ripe old age of ninety-seven on January 10, 2007. If ever there existed a dying breed of real pioneer men, Brad Washburn was surely one of the last.

Henry fleetingly imagined encountering a barroom brawl down at the Roadhouse, where Daniel and he hoped to share a cup of tea. Yes, Henry could see

---

77   Web link: *Welcome To Beautiful Downtown Talkeetna.* http://farm1.static.flickr. com/70/186873168_3565bbadf5_z.jpg.

The West Buttress Route pioneered by Bradford Washburn in 1951 is the way most climbers ascend Denali today.

Photo: Bradford Washburn Collection, Courtesy Decaneas Archive, Revere, MA. Image scanned from Wager With The Wind: the Don Sheldon Story by James Greiner, Copyright 1974, Rand McNally & Company.

The old 'Welcome Beautiful Downtown Talkeetna' sign at the head of main street.

Photo: Jeff Babcock, from the family photo collection.

why the conductor had called this place, a quiet little drinking village, with a climbing problem.

Yet even in 1967, the streets of Talkeetna[78] were beginning to show signs of outsiders from the civilized world. Along with its handful of mountain climbers showing up on its main thoroughfare every now and then, much of the activity in Talkeetna during the summer months came from another new breed of Cheechakos, who had recently flown into town from the lower forty-eight called the Alaska tourist. Aerial sightseeing flights over the massive mountain were literally beginning to take off. Today, such adventures are often booked weeks in advance.

Yet an overwhelming fact remained clear to the present day;

---

78   Wikipedia link: *Talkeetna, Alaska.* http://en.wikipedia.org/wiki/Talkeetna,_Alaska.

all such activity to and from the mountain was solely dependent upon the potentially lethal whims of Mother Nature and the horrific storms that blast the upper slopes of the mountain.

Daniel and Henry entered the Roadhouse, and made their way to one of several rustic looking tables, scattered about the large room below it's high vaulted ceiling. A large stone fireplace at the back of the room gave a rustic, yet friendly appeal. Daniel ordered tea from a cute waitress, and then the two men both sat quietly across from one another.

Henry knew that Bonnie wasn't very happy about Johnny being away from home, any longer than he needed to be, so why hadn't he chosen this quicker route up the mountain? Henry too reflected upon his own father's absence from his life during his early childhood years.

"Why didn't we go this way?"

"Well, your brother's a purist. Johnny wanted us to do it from the bottom to the top. You know, the same way the Pioneers did it, back in the beginning."

Daniel scratched his head, and then he smiled. "Well, come to think of it, I guess I feel that way, too. If I'm gonna climb Denali, I'd just as soon do it the same as Harper and the rest of those guys did it, back in 1913."

"'Course, you know Walter Harper was an Alaska Native?"

Henry wanted to impress Daniel with his historical knowledge of the mountain.

"Believe it or not, I sat next to an old Native woman on the plane who actually knew Harper when she was just a child."

"No kidding. Well, actually Harper[79] was only half-Athabaskan. His father was white."

Daniel hesitated a bit, and then he shrugged.

"You know, If I make it to the top, they say I'll be the first Eskimo tah ever get up there."

"Really. Wow! Johnny never told me that. That's really something, Daniel!"

"Oh, I dun no ... I suppose." During the course of the next couple of months, Henry's respect for this humble, strong, and very kind man grew with the passing of each day, and Henry came to realize what a great asset Daniel Sheath would become, not only to his brother Johnny, but also to Henry, himself.

By the time Daniel and Henry had returned to the train, the conductor was standing outside, ready to fulfill that time-honored tradition that conductors have done since the Railroads of the east met with those of the west at Promontory Summit, Utah, in 1869 becoming the first transcontinental railroad in North America.

---

79   Wikipedia link: *Walter Harper*. http://en.wikipedia.org/wiki/Walter_Harper.

President Warren Harding on Board Presidential train in Talkeetna, Alaska. S&C. Hoover, Sec. Wallace, Sec. Work, and Mrs. Harding included in Presidential Party. 1923. Harding became the first president to visit Alaska. He hoped that with completion of the Alaska Railroad, WWI veterans would return to their home territory and any impoverished workers in the lower states could come to Alaska and make or find their own employment. On July 15, 1923, President Harding drove the golden spike on the north side of the steel Mears Memorial Bridge, that completed the Alaska Railroad. President Harding died in the middle of a conversation with his wife at 7:35 PM on August 2, 1923 in San Francisco, from what was concluded a heart attack. Harding and John F. Kennedy are the only two presidents to have predeceased their fathers. Harding's term of office was the shortest of any 20th century president.

Photo: Unknown, Library of Congress, Creative Commons Attribution 3.0 License.

Like Dr. Cook, Belmore Browne, and Bradford Washburn, here was another breed of pioneer, performing one of the key vestiges of a job his father had done before him. Even after U. S. President Warren G. Harding[80] had driven the golden spike that completed the Alaska railroad on July 15, 1923 the conductor on his train performed the same task, which Henry was about to witness for the first time. The man in front of Daniel and Henry looked down at his pocket watch.

"Well, gentlemen. You're right on time. I said we'd be here in Talkeetna, for about a half hour, and by golly, it's been exactly twenty-nine minutes since you two stepped down from these steps."

---

80   Web link: *Golden Spike Driven*, July 15, 1923. http://www.alaskarails.org/golden-spike/ spike.html.

The conductor pointed to the two-step corrugated iron steps that gave Henry and Daniel entry to their coach.

"Climb aboard, gentlemen, the engineer's just about ready to give her the ole full steam ahead."

Henry looked back over his shoulder as the middle-aged man with a twinkle in his eye waved an open palm toward the front of the train, and then Henry heard the conductor shout aloud that familiar time-honored phrase.

"All aboard! All aboard!"

Once the train was again underway, Henry tried to settle in for a little snooze. Daniel was already counting mountain goats in his mind a few seats in front of Hans and Barney, who were now occupying themselves by playing a game of cards.

"Come on Henry. Let's see if you're any better at cards, than you are at climbing?"

"No thanks, Hans. I'm not much for cards." The last thing Henry wanted to do was to get involved in a game of cards with Hans and Barney. They had become increasingly adept at robbing Henry of his last shreds of self-confidence, and Henry certainly wanted to avoid any further erosion of self-esteem; it was something he simply could not afford at this stage of the game.

Hans smiled at Barney. "Hah. Yah. Just a good little momma's boy. Right?"

Henry nodded and made a feeble attempt, at defending himself. "Sure, Hans. That's right. My mother and I never played anything more risqué than Old Maid. Well, once she tried to get me to play Crazy Eights, but that was just plain too scary for me."

They 'snickered and guffawed,' as Henry's father would have said, 'like a couple of wild hyenas,' then Henry continued down the aisle and again retreated to his small platform between the two cars.

As the train rocked from side to side, Henry noticed they were traveling alongside the gushing rapids of the Chulitna River, reminiscent of those frigid waters he had encountered while crossing the Eklutna.

The train slowly began to climb up a steep and mountainous terrain. A thick blanket of snow now covered the hills on either side of the tracks. Yet, the towering peaks of the Alaska Range remained hidden beneath the clouds. Surely, Henry thought to himself, they would sooner or later get to see their Castle in the Clouds.

Or, would they end spending the bulk of their time on Denali wandering around in a blanket of fog, as Henry remembered seeing his Aunt Sophie, Aunt Hazel, and even his own mother Katherine do from time to time, stumbling about the house in an alcoholic stupor.

Finally, a small-dilapidated Lincoln Log cabin appeared out of nowhere. Henry could see the small rustic structure about one hundred yards ahead, and set back from the tracks in a small cluster of Alaska spruce. From his small perch between the cars, Henry noticed another sign up ahead, similar to but even more weathered than the old wooden Talkeetna sign he and Daniel had walked past.

The words however were barely legible, perhaps this was the original Railroad sign posted here alongside this desolate whistle stop some forty years earlier. It's faded white-stenciled letters, on an equally pale blue metal background read Colorado.

Slowly, the blue and yellow string of passenger and boxcars came to an un-scheduled stop. Daniel, Henry, Hans, and Barney had come to the end of their train ride, and the beginning of their assault on Denali.

CHAPTER 10

The Train

By now fat snowflakes fell from a darkened sky overhead, turning the sleeve of Henry's green cotton parka, the one Johnny had bought him from the Army/Navy store on 4th Avenue in downtown Anchorage, into a thin layer of white.

The side door of the baggage car slid open, and above Daniel and Henry stood the conductor, Barney and of course, Hans. Like the German climbers in Talkeetna, Hans and Barney began handing down the team's collective gear: backpacks, food containers, sleds and other miscellaneous items, which they would need for their trip up the West Fork of the Chulitna River.

"You know, in all my years on this run, I've seen a lot of climbers get off to climb Denali, but that was either in Talkeetna or up at the park. No one's ever gotten off here before! You sure you fellows know where you're going? Whose route are you following, again?"

"Belmore Browne," replied Daniel. "His team came through this way, in 1912, 'bout sixty-five years ago."

"Sixty-five years ago?"

"Ah, course, they were using dog teams, back then. Not the train. Your railroad crews didn't finish putting in the bridges and laying all the track until ten years later, right?

The conductor brought his hand up to his chin, and then he said, "Yah … That's 'bout right. Come to think of it."

Hans and Barney jumped down from the boxcar.

"Who cares about dah past? Let's get dis stuff moved to dat cabin up dare avay from dah tracks. Dah last ting I want is to get run over by anudder train."

Hans and Barney shouldered their packs and headed toward the snow-covered remains of the ramshackle log depot. Daniel and Henry joined them and

Alaska Railroad Baggage car with gear for the MCA team loaded on the old original Alaska Railroad cargo wagons.

Photo: Gayle Nienhueser

began ferrying gear up to their first cache,[81] which Hans and Barney had begun to establish along side the abandoned cabin that was now completely boarded up, windows and all.

As the train lurched forward, the conductor waved from the open doorway of the boxcar.

"Good luck, gentlemen." The conductor shook his head, and the he cupped his hands over his mouth.

"You're going to need it. You've got about fifty miles to go, before you even get to the mountain, let alone climb it."

Henry waved back, as Daniel, Hans and Barney began to set up their two tents. Henry looked at the gray sky overhead. The snowflakes had become smaller now, and it appeared as though they were in for a good snowfall.

That night the four men had their first meal on the trail, a hearty moose sausage stew made from a can of Corned Beef, several slices of moose sausage, a half a stick of margarine, a bag full of white rice, two packages of Vegetable Beef Lipton Soup, and several large scoops of fresh snow. All of these items simmered slowly in a large three-quart pressure cooker pot.[82] Hot tea and some homemade brownies that Daniel's sister Rachel had made in celebration of their departure topped off the meal.

By now the snowfall had tapered off and the crackling campfire before the men shot sparks upward into the dark sky over their heads. Tomorrow the laborious task of putting in a trail for the dog teams would begin. In two or possibly three days Johnny and the remaining climbers … Gene and Grace … and the two dog teams manned by Grace's husband, Vin and Billy McAlpine, the Native musher from Galena would be hopefully catching up to them.

"Well, gentlemen. I don't know about the rest of you. We all have a big day ahead of us tomorrow. I'm gonna call it a night, and try to get some sleep." Daniel

---

81   Definition: Associated with the wilderness, a *cache*, as in a food or equipment, is a safe place to store such items while traveling in the backcountry. http://www.wildernesscache.com/

82   Pressure Cooker Pot. http://www.wisementrading.com/campcookware/pressurecooker.htm
     Note: Though not identical, this contemporary Pressure Cooker is very similar to the model used by the MCA team in 1967.

checked the small metal thermometer, which he had attached to his and Henry's tent zipper.

"The temperature's not all that bad. 18 degrees F. above zero."

When the team awoke the next morning, Daniel's thermometer registered a chilly 10 degrees F. below zero. After a breakfast of hot cereal with raisins, cocoa, and tea the men headed down to the Chulitna River on snowshoes, while dragging small sleds behind them.

Belmore Browne's team had mistakenly traveled up a river basin a few miles below the West Fork of the Chultina called Ohio Creek, which unfortunately brought them into what appeared to be a dead end, a box canyon with no passage to the North side of the Alaska Range. After a fairly treacherous climb (with their sleds and dogs) up a steep couloir, they were able to cross over and drop down into the West Fork of the Chulitna. Henry's brother wanted to follow Browne's route, but chose not to make the same mistake Browne's team had made back in 1912 by traveling up Ohio Creek.

They would cross through Anderson Pass, named after Pete Anderson, one of the two early pioneers who had climbed to the top of the North Peak in 1910. Belmore Browne had taken his team along this route in 1912, and now Johnny Locke would be doing the same with his Mountaineering Club of Alaska (MCA) team.

In the spring of 1967, the MCA group would join their ranks at the tail end of those glory days of the pioneer climbs on Denali, and their story, like many before them, would be added to the annals of Denali mountaineering legend; their adventure marked by the profound tragedy that lay ahead, had finally begun to play itself out.

If Henry only knew then what he was getting himself into, he would have taken his mother's advice and stayed home that summer and worked as a Lifeguard at the Lamphier's Cove beach. Instead, Henry was embarking upon the worst nightmare of his life.

As the men plodded their way down through the deep snow, while dragging their small sleds behind them, one thought kept flashing itself repeatedly, inside Henry's head.

"You'll probably gonna get yourself kilt, too. You know, Denali takes one or two every now and then." It was the old Native woman's voice from the plane.

During the next few days, the lead team encountered deep snow, open water, and in two different locations along the way, they were forced to cross seemingly tenuous bridges of snow and ice, which spanned the frigid waters of the Chultina River. Henry thought of the children's story of *Three Billy Goats Gruff*, and imagined the imminent danger of some grizzled troll reaching up from beneath each bridge and dragging him down into the icy waters below. With each safe crossing

Henry breathed a sigh of relief having crossed to the other side without harm, as the men relayed gear back and forth over the river.

At night they camped around blazing wood fires, amidst patches of spruce and alders alongside the river's edge. Nevertheless, Saturday came and went, and there was still no sign of Johnny and the others, or the dog teams. The men's anxiety heightened with each passing day and Hans became less and less agreeable to be around, which didn't surprise Henry. In fact, Hans was even beginning to get on Daniel's nerves.

"This is not right, Daniel. Johnny and de udders should have caught up vith us by now. Somethin's got tah be wrong."

"Let's give it another day, Hans. If no one shows by tomorrow night, you and Barney can head back and check things out. Henry and I will keep pushing through the trail."

"Vell, somethin' better give. Ver running low on food, in case you hadn't noticed. Vee can't keep push in on vithout any food!" Hans rose to his feet and tossed a small log onto the fire, which again caused sparks to fly up into the dark sky. Henry looked to Daniel for some sign of relief, but his eyes too showed only concern.

"Well, Henry. Guess we should call it a night too? All we can do is wait." Then he said it, and it took Henry by surprise.

"Time will tell."

Somehow, hearing his father's words spoken by Daniel made Henry feel better, but deep down inside, he too, like Hans and even Barney, felt something was terribly wrong.

≈

A large seemingly abandoned hotel[83] (Mile 188.5 on Parks Highway) came into view from high overhead as a bald eagle,[84] the iconic symbol of freedom for the USA, swayed gently in the wind gliding back and forth from one side of the valley to the other. To the eagle the white dome-like structure below seemed totally out of place in the otherwise pristine wilderness setting.

The bird gazed down upon the bizarre looking structure, a giant four-story-high white igloo, which was located just three miles north of the MCA team's starting point, the Colorado whistle-stop.

---

83   Cantwell, Alaska. *Giant Igloo-Shaped Building*. http://www.roadsideamerica.com/tip/4 Note: This building was constructed sometime after completion of the Parks Highway in 1971, and therefore offers an event that occurred during the author's second Denali climb in 1977.

84   Wikipedia link: *Bald Eagle*. http://en.wikipedia.org/wiki/Bald_Eagle.

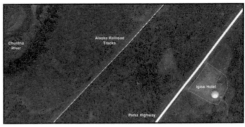

In Cantwell, Alaska along the George Parks Highway this abandoned four-story igloo-shaped hotel has become a roadside attraction. It was from here that the MCA dog teams began their ill-fated journey.

Photo: Garnet Roehm

This aerial photograph shows the close proximity of the Igloo Hotel at mile 188.5 on the Parks Highway to the Alaska Railroad tracks.

Photo: Website wikimapia: http://wikimapia.org/12502583/Igloo-City-Abandoned-Igloo-Hotel) On page 146 of manuscript.

The huge building looked as though it had been constructed by some misguided set designer from the 1960 wilderness epic film entitled *The Savage Innocents*,[85] a remake of Robert Flaherty's 1922 classic *Nanook of the North*, which starred a young and handsome looking Anthony Quinn.

Gliding down from above, the eagle noticed something in the parking lot that was new and different about this outstanding landmark. Two dogsled teams were preparing to cross the Parks highway.

The barking dogs and their manned dogsleds crossed the highway then moved quickly over a small span of tundra[86] on the far side of the road. Within minutes the two teams were approaching the tracks. The sleds turned south, and were seen to move quickly down the three-mile stretch of railroad tracks, headed for the small whistle stop of Colorado.

Johnny, Grace, and Gene had already removed their snowshoes, and were now seen walking

In the spring of 1967, the building was one of the few places along the Parks Highway where the railroad tracks nearly paralleled the newly completed Alaska wilderness road. The Parks Highway allowed tourists to travel by car from Anchorage, not only up to Mt. McKinley National Park, but also another 121 miles north to Fairbanks.

The Igloo was now boarded up, the gas pumps were gone, and a few of the dormer windows had begun to collapse inward. The structure, it was said, could be seen from 30,000 feet by passing planes.

---

85   Wikipedia link: *The Savage Innocents*. http://en.wikipedia.org/wiki/The_Savage_Innocents .

86   Wikipedia link: *Tundra*. http://en.wikipedia.org/wiki/Tundra.

down the tracks in their climbing boots, as Vin (Grace's husband) pulled his dogsled alongside them; Vin was a short, stout, and energetic looking middle-aged man (a *James Cagney* type). Billy McAlpine, the native musher from Galena passed by Vin's sled and took the lead, as he and his dog team continued down the tracks.

"McAlpine and I will push on up the valley and find Daniel and the others. We'll unload and be back to get you, Gene, and Grace, probably sometime late this afternoon."

"Okay, Vin. We'll plan on seeing you two sometime, later. Maybe join you for a late lunch." Johnny smiled. "Or an early dinner."

Grace Jensen Hoeman,[87] an attractive looking woman in her mid forties, spoke with what appeared to be a thick Swiss/Austrian accent. Her parents, however, had moved to the states from Czechoslovakia prior to WWII, and took up residence in Silver Beach, Washington, where Grace was born in 1921.

Grace was educated in Holland and Germany, receiving medical degrees from the University of Berlin (M.B. 1944) and the University of Utrecht (M.D., 1948). Grace returned to the U. S. in 1950 and worked as a physician in upstate New York before earning a master's degree in public health from Yale University in 1953. She then taught preventive medicine before entering a residency (1960-1962) and assistant professorship (1962-1965) in anesthesiology at Syracuse Hospital Upstate Medical Center. She came to Anchorage, Alaska, in 1965, where she met and married Vin Hoeman.

Grace had always been an avid outdoors person, and it was here in the mountains that she met her future husband, who then served as the president of the Mountaineering Club of Alaska.

Vin first came to Alaska in 1960 while serving in the U. S. Army at Fort Richardson and Fort Greely. He then worked for the Arctic Health Research

Grace Jensen Hoeman was the sole female on the MCA team, and she was also the team's doctor.

Photo: Gayle Nienhueser, Copyright Courtesy of Gayle

87   Website link: *Grace (1921-1971) and John Vincent Hoeman (1936-1969)*, http://www. consortiumlibrary.org/archives/CollectionsList/CollectionDescriptions/hmc-0887cd.html.

Center in Anchorage and the Smithsonian Institution (Pacific Project). Vin started mountain climbing in 1949, scaled the highest points in all 50 states, and reached both summits of Mt. McKinley in 1963. Vin also did extensive research on climbing in Alaska and the Yukon Territory.

Grace was a great asset to Johnny as the team's doctor, as well as being a free meal ticket for her adventurer husband who often traveled to the Himalaya on various climbing expeditions.

"Take it easy, darling, and remember. No svimming in dah river."

Vin smiled, gave Grace a peck on the cheek, and mushed his team down the tracks. Billy McAlpine, the pro musher from Galena, was about fifty yards in front of Vin.

From high above, the three-mile stretch of tracks could be seen to span ahead to the Colorado whistle stop. Continuing west from this eagle-eyed perspective an unexpected surprise came into view. A mile below Colorado, a locomotive was seen chugging along up the tracks, pulling a long string of cars behind it. The train reached Colorado and clicked past its dilapidated log cabin depot like a ticking clock, as it barreled full steam ahead up the rails.

Billy McAlpine, the large muscular native man controlled the lead sled, as it sped down the tracks. Vin trailed close behind Billy. To their dismay, the two mushers entered a narrow section of track, with *ten-foot snow walls* on either side. The echo of barking dogs and the rough scraping of sled runners over the trestles foreshadowed the approaching disaster.

Man standing beside Alaska Railroad tracks in 30 foot deep trench of snow in Alaska, with snow shed in distance. 1920s.

Photo: John Urban, Courtesy of Anchorage Museum at Rasmuson Center.

Billy glanced back, over his shoulder.

"Vin! Vin! I sure hope we get outta here fast. I wouldn't want tah run into a train coming the other way."

As the train closed in on the mushers, the engineer chatted with his assistant, then turned and saw McAlpine's team approaching dead ahead in the middle of the tracks.

The engineer quickly yanked a cord, blasting the train's whistle in rapid succession, as he pulled a lever backwards in an attempt to slow down the onrushing train.

Hearing the whistle, the very same Conductor from Daniel and Henry's train ride a few days before, was seen leaning out from a platform between two cars and he too saw the dog teams in the bend ahead.

A close-up of Johnny's face came into view. After the first whistle blast, he turned and looked at Grace. Again, they heard in the distance, this unexpected shrill sound cutting into the cold desolate silence and they felt the screeching of metal on the surface of the tracks over which they stood.

Johnny, Grace, and Gene quickly lowered their packs to the ground, unhooked from their sleds and began to run down the tracks.

McAlpine froze in terror, as the train barreled down the tracks headed directly for him. A horror-stricken expression fell across McAlpine's face; the same terror-stricken gaze was seen in the eyes of the Engineer, his assistant, and the Conductor.

The engineer pulled hard upon the lever and tried frantically to stop the train, as the moose catcher crunched into McAlpine's dogs and sled. McAlpine leaped from his sled and smashed into the wall of snow at his right.

The dogs yelped and cried as the train dragged them alongside the tracks. The screeching wheels of the train finally came to a stop, as clouds of steam fill the air. Two dogs lay near the tracks wincing in pain, as they attempted to stand up. One dog hobbled around in circles; another lay dead in the blood stained snow, mangled and unrecognizable.

Johnny and the Conductor continued to run down the tracks toward the accident, from opposite directions.

The Conductor stopped running when he saw McAlpine sitting near his demolished sled, holding a dog in his lap. The large muscular man appeared to be crying.

Johnny passed by Vin's sled as he headed toward the terrible accident. Jogging close behind Johnny, Grace finally reached Vin, who had somehow managed to keep his sled and dogs out of harm's way. Grace leaned over at the waist, trying to catch her breath. She rose up into her husband's embrace still gasping for air.

From high overhead the accident below continued to play itself out amidst the confusion, the sadness, and the despair.

Hans' fears had become realized. An unforeseen accident with the Alaska Railroad's daily run to Fairbanks was the reason for their delayed rendezvous with the others. None of the men had even imagined the disastrous scene that had sadly unfolded at the onset of their journey.

However, the train accident was only the beginning. The terror that Henry and the others would eventually feel, and the sheer brutality of what they would experience on the upper slopes of Denali would make them nearly forget that the train accident had ever happened. Like Katherine's and the old Native woman's prophetic warnings, the train disaster was merely another imminent foreshadow of what lay ahead for Henry, his brother Johnny, and the rest of the MCA team.

CHAPTER 11

Ghost Riders In The Sky

A frozen campsite of three pyramid tents and one smaller tent came into view below Anderson Pass, the key cross over gateway to the north side of the Alaska Range. Named after Pete Anderson, one of the two Sourdoughs from the 1910 Expedition who actually made it to the summit of the North Peak, the pass lay fifteen miles east of Denali, which now glistened in the setting sun. A sickly grayish-yellow mass of storm clouds, however, approached Anderson Pass and the tiny campsite of the MCA team, which was now seen from high overhead.

All seven climbers of Johnny's team were seated outside their tents eating dinner. Two camp stoves were simmering beneath pots of boiling water.

Henry was wondering if their trip plans had changed much since the horrific occurrence of the train accident.

"Are we still gonna be able to complete the traverse?"

Johnny's original plan was to use dog teams all the way to the base of the mountain, following pretty much the same route that Belmore Browne had done in 1912. This endeavor was supposed to take them about a week to accomplish.

"Well, the train accident put us behind at least two weeks." Johnny's estimate was about right, yet the team still had to make their way across the tundra to the Wonder Lake Ranger Station.

Hans, however, was less optimistic about the future of their climb.

"Yah. Dah last ting we needed was to have dah dog teams turn back on us now."

Everyone could tell that Hans was just starting to warm up. By now, his skepticism had turned to serious doubt. Worrying about Henry had become the least of his worries.

"Well, with three of Billy's dogs dead and his sled demolished, there really wasn't much choice." Daniel offered his very straightforward opinion of the tragedy that had befallen their team, ten days earlier.

'As the riders loped on by him he heard one call his name

If you want to save your soul from Hell
a-riding on our range

Then cowboy change your ways today
or with us you will ride

Trying to catch the Devil's herd,
across these endless skies.'[88]

---

88 Answers.com, WikiAnswers. *Ghost Riders in the Sky.* http://wiki.answers.com/Q/Who_
recorded_Ghost_Riders_in_the_Sky.

Anderson Pass was named after Pete Anderson, the big Swede, a miner from the Kantishna area. It was Pete and Billy Taylor that went all the way to the top of Denali's North Peak in April of 1910.

Photo: Unknown, cropping of original photo, courtesy Historical Photograph Collection, University of Alaska Archives, Fairbanks.

Belmore Browne's team approaches 'Anderson Pass' (left of center) in the distance.

Photo: Merle LaVoy, image scanned from Belmore Browne's The Conquest of Mount McKinley, 1913, with copyright permission from Isabel Driscoll, Belmore Browne's granddaughter.

The MCA team camped on the West Fork Glacier of the Chulitna River. The snow walls helped to protect the tents from severe winds that funneled through Anderson Pass.

Photo: Jeff Babcock.

"Yah, but the deal vuz to get all of our gear to dah base of the mountain! From vhut I could see, day only made it about five miles. Its gonna take us anudder month to get to dah mountain!"

Johnny interrupted, attempting to quell Hans's tempest.

"Look Hans, I still think we'll be okay. It might be a little tight up top, with food. But, if the weather holds, we should be able to make the summit, then get down safely to a lower altitude and come back out to Wonder Lake, instead of doing the traverse."

Hans grumbled as he rose from the campfire.

"And I suppose we still got tah check in vith Dah Park on dis side of the mountain, don't we?

"Yeah. There's a Park Ranger at Wonder Lake,[89] some fellow named Wayne Merry. He's expecting us; something to do with Brad Washburn, I think."

"Vell. If you vant my opinion, I tink vee should keep right on going up dah Muldrow once vee drop down through Anderson Pass."

Hans looked up toward the cloud-streaked sky. "I'm going to hit dah sack. Doze clouds don't look good to me, at all. I tink ve're gonna be in for some bad veather tonight."

"That's the best idea you've had in a long time, Hans. I'm going to follow right behind you, and I think you're right. Those clouds don't look good at all."

Johnny and Hans headed for their respective tents, to join the others who had already begun to crawl inside.

"Make sure your guy lines are tight." Johnny yelled to the others. Henry saw his brother look toward the angry sky. Johnny gazed toward Henry and Daniel.

"I agree with Hans. I'll bet were going to be in for some big winds tonight."

Daniel and Henry remained outside for a few minutes longer. Above their camp, the moan from the winds grew louder, as the approaching storm clouds continued to streak through Anderson Pass, like ghostly spirits from the past.

Henry thought about Belmore Browne and his good friend Herschel Parker, and of course Pete Anderson and the rest of his Sourdough team. They were all now dead and gone, part of Denali's colorful past. Henry looked at the strange clouds that seemed to splash across the dark sky overhead, funneling their way through Anderson Pass.

"Do you believe in ghosts, Daniel?"

"What do you mean ghosts?"

---

89   Web link: *Wonder Lake Photos*. http://www.wildnatureimages.com/DNP%20Wonder%20
Lake%201.htm.

"Oh you know. When someone dies, do you think their spirit or whatever's left behind, sometimes still remains here on earth, or maybe comes back to visit some place they really liked when they were alive."

"Well, my great grandmother surely believed in the spirit world. In the Inuit culture[90] humans have souls that can be lost or stolen. When that happens a person could become very ill, or even go mad. According to our traditions, humans are made up of three parts: a body, a name, and a soul. When a person dies, Eskimos believe only the body dies; the spirit and the name can continue living in a new body. The names of dead relatives are sometimes given to babies. I was named after my great uncle."

"What about those spirits and names that are not given to anyone?" Do their spirits still roam about?"

"Well, I guess maybe so. I suppose its possible."

"Now that would be something, wouldn't it? Maybe there really is an after-life, in which each of us has the chance to re-visit our favorite old stomping grounds from the past? One of the spots I would go back to would be the beach at Lamphier's Cove, where I grew up as a kid."

Daniel smiled.

Then a strange thing happened. Henry looked up toward the pass behind Daniel, and he saw something? Henry rubbed his eyes, and looked again. The shadowy figure of a man seemed to be walking through Anderson Pass, high above their desolate and lonely camp. This shadowy figure seemed to disappear into the clouds above, as he apparently had crossed to the other side of the pass.

"Who's that?" Henry pointed toward the pass, hoping that Daniel too would see what Henry thought he had just seen.

"Who's what?" Daniel looked toward where Henry was pointing.

"I thought I just saw someone, up there, in the clouds, near the pass. Did one of our guys hike up there?"

"Nope. Don't think so. Everyone's down here, they've all gone to bed. Daniel gazed again, up toward the clouds and snow funneling through Anderson Pass. "I don't see anything up there. Come on Henry, the weather's taking a turn for the worse. Let's call it a night.

"Huh? I could have sworn I just saw someone up there cross to the other side of the pass."

Daniel smiled. "Maybe it was the ghost of Pete Anderson."

As the wind continued to drone its eerie moan, echoing throughout the near-by peaks and hills, Henry smiled and said, "Damn, this whole trip is starting

---

90   Web link: *The Inuit. The Spirits.* http://firstpeoplesofcanada.com/fp_groups/fp_inuit5.html.

to turn into one scary ghost story; the train accident, dead sled dogs, and now pioneer ghosts from the past."

"I wonder how many other pioneers spirits we're going to run into, up here?"

Daniel laughed, and then he and Henry both retired to the shelter of their small orange pyramid tents, while the building storm continued to fume over their heads. Soon they were in the midst of their first major mountain tempest.

Later that night Henry awoke to the howling blasts of wind against the walls of his, Johnny, and Grace's tent. He whispered to his brother.

"Johnny, psst. Are you awake."

Johnny smiled and opened his eyes.

"Jeez, Johnny. Does it get much worse then this? Up on top?"

Johnny chuckled to himself. "Ha. This is nothing more than a gentle breeze compared to what we might get up on top." Then he rolled over.

Henry looked at Johnny's backside with a worried expression. "What do you mean?"

"Come on, Henry. Go back to sleep. We've got a hard day ahead of us tomorrow."

Henry closed his eyes and soon his thoughts took him to the water's edge on the beach at Lamphier's Cove. He saw himself building a small mountain of sand with his little red shovel and bucket.

Bunny was at his side. Little Henry and his very own *Velveteen Rabbit* had conquered many mountains in the past. Henry remembered and felt the good feel-

The author as a child playing on the beaches of Lamphier's Cove in Brockett's Point, Connecticut.

Photo: the author's mother, courtesy of the family's collection.

ings in his dream from those happier times with a younger looking and happier Katherine, his other brother Skipper, and of course, Johnny, who was just then burying Skipper in the sand up to his head.

"Come on Henry, it's time to go home. Your father flies in from Miami tonight, and you know how he likes to have everything ship shape back at the house. You boys will need to straighten up your rooms."

Yet, a nagging sense of fear kept prodding into the inner workings of Henry's mind, blasting away these fond memories from his past, as the pulsating force of the locomotive winds pummeled against the sides of their frail pyramid tent.

The icy wind continued to moan above their camp, as if the voices from the dead spirits of Denali's past were now beckoning a warning to Henry and the others, as the tempest funneled through Anderson Pass and swept across the frozen surface of the West Fork glacier.

CHAPTER 12

A Gut Feeling

T he sound of falling rain and the occasional rumble of distant thunder
echoed across the tundra. Drifting down through clouded skies, an
opening below showed a fairly large and picturesque lake situated within
a broad expanse of the Alaska wilderness.

The tundra[91] was an area where the tree growth was hindered by low temperatures and short growing seasons. The term tundra came from Kildin Sami, (the
Russian language) meaning an uplands, tundra, treeless mountain tract'. In tundra, the vegetation was composed of dwarf shrubs, sedges and grasses, mosses,
and lichens. Scattered trees grew in some tundra. The ecotone (or ecological
boundary region) between the tundra and the forest was known as the tree line
or timberline. The remote body of water seen below, surrounded by tundra, was
called Wonder Lake.

Panning down across this desolate terrain the Wonder Lake campground
came into view, one of the most distant camping areas in Denali National Park,
aside from those established by climbers on the glaciers and mountains themselves. Wonder Lake was situated at the end of an eighty-mile long dirt road leading into the park. Though the ground was still covered with a thin layer of snow,
Denali Park Ranger, Wayne Merry and his wife were now in the process of getting the campground ready for the upcoming hoards of summer tourists.

Johnny, Henry, and Daniel were seen leaving their campsite of three orange
pyramid tents, perched about a mile or so above the lake. It was still cloudy,
and a slight drizzle of slush and rain continued to fall from the sky above. They
were headed up a dirt road for an evening visit with Wayne and his wife at their
Ranger cabin. The three men arrived at their destination and were greeted by

Mt. McKinley and the Alaska Range, as seen from From Wonder Lake.

Photo: National Photo & News Service, Eugene Omar Goldbeck, Library of Congress Prints and Photographs Division, No known restrictions on publication.

an attractive young woman, who opened the door. Johnny, Daniel, and Henry entered the small cabin.

Our view changed and this time it took us through an open window, which faced the lake. From this perspective it was seen that this structure was the Real McCoy … the Lincoln Log style cabin of Henry's childhood fantasies. Entering through the window, Henry and Johnny were seen seated at the kitchen table of Wayne's two-room cabin. Wayne's wife stood at the kitchen sink. Daniel sat on a nearby stool.

Johnny was looking through a 3-ring binder notebook, which had been given to Park Headquarters by Dr. Bradford Washburn of the Boston Museum of Science, showing a selection of Black and White photographs, taken from the air, which clearly showed the early Pioneer's routes up Denali.

≈

Denali's chief historian, cartographer, pioneer climber and director emeritus of the Boston Museum of Science is, and would be until his death in 2007, the renowned explorer Dr. Bradford Washburn. Brad was enlisted by the U. S. War Department in the spring of 1941[92] and was asked to test cold weather clothing and equipment in a locale that would prove equal to those winter conditions encountered by U. S. troops on the European front during WWII. Washburn could think of no better arena than the upper slopes of Denali. By 1941, his mountaineering accomplishments and leadership capabilities were well known,

---

92 Brad Washburn and David Roberts. *Mount McKinley-The Conquest of Denali*. Abradale Press, Harry N. Abrams. Inc., Publishers: New York, 1991. First Edition. 206 pp, 120 photos, 41 color, 77 duotone.

so thirty-one-year-old Brad Washburn was acknowledged by all as the perfect choice for the task at hand.

Brad's team became the first to conquer both summits, and to live in high altitude sub-zero, freezing conditions for nearly a month on the upper slopes of Mt. McKinley. They also became the third team to claim legitimate victory, following in the footsteps of Hudson Stuck's 1913 party, and the Lindley-Leik Expedition of 1932. They also had the honor of being the second team to summit the North Peak, after Pete Anderson, Billy Taylor and Charlie McGonagall had accomplished their *eighteen-hour* marathon assault in 1910. Add to this his close friendship with Browne, McGonagall and Harry Karstens; it is easy to see why many considered Brad Washburn to be one of the last great living explorers of the twentieth century.

In 1967, Johnny and Henry unexpectedly climbed into what might be called one of the darkest moments in Denali's pioneer history, aside from Frederick Cook's exploits, and in so doing they inevitably crossed paths with Brad Washburn.

Yet, as history has so often shown, all great men have their individual short comings or Achilles heel, so to speak, which invariably become apparent at the least opportune times, and this would certainly prove true for Dr. Bradford Washburn, though it would take another forty years before these character flaws would become revealed.[93]

By 1967 Dr. Washburn had already taken on one personal vendetta with his conviction to disprove Dr. Frederick Cook's false 1906 summit claim, a promise he had made to his dear friend Belmore Browne before he passed on in 1954.[94] In the summer of 1967, however, Washburn would become enmeshed in yet another bitter feud, one that would eventually taint the record of his amazing accomplishments and may very well have haunted him until his dying day.

Brad Washburn would become unwittingly involved with yet another explorer who not only reminded him of Dr. Frederick Cook, but who also bore an uncanny physical resemblance. The friction between these two men would spark a debate for many years that would never be resolved publicly before Brad's death.

Joe Wilcox, however, would live to experience a sense of private reconciliation when Dr. Washburn finally approached him after Joe finished his slide show presentation of the '67 disaster at the Mazama Club's annual mountaineering Symposium in 1998. Brad briskly walked up to Joe, (as he was often known to do with other associates and friends); Brad was always a man of action. He reached

---

93   James Tabor, *Forever on the Mountain*, New York: W.W Norton & Company, July 17, 2007.

94   Bradford Washburn, Peter Cherici, *The Dishonorable Dr. Cook: Debunking the Notorious McKinley Hoax* (illustrated). Mountaineers Books: Seattle, (September 2001).

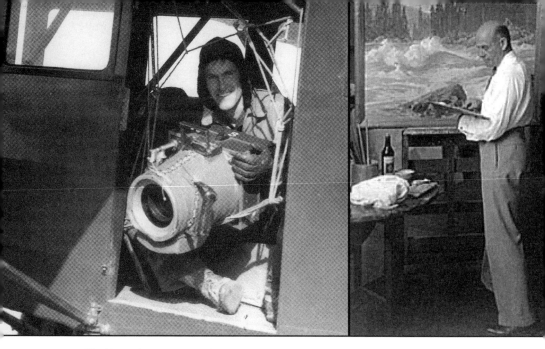

left Washburn sits in the door of Bob Reeve's Fairchild 71 holding his 50-pound Fairchild K-6 camera. He is roped to the other side of the cabin to keep him from falling out in turbulent air.

Photo: Bradford Washburn, courtesy of the Decaneas Archive, and Betsy Washburn Cabot.

right Aside from being a great mountaineer, Belmore Browne was also an accomplished artist, who is perhaps best known for his many paintings of the Canadian Rockies.

Photo: Courtesy of Isabel Browne Driscoll and Belmore Browne, from The Conquest of Mount McKinley, New York, 1913.

out his hand in a stilted yet sincere manner, which Joe thought was going to be a perfunctory acknowledgement of his overall slide show presentation.

Instead, Brad Washburn looked Wilcox in the eye and said, unabashedly, "Joe. Under the circumstances you did everything in your power to deal with that horrific event."

That was it. Yet to Joe, it was enough. From that moment on, as far as Joe Wilcox was concerned, an unspoken apology had taken place between the two of them, and in his mind, their thirty-one year old shooting match had finally come to an end. Nothing else was ever said, or written to retract the fairly outstanding blame strategy that had been perpetrated over the years against Joe Wilcox, largely by Brad Washburn himself. Joe was stunned and replied, "Thank you Dr. Washburn."[95]

---

95   This information was related to the author in a phone conversation with Joe Wilcox in the spring of 2004. The author's intent is simply to set the record straight. Mr. Wilcox however was not privy to this disclosure and the author can only hope that Mr. Wilcox takes no offense.

Yet, their well-publicized antagonism, fueled by bitter exchanges prior to the tragedy of 1967 has been thoroughly written about in not one, but three separate books, over a span of nearly forty years. *Should I Not Return* is a fourth attempt, a non-fiction novel loosely based upon the events that happened to author and his brother as described earlier in the Prologue.

More simply put, *Should I Not Return* represents an archetypal tale of forgiveness, acceptance, and love, not only for the author, but also for many of the characters portrayed throughout his story.

The book is also a vivid testament dedicated to all the brave men and women who have ever set foot on the icy slopes of Denali or its neighboring peaks, and have braved the untold hazards of conquering these lofty heights without recognition, and often at great expense. Aside from the personal satisfaction of feeding one of society's more acceptable addictions (namely, an addiction to danger and adventure), many of these explorers found that one quest after another would eventually lead them to an undeserved death, as was the case with the '67 tragedy.

Lastly, *Should I Not Return* represents the story of any adventurer, confronting death against insurmountable odds. It is the hero's journey, a story that has been told countless times, and with countless different names throughout time, be they Cook, Anderson, Harper, Browne, Washburn, or as destiny would dictate—Joe Wilcox.

≈

Johnny, Daniel, and Henry were seated around the table in Wayne Merry's cabin, and the purpose of this get together was largely due to a request from Dr. Brad Washburn, which was to show his latest compilation of photographs and written explanations to those teams ascending Denali on the north side of the mountain. Wonder Lake Ranger Wayne Merry had been given the task.

Wayne's young wife set two more cups of tea on the table, and then she sat beside Henry on the bench, who moved slightly to the left.

"Well, we all heard about the train accident. That must have been horrible."

"It sure was." Daniel spoke first. "It's set us back close to a month. At least we were still able to push on with our own little pulk sleds, even though we had to make three separate relays. Just took us a lot longer then what we had planned on, though."

Wayne's wife smiled and then she turned her attention to Henry.

"So, Henry? This is your first big climb? Isn't it?"

Reminded of his encounter with Bonnie, Hans and Barney at the depot, Henry looked down at his cup of tea, and replied with a sheepish grin.

"Yup. I'm the green-horn."

Henry began to wrap the string around the tea bag on his spoon. Wayne noticed what Henry was doing.

"Say, that's how I strain the last few drops of tea outta my bag, too."

Henry smiled, "Yeah, my mom showed me that one."

Johnny came to Henry's rescue and handed him Washburn's photo notebook.

"Here, Henry. Check this out."

Henry began to flip through the many pages of photographs clearly depicting the Pioneer's route across the fifteen-mile stretch of tundra, between Wonder Lake and the mountain, and those photos that detailed the route as teams moved higher up the mountain.

Washburn had written the names of different locations on each photo: Turtle Hill, McGonagall Pass, and Gunsight Pass... to name just a few.

"Seems to me, almost anyone could climb Denali, if they had this book with 'em." The photos almost made the climb seem easy to Henry.

Wayne looked at Johnny and smiled.

"Well ... maybe so. I'll tell you though, I didn't feel all that good about this last crew that went through here, a week or so back."

"Oh yeah? Why's that?" Johnny's curiosity had been aroused.

"Well, for one thing, they're not just one team, there's two. Two groups sort of merged together, to make up one team."

Dr. Washburn was interested in getting feedback on the condition of the Muldrow/Karstens route, so that this information could be incorporated into a new book Brad would eventually call *Mount McKinley: The Conquest of Denali*, published by Abradale Press, Harry N. Abrams. Inc., Publishers, New York and finally released to the public twenty-four years later in 1991. Several pages of this book, (Chapter Twelve: Triumph and Tragedy, pages 145-149) offer a detailed explanation of the events in which Henry and his brother would soon become involved.

These pages also document a clear strategy of blame by Washburn toward Joe Wilcox, who would then go on to spend the better part of his adult life, in an attempt to vindicate himself from what Washburn called "tactical blunders and poor leadership" as the main cause underlying the demise of seven men.

Johnny and Daniel both looked at Wayne with a puzzled expression.

Wayne continued, "Well, there was a car accident back in the states, and the park wouldn't let this one group from Colorado climb the mountain with only three guys. That's one of Headquarters unspoken rules these days."

Henry's ears suddenly perked up. "Colorado? That's interesting." Henry looked at Johnny and Daniel. "You know? Like the place we got off at from the train?"

The Muldrow Glacier/Karstens Ridge approach on the north side of The Alaska Range was the route the MCA team would take, as did the Sourdoughs, Belmore Browne and Hudson Stuck's team. Also, it was the route that the Joseph Wilcox Expedition took in the summer of 1967.

Photo: Bradford Washburn, courtesy of the Decaneas Archive, and Betsy Washburn Cabot.

Daniel and Johnny both nodded. Then Daniel spoke.

"So, these guys from Colorado joined up with the Wilcox group?"

"Yup. That's what headquarters suggested. The Joseph Wilcox expedition is now a party of twelve."

The expression on Wayne's face, however, was not one of confidence, as he began to wrap the string around the tea bag in his cup.

"With two leaders?" Wayne frowned for a brief second. "Though, I believe Joe is calling the shots.'"

"Why do you feel a bit uneasy about these guys?" Johnny was still curious.

"Not all of 'em. Most of 'em seemed okay to me. Just one or two maybe seemed as though they might have bit off more than they could chew."

Wayne looked at Daniel. "Yah know what I mean? Sometimes, you just have a gut feeling, you know? That something's not quite right."

"Well, some of our guys felt that way about ole Henry, here too, at least back in the beginning."

Daniel looked at Henry with an encouraging smile.

Henry however was still doubtful about how he was really perceived by the other members of their team, especially after Han's continual prodding.

Daniel noticed Henry's anxiety.

"Uh … but he's done real good on our, uh … our practice climb back in Anchorage, and also in getting this far over the past month. He's gonna come through real fine. I'm sure of it. I'm not worried about Henry, at all." Daniel looked at Henry and winked. "At least, not anymore."

Wayne smiled grimly, shrugged his shoulders and said, "Well, the Wilcox guys are all on mountain, by now. I guess we'll just have to hope for the best and just wait and see what happens."

CHAPTER 13

The River's Edge

The following morning the MCA team again awoke to drizzling rain and clouded skies. They had yet to be given that golden opportunity of viewing their adversary from the pristine surroundings of Wonder Lake. Many photographers had tailored such vistas of Mt. McKinley into postcard images like the ones John alluded to during his and Henry's train ride to Talkeetna.

Hans was grumbling to himself as he, Daniel and Henry made their way down to the river.

"Man, are vee ever gonna get to see dis god forsaken mountain!"

The three men were headed down to edge of The McKinley River,[96] a mile wide series of glacial streams, which presented the first major obstacle on their fifteen-mile trek across the tundra. As they got closer, the distant churning of rapids over rock signaled their approach. Henry reflected again upon his childhood, and some of the stories Katherine had read to him about knights slaying dragons and the tales of King Arthur.

Henry smiled to himself. The sound of the rushing waters steadily grew louder and seemed to Henry as if they had awoken a sleeping dragon that lay hidden beneath the Mysts of Avalon.

Daniel, Hans and Henry finally arrived at the river's edge. A low fog bank hung like smoke over the rushing currents, blocking their view to the other side of the river. A huge pile of gear, Henry imagined a dragon-shaped cache of food cans and climbing gear, which lay before their feet, the end result of the previous day's effort of relaying gear down to the river's edge. The men loaded up their empty frame packs, and got ready to push a trail across the first glacial stream.

---

96   Web link: *without baggage / accepting wet feet.* http://withoutbaggage.com/essays/alaska-mckinley-river/

PICTURESQUE MIGHTY MAC (MT. McKINLEY)
Showing a lone Caribou in foreground
Color by Mal Lockwood, Fairbanks

Dear Mom,

I haven't written because
I have been fire-fighting
for the past 10 days. I
earned $250. I have one
other job opportunity here
in anchorage + numerous
possibilities in Fairbanks.
However, I figure I'll be
leaving for home within
a week or so.

Love, Jeff

POST CARD

Mrs. R.F. Babcock
P.O. Box 363
Clinton, Conn.
06413

top A copy of a postcard written by the author and sent to his mother
dated August 2, 1967.

Courtesy of the Babcock Family Collection.

bottom The front of the postcard showing Mt. McKinley taken from the
north side of the mountain in Mt. McKinley National Park.

Photo: Mal Lockwood, Fairbanks by ColourPicture, Boston MASS.

Daniel turned to Hans. "Where's Barney? I thought he was going to be helping us put in the route across the river?"

"Nah, Daniel. Barney said he'd be coming down with dah others, in about an hour. I don't know. I tink he had to fix somethin' on his pack."

Henry was a bit hesitant to be a member of the first team to begin forging a route over this mysterious body of water. He trusted Daniel's judgment, but wished Johnny was here, too. Begrudgingly, Henry picked up a handful of wands, the small bamboo poles with red surveyor's tape attached to one end. They would be used as markers as the river team put in a pathway across the mountain's first major obstacle.

"Shouldn't we wait until the other's catch up?"

"No. We'll be okay. Johnny said for us to go ahead and start putting a route across. They'll catch up with us soon enough." Daniel approached the first of many off shoot streams. The river's roar had increased twofold, as Daniel, Hans, and Henry began to make their way across the rock-strewn river basin.

The first major problem that teams encounter while climbing Denali from the north side of the mountain is crossing the frigid waters of The McKinley River.

Photo: Courtesy of Joe Wilcox, author of White Winds. Publisher: Hwong Publishing Co ... 1981.

"Okay, Henry. I'll be looking for shallow water. Hans will follow me … then, you stay right behind him. Okay?"

Henry nodded his head in agreement. The first couple of river crossings were not bad. The frigid waters rose to just below their knees. It reminded Henry of the Eklutna crossings. Then, Daniel forged another stream, one that gushed nearly up to his thighs. He turned and looked back at Hans and Henry.

"Man, this water is cold! And deep!"

Hans and Henry waited, as Daniel crossed diagonally from the top of one shoal, to the top of another rocky island, twenty yards beyond. He barely made it the last few feet, whereupon the water nearly reached his waist.

Daniel threw his pack to the ground, after scrambling up onto the gravel bar upon which he now stood. Daniel was shaking from the frigid cold, and his pants legs were drenched. Hans and Henry planted another bamboo marker, anchoring it to the ground with a small cairn[97] of rocks. Daniel called back to Hans.

"Okay, Hans. Give it a try. But it's deep, so go slow and be careful."

"I'll be okay. Don't verry about me."

Hans turned to Henry sharply and barked above the loud flow of the surrounding waters. "All right, Henry. Watch exactly veer I go, and then you do the same. Got it?"

"Yeah, Hans. I understand."

Hans crossed diagonally down the river, the same way Daniel went. Henry saw Daniel once again shoulder his heavy pack, and begin to move further across the wide rock-strewn basin, looking for the next safe crossing. Henry watched closely, as Hans began to struggle to keep his balance.

Hans fought the freezing currents, but since he was smaller and lighter than either

---

97   Wikipedia link. *Cairn*. http://en.wikipedia.org/wiki/Cairn.

Daniel or Henry, he was being pushed along by the rapidly flowing waters, and Henry could see him stumbling on the unseen rocks below its silt ridden surface.

"Oh, no. I'm falling. I'm going over." As Hans fell backward into the deep water just this side of the rocky shoal, Henry yelled to Daniel, but the noise of the rapids was too loud. He could see that Daniel had not heard his cry for help.

"Daniel! Hans is going over! He's in trouble!" As Hans fell into the water, his heavy backpack became waterlogged, and it soon began to drag him beneath the surface of the water. Henry could see that Hans was in serious trouble.

Henry quickly lowered his pack to the ground, and then he ran down the rocky bank of the river, following Hans who was now being carried along by the rapids. Hans was struggling desperately, trying to remove his pack, but his arm had become pinned tight beneath one shoulder strap.

"Help. Help me, Henry." Hans was coughing, and gasping for air, barely able to catch his breath. "I can't get my pack off."

Henry reached the end of the rock-strewn island and then without thinking, he dove into the frigid waters. At first, the heavy force of the rapids pushed him several feet beneath the surface to the bottom of the river.

In addition to the hypothermic temperature of the water, there were dangerous quicksand areas formed by the flow of the water at the downward end of each of the sand bar islands in the middle of the river. When Henry tried to stand, he found himself sinking into one of these quicksand pockets.

Henry soon realized that he, like Hans, was in serious trouble. The frigid waters of the McKinley River rolled him along the bottom, smashing his frail human form into sharp rocks along the way.

Finally, with a rush of adrenalin pulsing rapidly throughout his body, Henry pushed upward and was able to get his head above water. Henry spotted Hans gasping for air, about ten feet below him, his nearly useless arms dog paddling to stay afloat.

To the left, Henry saw Daniel running along the far bank. At last, Henry reached Hans and grabbed hold of his frame pack, pulling his head out of the water. Hans was by now clearly hypothermic and could barely move.

"Help me, Henry." Hans sputtered, as his head again fell beneath the water. He jerked upward for another gasp of air.

"Help me. I can't get up. Hans gasped what seemed his final plea for help. "Get me outta here."

Henry dragged Hans to the far side of the river. Daniel jumped in behind the two men and helped Henry pull Hans's limp and thoroughly drenched body up onto the shore. The three men collapsed on the rocks. An open bloodstained wound soaked bright red through the pant leg on Henry's left knee. Daniel saw this, and reacted accordingly.

The author at age twenty rests on the far side of The McKinley River, as the MCA team begins its journey from Wonder Lake across fifteen miles of tundra to reach the base of Denali.

Photo: Gayle Nienhueser, the photographer of the author's Mountaineering Club of Alaska team in 1967.

"Hold on, Henry. I'll go back to my pack and get the first aid kit."

Still gasping for air and exhausted from his ordeal, Hans looked up at Henry, and for the first time, since they had met on Eklutna Glacier, he gave Henry an honest, and what Henry believed to be a well-deserved smile.

"Tank you, Henry." Hans stopped talking and took in another deep breath, panting like marathon runner. "I tink you saved my life."

The near drowning of Hans in the McKinley River proved to be the team's second dramatic occurrence. Neither Hans nor Henry chose to broadcast the incident to any of the others; even Daniel remained silent about the mishap. Everyone was more interested in reaching the mountain, trying hard to minimize the drama they had already experienced with the train. Never the less, on adventures of this caliber, a desire to avoid drama proves often to be nothing more than a case of wishful thinking.

CHAPTER 14

A Real Monster in the Fog

Two days later, Johnny and Daniel hiked down a steep embankment at the fork of the two adjoining rivers of Clearwater and Cache Creek. A clear view of Denali, however, still remained blocked by a low cloud ceiling and the seemingly endless drizzling rain and sometimes wet snow.

When the precipitation did stop however another of McKinley Park's annoying realities, hampered the over-all spirit of the team even further, a cloud of a different kind—the infamous McKinley mosquitoes. Add to this, the cold, wet clothing and water soaked hiking boots; the possibility of any sign of relief seemed almost non-existent.

Johnny and Daniel were now returning from a reconnaissance trip, since the team had run into a snag. Johnny, along with everyone else was in doubt as to which valley the team needed to proceed up, in order to find McGonagall Pass, the gateway approach to the Muldrow Glacier. This pass provided an opening through the foothills similar to Anderson Pass, which was now situated nearly nine miles east of McGonagall, if one chose to follow the Muldrow Glacier clear to the end of its snout. This was the route that Hans wanted the team to follow to McGonagall Pass, instead of taking Browne's route back down into the tundra toward Wonder Lake.

Johnny and Daniel threw down their empty backpacks, as a mosquito landed on Henry's cheek. The comparatively large insect, which looked more like a small dragonfly, began to draw blood. Henry slapped the pesky insect hard, splattering a large red blotch across his small scar, Henry's red badge of courage from his glacier mishap. Johnny let the team in on what he and Daniel had discovered.

"Dan and I think we've finally gotten us back on track. Right, Daniel?"

"Yeah, Johnny. When I went into McGonagall last summer, this is pretty much the route I remember taking." Daniel looked up at the sky overhead, which was still blocked by clouds and a light drizzling rain.

Members of the MCA team approach the gushing waters of Clearwater Creek as they forge their way across the tundra in search of Cache Creek Valley.

Photo: Jeff Babcock. Taken during the author's "Traleika/Karstens Ridge Expedition" of 1986..

"I just wish we could see our surroundens' a little better."

"We dropped our loads 'bout two miles up the bluff. We'll make a carry up to there, then just keep pushin' on up the valley. If we're lucky, we should reach McGonagall late tonight."

Johnny, like the rest of the team, was anxious to finally get to the base of the mountain. The group had now been traveling into the wild for more than a month. Hans had recovered from his river mishap, and once again he began to add his usual critical appraisal to the already dismal prospects that lay ahead for the group.

"Johnny, so far dis veather has been for the shits! I hope you know veer dah hell you're goin'. The last ting I vant to do is carry a bunch of crap up the wrong valley."

"Listen, Hans. I wish we had a clear blue sky, a cool breeze, and sunshine. But we don't. What else can I say?"

"Yeah, yeah. Just do your job, and get us in dah right valley."

Henry winced, as he saw his brother finally lock eyes with Hans. He had seen Johnny lose his temper more than once, back east, and it was not a pretty sight.

Whenever Johnny had located one of Katherine's hidden stashes of bourbon, his explosive nature would click in. Henry remembered how Johnny once ran out into the back yard and tossed a nearly empty bottle of Old Grand-Dad high into the air. Henry watched from the porch as the bottle sailed like a football into a cluster of sturdy oaks. Henry recalled the sound of glass smashing on the rocks beneath the trees behind their Brockett's Point house. It was one of the few times he ever saw his older brother break down and start crying out of rage and sheer frustration.

Another time Johnny put one of Branford High's so-called hoodlums into the hospital, when the kid pushed Johnny so far that a fist fight broke out between the two in a small fire escape near the parking lot in the back of the high school. Had Tommy Coolock, Branford's only Polish cop on the beat (who was also a good friend of their father's) not intervened, some folks said Johnny might have beaten the young punk to death.

Henry could tell that his brother was nearing this breaking point.

"And you do yours, Hans! Why didn't you say something to me about nearly drowning in the river, the other day?"

For once, Hans was caught off guard and remained speechless.

Standing in front of their Brockett's Point home *(left to right)* the author's older brother, Captain Reggie, Reggie, Jr. and the author.

Photo: Courtesy of the author's family Collection.

Johnny fumed. "I just hope that gash on Henry's knee heals before we get onto the mountain."

Henry saw a glimmer of fear creep into Hans' eyes, as he backed off, and sauntered toward his ally Barney. "Yeah, yeah. Just get us in the right valley, big boy."

Daniel smiled and almost chuckled to himself. Like the others on their team, Daniel was glad to see Johnny assert himself by finally confronting Hans. Daniel decided to intervene on Johnny's behalf.

'Come on everyone, let's get going. I'll show you the way."

Henry shouldered his pack, as did Gene and Grace. Within minutes the team slowly plodded up the steep tundra shoulder above Clearwater Creek, following in Daniel's footsteps.

Johnny hung back, waiting for Hans and Barney to move out. Johnny had decided to take up the rear. Hans and Barney however did not make a move. Finally, Hans spoke.

"Go ahead, Johnny boy. Go ahead. We'll be coming along shortly! You don't have to wait around here for us. Vee don't need a baby-sitter." Hans looked at Barney and muttered something under his breath.

"Like some people on dis team! Don't vorry! Vee von't get lost!" Johnny shook his head, and decided to let it go, as he trudged up the steep bluff to join the others.

About an hour or so later, Hans and Barney were hiking in the thick fog, while a cloud of mosquitoes buzzed around their heads. Peering off into the gloom

Grizzly Bear in autumn in Denali National Park and Preserve.

Photo: Jean-Pierre Lavoie, 2004, Copyright from Permission is granted to copy, distribute and/or modify this document under the terms of the GNU Free Documentation License, Version 1.2 or any later version published by the Free Software Foundation; with no Invariant Sections, no Front-Cover Texts, and no Back-Cover Texts. Wikimedia Commons.

Hans saw something ahead of him, which later made Henry think of that shadowy form he had seen above Anderson Pass.

Hans and Barney related the story to everyone of what had happened, while their team members were cooking dinner two days later at McGonagall Pass.

"Damn," Hans said, "I taught it vuz one of you guys, coming back to check on us."

As it had happened, two days earlier, Hans gasped, turned around, and stumbled backward toward Barney.

"Dat's not one of us! I tink it's a bear!" Barney quickly moved up the trail to have a look for himself.

"Are you sure, Hans? Are you sure?"

Barney saw very clearly what lay ahead of them. He froze in his tracks and took in a deep breath. A large grizzly was lumbering toward the two terrified climbers, not more than a few yards away.

"Damn! Damn it! Hans! It's a brownie."

"Barney! Vhut are vee gonna do?"

"Oh, ...Uh ... Don't panic! Uh ... drop your pack, Hans! Uh... Drop your pack."

Hans and Barney slowly lowered their heavy packs to the ground. Hans glanced to his left, then to his right and then he looked up at the sloping bluff above them.

An explanation is needed between the bear story and the MCA's arrival at McGonagall Pass. In fact, Johnny and Daniel did lead the team up the wrong valley, which put them at least two or three days behind the Wilcox group. Had Johnny's group not been delayed by this error in route-finding, the MCA team would have been caught up on the Harper Glacier along with the Wilcox climbers when the terrible nine-day storm hit the upper slopes of Denali. It is anybody's guess as to what the outcome might have been, had the MCA team been high on the Harper during this horrific event.

"Let's get to dah top of that bluff. Come on, Barney. Go slow. Don't run. Move slowly, Slowly! We got tah get out of dis guy's way!"

The bear was now about five yards away, heading directly toward them, when he finally noticed the two climbers. The huge animal rose upward abruptly upon his two hind legs, towering high above Hans and Barney, and then suddenly the huge animal let out with a ferocious roar. Then, the Grizzly fell to the ground, and began to lumber forward toward the two men.

View of Mt. McKinley
from twenty miles away.

*Photo: Belmore Browne,
Courtesy of Isabel Browne
Driscoll and Belmore Browne,
from The Conquest of Mount
McKinley, New York, 1913.*

The men scrambled to the top of the bluff, as if there would be no tomorrow, and then once on top they quickly dropped to the ground, terrified by the very real possibility of being mauled to death. Hans and Barney cringed in fear, hoping that if they played dead, their assailant would leave them alone.

Yet, nothing happened. Apparently, the bear for some reason unknown to them had given up the chase.

Slowly, the two men inched their faces over the edge of the bluff and peered downwards. Below them, they saw the huge animal sniffing at their packs, making occasional grunts and snorts. The bear gave one of the heavy packs a violent WHACK with his paw, sending it sailing across the ground as if it were made of Styrofoam.

Then the huge animal bit into and violently shook the other fully loaded pack. The bear released the pack, as drool dripped from its jaws, and once again he looked up the bluff, directly toward Hans and Barney. Their eyes met. Again, the bear rose to its feet, and let out with an even louder ear-piercing roar.

Hans and Barney quickly moved back from the edge of the bluff, and cowered with their faces pressed to the ground. A minute or two went by, and again, the bear failed to show, or so they believed.

With sheer trepidation, the two men peered once more over the bluff. Yes, it was true, the bear was nowhere to be seen. It had moved on off into the fog.

"Oh, … Barney. Aw … ! I taught vee were goners. My heart is beatin' like a drum! I tink I'm gonna die."

"Take it easy, Hans. Take it easy. We're okay. The bear's gone. He's gone."

Hans rolled on his back. "I don't know, Barney. I don't tink I'm cut out for dis kind of crap! Dis is too much for me. My heart can't take dis kind of excitement."

Slowly the two men rose to their feet, descended the bluff to retrieve their packs, and after a few minutes of hesitation, Hans and Barney continued on in what they hoped was the opposite direction from the bear, on their way to join the others at McGonagall Pass.

CHAPTER 15

Amazing Grace

enry swatted aimlessly at the cloud of mosquitoes that encircled his head, as he slowly made his way up to the top of McGonagall Pass.[98] A cool breeze blew across his face as he crossed to the other side, and miraculously the mosquitoes vanished before his eyes. Twenty feet below, Henry saw Johnny seated upon a large slab of rock.

"I think we've seen the last of the mosquitoes. From here on out, it'll be cool breezes and nothing but rock, snow, and ice." Johnny smiled. "And hopefully, not too many big storms."

Henry walked down to his brother and carefully lowered his heavy pack to the ground with a thud. Rising slowly to his feet, Henry gazed across the huge valley before him at the snow, the ice, and the rock-strewn moraine of the Muldrow Glacier. Henry stared with complete awe.

High above in the crystal clear blue sky, the soaring ridgeline of Mount Tatum extended upward to the glistening slopes of Denali's two summits. The pyramid shaped North Peak soared magnificently at the far end of Pioneer Ridge, which bordered the north side of the Muldrow. The South Peak's summit dome was still hidden behind the frozen walls of Mount Carpe and Mount Koven, two other high points located along the ridgeline, which extended beyond Mount Tatum. Not until the MCA team was higher on the mountain would they be able to get a glimpse of their final destination.

"Whoa... That's amazing! What a view! What an incredible view! Johnny, this is unbelievable!"

"Yeah. It's something else, isn't it?"

It was truly a wonder to finally be camped at the foot of this magnificent

---

98   Web link: *nps.gov / Unit 20: McGonagall Pass*. http://www.nps.gov/dena/planyourvisit/unit20.htm.

Members of the MCA team stand around two Pyramid tents at McGonagall Pass. Notice the footprints in the snow above the smaller tent, made by the Wilcox team ten days earlier.

Photo: Gayle Nienhueser, the photographer of the author's Mountaineering Club of Alaska team in 1967.

mountain. It was hard for Henry to believe, but he had now been in Alaska for more than a month, and their journey to the top of North America was finally within reach. Here he was camped at one of the most amazing spots on earth, in the midst of Mother Nature, in all her glory. Henry sat down beside his brother and breathed a sigh of relief.

"Well, we made it. You know Johnny, I almost thought we we're never going to get here."

Johnny smiled, "Yup, we're here. Now the fun begins."

Henry awoke the following morning feeling warm, snug and cozy inside the warmth of his New Zealand down filled sleeping bag. Henry stared at the orange material on the inside of their pyramid tent, as it swayed in and out from a gentle breeze which blew down from the icy slopes above.

Most of his teammates were still asleep, when Henry noticed a strange rustling of activity, which sounded as though someone outside was dismantling one of their team's three tents. Soon, Henry recognized the hushed voices as being those of Hans and Barney.

"You sure this is what you want to do?"

"Damn right, dis is vhut I vant to do. I've had it vith dis bunch."

"Quiet, Hans. You'll wake up the others."

"I don't care, anymore. Even if dah great Johnny Locke hears us. Who dah hell cares? I know I don't."

Johnny's eyes too opened to the furtive sounds being made by Hans and Barney. He rolled on his side and looked at Henry. Johnny turned slightly and looked toward Grace, who lay between the two brothers with her head down by their feet. Johnny put a finger in front of his lips, indicating that they too should speak in hushed tones. Grace, remained asleep, blissfully unaware of what was to become Hans and Barney's secretive departure.

"Sounds like Hans and Barney?"

"Yup. I suppose I should go and see what's up."

"You want me to come along?"

"No. I'll handle it." Johnny quietly slid into his mukluks[99] Then, he crawled slowly through the entrance of their tent to confront Hans and Barney. Henry could hear the sound of his fading footsteps as Johnny approached the two men.

> Mukluks are combination canvas outer shell with a thick leather sole, a wool insole, down bootie, and heavy wool sock— similar to the traditional Native footwear worn by Alaska's Eskimo people.

"Nice going, Hans. Now you've done it. Here comes Johnny."

"I told yah. I don't give a damn."

Johnny slowly made his way to Hans and Barney. Hans was fastening their tent sack to top of his pack, being careful not to make eye contact with Johnny. Henry strained his ears and held his breath, but could only hear the gentle sound of the wind as it brushed against the walls of their tent.

Barney had already lifted his pack onto his back, and hoped to get moving before Johnny had a chance to say anything.

"Okay, guys. What's going on?"

Hans's voice exploded in Henry's ears, and seemed to echo throughout the camp and the surrounding valley.

"Vee've had it, Johnny! Vith you and your half-baked expedition! I'm fed up. Dah train crap put us two veeks behind schedule. Den vee finally get here, and you end up taking us up dah vrong valley!"

"Easy, Hans. Slow down."

"On top of all dat, you ask your little baby brudder to come along for dah ride, as if he's gonna be some kind of an asset to our climb!"

"Well, I think he was somewhat of an asset to you, down on the river the other day. Wasn't he? Last week?"

Johnny had stopped Hans's tirade.

"If you remember."

Hans caught his breath, and slowly he began to breathe in and out; then came a couple of deep sighs.

---

99   Web link: *Canvas Mukluks.* http://www.mollymacpack.com/canvas.htm.

"'Vell, Johnny." Hans took in another breath. "You've got me dare, Johnny. You've got me dare." At last, Hans began to simmer down. The wind had gone out of his sails, not to mention his lungs. His voice returned to normal.

"But, I've still had it Johnny and I'm just fed up vith dah whole damn ting. Barney and me are getting outta here, before it's too late. Before somebody else almost gets killed."

Henry looked at Grace who was still snoring away.

A few seconds of silence went by. Henry wondered what was going on?

"That's your choice, Hans."

Johnny turned to Barney. "Do you feel the same way, Barney?"

Barney was less enthusiastic. "I don't know, Johnny. I don't know. I think the bear episode, the other day, just about did me in. Plus, I've been thinkin' a lot about my wife and kids."

Barney turned and looked up at the huge mountain before them. "I think this is just turning into something more than I bargained for. I'm sorry but I'm stickin' with Hans."

Henry heard Johnny's reply. "Okay … okay. If that's how you guys feel. I understand."

Then, it was quiet. The breeze billowed the tent material above Henry's head, as the three climbers apparently, as far as Henry could tell, just stood there for a few seconds, in silence. Then, Johnny spoke again.

"Well, if you two want to pull out of here, I can't stop you. I'll try and work out the finances with you when we all get back down from the mountain."

Henry crawled to the entrance of their tent and slowly poked his head outside, just far enough so he could see what was happening.

By now, Hans seemed much calmer, almost passive. Before shouldering his pack, he crossed to Johnny, and Henry saw Hans extend his hand. Johnny and Hans shook.

"Good luck, Johnny. I'm sorry dat tings ended up like dis. I hope everyting works out okay for you guys, up on top. We'll see you vhen you get back down."

"Thanks, Hans."

Hans started to leave but then he stopped again, and he turned around for one final comment.

"Johnny, I'm sorry I've been such an ass. Dis whole ting has just become a real nightmare for me. You don't need me tagging along, making tings worse for everbudy else."

When he saw Hans point toward their tent, Henry quickly ducked back inside.

"Especially, for Henry. He's a good boy, Johnny, and he's gonna do just fine on dah rest of the climb. You take good care of him up dare. Okay?"

Members of the MCA team gather around tents on the Muldrow Glacier at their camp not far from Gunsight Pass.

Photo: Gayle Nienhueser, the photographer of the author's Mountaineering Club of Alaska team in 1967.

"Right, Hans. I will. I'll do my best."

Henry could hardly believe his ears. Slowly he again inched his head through the tent opening and looked toward his brother. Hans lifted his heavy pack onto his back, just as Barney waved a silent goodbye to Johnny. Together, he and Hans slowly began to plod their way step by step, back up toward McGonagall Pass.

After a few minutes, Hans and Barney were gone from sight as they moved down the other side of McGonagall Pass. Henry knew the two men would trek the fifteen miles back across the rolling tundra to the Wonder Lake campground, where they would hope to work out transportation with Wayne Merry back over the eighty-mile stretch of dirt road to Park Headquarters and the Park's Alaska Railroad depot station. Passenger cars packed with tourists from Anchorage and Fairbanks would soon be getting off there in another two or three weeks to enjoy the wonders of Mt. McKinley National Park. The summer season would be kicking off, as hoards of visitors from all over the world would arrive with the expectation of enjoying the ultimate journey 'into the wild,'[100] on The Last Frontier in Alaska's Mt. McKinley National Park.

Later that morning Johnny sat outside his tent cooking breakfast, while Grace and Henry sat nearby on their ensolite pads.[101]

---

100 *Into The Wild*, John Krakauer, Publisher: Anchor, First Edition (January 20, 1997).

101 Web link: *Ensolite Sleeping Pads*, Uncle Sam's Army Navy Outfitters. http://www. armynavydeals.com/asp/products_details.asp?SKU=SBPADOD&ST=2.

Johnny turned off the stove and passed one of their team's two-quart pressure cookers, in which Johnny had prepared a tasty mixture of brown sugar, fruit, powdered milk and hot cereal. Grace and Henry were eager to fill their large plastic cups.

Ensolite is a special heat retaining half-inch thick, spongy material that climbers used between themselves and the cold ground. Sleeping bags were also laid out on top of an ensolite pad, which in turn offered insulation protection from the frigid temperatures of ice and snow.

"Yeah, Grace. Hans and Barney left early this morning. I don't think either of them ever forgave me for leading us up the wrong valley."

Henry quickly came to his brother's defense. "It wasn't your fault. We couldn't see where we were going."

Today, science has come up with a large variety of different materials comparable to ensolite, but in 1967 it was considered the standard used by most outdoorsmen and mountaineers.

"Well, it's probably just as well they turned back. If your heart's not into it, you shouldn't be here in the first place. In fact, that's pretty much what Hans and Barney told me."

Climbers also used the ensolite pad for sitting upon outside their tents, as Grace and Henry were now doing.

"Vell, Johnny. Hans vuz always a vorrier. I'm glad he turned back now, instead of vaiting until we all got on dah mountain. Everyting always vorks out for dah best, if you ask me."

Grace reached into her personal medical kit (separate from the one she had prepared for the team) and she took out a tube of zinc oxide and a small metal mirror. Henry watched with curiosity as she started rubbing the white cream all over her nose and cheeks.

Henry smiled to himself, as he noticed a peculiar transformation begin to take place before his very eyes, which reminded him of one time when Katherine and his father had taken Skipper and him to the Barnum and Bailey Circus in down town New Haven.

Even then, Henry had never been particularly fond of circus clowns, but when he saw Grace painting her face with this white ointment, she gave him the distinct impression of a rather bizarre looking circus clown. Before he knew what was happening, Henry began to lose control, chuckling quietly at first to himself at the sight of Grace's humorous facial.

"So, vhut is the plan for today, Johnny?"

By now, Johnny had picked up on Henry's silent hysteria and he too started to snicker uncontrollably himself.

"All right you guys? … Vhut is so funny? Vhut seems to be dah matter?" Grace took another look at herself in the hand mirror. "Oh, I see. You tink I look a little silly, don't chew?"

Johnny could barely contain himself. "Well Grace, now that you mention it."

Both he and Henry broke into total hysterics. They couldn't help themselves. Grace's clown-like features were more than either of them could handle.

'Vell, go ahead and get a good laugh."

Grace smiled and remained unfazed by their lost sense of humor. "Go ahead! You know vhut day say don't you? Laughter is good for dah heart. It is dah best medicine. It gets dah endorphins flowing."

Grace Jensen Hoeman would not be making it to the top of Denali on this trip. As it turned out Grace was one of those people who suffered greatly with the problems associated with acute mountain sickness when it came to high altitude climbing. When her husband Vin was tragically killed in an avalanche on Mt. Dhaulagiri in Nepal in 1969,[108] Grace pretty much lost her zeal for life, and needless to say, her sense of humor. Yet, she persevered and went on to lead the first all female expedition on Denali in 1970,[109] and at long last she finally made it to the top on July 6, via the West Buttress.

Grace and two other climbers would spend the night in the Pitchler's Perch A-frame a year later in the fall of 1971, and when the weather turned bad, the three ski-mountaineers would give up their plans for a traverse to Girdwood, and would opt to descend the five hundred foot slope upon which Henry had first learned to self-arrest. Sadly, for Grace and one of her companions, Hans Van der Lann, they both died in another avalanche accident,[110] which they probably set off themselves as they descended the steep slope. It was believed that Grace had actually entertained thoughts of dying in the mountains herself, a kind of self-fulfilling death wish, after her husband Vin had passed on.

None of her friends would ever know what really happened. It's always difficult to piece together the aftermath of a tragedy, when all is said and done.

Johnny and Henry however were both on the rescue team that probed for their bodies on that Thanksgiving Day weekend in 1971. They searched for two days, along with other members from the Alaska Rescue Group, but were unable to locate their bodies, which were eventually discovered the following spring, after the snow had melted below Pitchler's Perch by another party of hikers attempting the Eklutna to Girdwood traverse.

102 Web link: *highpointers.org*, Vin Hoeman Award. http://highpointers.org/archives/10.

103 Web link: *Denali Facts and Statistics*, First all female ascent. http://www.greatadventures.ca/about_denali.htm.

104 Web link: *Historical Manuscripts Collection List*. Grace and John Vincent Hoeman. http://www.consortiumlibrary.org/archives/CollectionsList/CollectionDescriptions/hmc-0887cd.html.

The two summits of Peril Peak loom in the background, Eklutna Glacier is seen at right, and the snow slope that killed Grace is seen at left in the spring

Photo: Jeff Babcock, leading a team of climbing students from Anchorage Community College.

Grace joined in the humor, and even came up with her own joke. "I should have tried out dis look on Hans and Barney. Den maybe day vood still be vith us."

After a minute or so, Johnny, Henry, and Grace's frivolity began to subside. Johnny turned his attention to the map he had spread out before them on his ensolite pad, a map that had been designed by Bradford Washburn. Gene and Daniel were beginning to crawl from their tent, curious to be let in on the joke.

"Okey dokey? Now what's going on out here? Who's ticklin' whose funny bone?" Gene was always one to enjoy a good joke.

"Johnny and Henry just aren't used to having such a good looking voman on dare team. Dat's all."

After a short time, everyone settled in to listen to what Johnny had to say. "Well, here's the plan for today."

Johnny pointed to specific locations on the map. "We'll drop down here onto the Muldrow, and then, we'll move camp as close as we can to the Lower Ice Fall." Again, he set his finger down upon a specific point on the map. "Right about here." Then he looked up at the others, who were all still huddled about the map. "By the way, did any of you notice the Wilcox trail down by our cache?"

"Yeah, I did." Henry replied. "I wondered if those footprints were made by them." After Hans's affirmative departing comments, Henry was at long last beginning to feel as if he was really part of the MCA team.

Johnny looked Henry in the eye and smiled. Then he looked at the others and slowly nodded his head up and down.

"I figure they must be about ten days ahead of us. I wonder how they're doing."

CHAPTER 16

Harper Icefall

B ack in the early days when the Sourdoughs, Belmore Browne, and then finally Hudson Stuck's team made their way up the Muldrow Glacier, things were pretty much the same as when the MCA team proceeded over the same route.

Charlie McGonagall of the 1910 Sourdough Expedition had discovered the crucial entry point down onto the Muldrow Glacier, which was bordered on both sides by the towering steep slopes of Pioneer Ridge on the west and the NE ridgeline on the east side of the glacier, which now bore the names of some of those early climbers. Mt. Tatum rose magnificently into the blue-sky overhead as the climbers looked down upon Johnny's map.

As teams started to move slowly up the Muldrow glacier, the massive wall street, as Charlie McGonagall had nicknamed it back in 1910,[105] could be seen towering overhead on each side rising slowly to the upper slopes of the mountain. Two separate ice falls blocked easy access to the upper end of the Muldrow, while the North Peak glistened far above in the blue-sky overhead. The South Peak remained hidden, as before behind the avalanche-ridden slopes of Mt. Carpe and Mt. Koven on the left side of the Muldrow.

Once teams had maneuvered their way through and around The Lower Icefall and The Hill of Cracks, a massive jumble of crevasses and ice blocks called The Great Ice Fall presented further difficulties.

Finally, as climbers passed through and above this last seemingly insurmountable blockade, a huge pyramid shaped formation called The Flat Iron came into view. Now, across from this large pyramid, somewhat reminiscent of Peril Peak,

---

105 Bill Sherwonit, *To The Top of Denali: climbing Adventures on North America's Highest Peak.* Alaska Northwest Books, 1990, revised Second Edition, 2000. http://www.billsherwonit. alaskawriters.com/book10.html.

top Harry Karstens pushes the route ahead on the Muldrow Glacier in 1913.

Photo: Hudson Stuck, from 'The Ascent of Denali,' Publisher: New York Charles Scribner's sons, 1914.

bottom Members of the MCA team are seen in approximately the same location on the Muldrow as in Hudson Stuck's photo above.

Photo: Jeff Babcock. Taken from 'The Anderson Pass Expedition' of 1977 photo collection.

Within the aerial photo:
BROWNE TOWER 14,600'
NORTH PEAK
MT. KOVEN
HARPER ICEFALL
12,200'
11,000'
MT. CARPÉ 12,550'
FLATIRON SPUR
AVALANCHE DANGER
Old route 1910, 1912, 1913-1932
Route since 1947
GREAT ICEFALL
8,500' campsite (1947)
PIONEER RIDGE

top Aerial Photo showing the various Pioneer routes taken over the years between 1910-1947.

Photo: Bradford Washburn, courtesy of the Decaneas Archive, and Betsy Washburn Cabot.

bottom The MCA trail meanders around several gaping crevasses. On the right is Pioneer Ridge leading to the North Peak. On the left are Browne Tower and the Upper Harper Glacier.

Photo: Gayle Nienhueser, the photographer of the author's Mountaineering Club of Alaska team in 1967.

Harry Karstens and Charlie McGonagall stand outside a building in Fairbanks when this photo was taken in the early 50s.

Photo: unknown, Courtesy of Alaska and Polar Regions Collections, Elmer E. Rasmuson Library, UAF.

the footsteps of the Wilcox trail came into view once again, veering to the left, which led up to the base of a treacherous looking knife-edged ridge.

'Karstens Ridge'[106] rose nearly four thousand vertical feet and it provided the early Pioneers with the only feasible access to the upper slopes of the mountain. It was named after Harry Karstens,[107] who served as the first Superintendent of Mt. McKinley National Park from 1921-1928. Karstens was also the lead trailblazer and climbing guide of the first successful ascent team of Mount McKinley in 1913, with expedition members Hudson Stuck, Walter Harper, and Robert Tatum.

The team's organizer, Archdeacon Hudson Stuck would later name what was then called the Northeast Ridge after Harry Karstens. As mentioned before, Brad Washburn was a close friend of Harry's right up until his death on November 28, 1955. It is a fitting coincidence, perhaps even a tribute that Grace Jensen Hoeman would pass on to her greater reward fifteen years later to the day.

A small campsite of five crowded tents was pitched precariously on the 12,100-foot snow shelf, about half way up Karstens. Above this fragile camp, a string of twelve climbers stretched out in three, perhaps four sets of rope teams near the top of the ridge. These men, members of the Joseph Wilcox Expedition are ascending the massive upper ridgeline of Karstens called The Coxcomb. It was an impressive sight, though in comparison to the massive mountain that dwarfed them, the twelve climbers seem no more significant than a string of tiny ants slowly making its way up a huge white, domed pyramid of sand.

A loud booming crack echoed across the broad basin of the Muldrow Glacier below, reverberating back and forth from one side of the mountainous walls to the other.

Dennis Luchterhand, a young twenty-year-old climber, not unlike Henry, was in the lead position on his respective rope team. Dennis was one of the twelve men from the Joseph Wilcox/Howard Snyder Expedition. Dennis gazed in awe, at the huge house-sized block of ice that was now crashing down from the massive, near

---

106 Web link: summitpost.org, Karstens *Ridge & Harper Glacier.* http://www.summitpost.org/the-awesome-karstens-ridge-harper-glacier-mount-mckinley-ak/364784/c-150199.

107 Wikipedia link: *Henry Peter Karstens.* http://en.wikipedia.org/wiki/Harry_Karstens.

left An avalanche plummets down from the Harper Ice Fall to the head of the Muldrow Glacier.
Photo: Jeff Babcock. Taken from 'The Anderson Pass Expedition' of 1977 photo collection.

right Climbers from the Wilcox Expedition move up Karstens Ridge. Behind them are
Mount Koven and Mount Carpe.
Photo: Dennis Luchterhand, Courtesy of Joe Wilcox, author of White Winds. Publisher: Hwong Publishing Co ... 1981.

vertical icefall to his right, called The Harper Icefall, which Stuck had quite natu-
rally named after his young half-Athabaskan protégé, Walter Harper.

This house-sized chunk of ice crashed down upon the head of the Muldrow
Glacier, and then it surprisingly continued to roll down the snow-covered surface of the glacier. The climber below Dennis, whose name was John Russell,
screamed at the top of his lungs.

"Man! Do you see that, Dennis! What a honking chunk of ice! It must be as big as
a house, and look! Look! It nearly made it all the way out to where we were camped."

Steve responded with a fearful look on his face. "Yeah, I see it."

He paused and took in several deep breaths in the now rarified air. "I see it."

As the house-sized chunk of solid snow and ice sheared off its snow-covered
skin, something entirely unexpected was revealed underneath, as the ice crusted
surface of the Muldrow Glacier and the massive walls surrounding it suddenly
merge into a familiar, yet entirely different scene.

Moving in closer to the swirling mass of whiteness, the ice block took on a familiar shape, one you may recall from an earlier scene, that of an actual house. As the rolling wooden structure came to a gradual stop, it was seen to be Johnny and Bonnie's home, back in Anchorage on the corner on Ingra and 9th Avenue.

Slowly our view changed and entered through the outside window above their back porch. Bonnie came into view standing in front of the kitchen sink. She crossed from the sink and sat at the kitchen table. Seated in a used old fashioned wooden highchair, one Johnny had purchased for $2 at the Salvation Army store on Northern Lights Boulevard, was their youngest child, a baby girl. Bonnie began to feed her smallest child from the Gerber baby food jar she held in her hand.

"Ooh, banana custard, Sweetie. That's one of your favorites. The one-year-old infant laughed and gibbered away as if giving her approval.

Also seated at the kitchen table were the baby's three siblings, who were still waiting for Henry to come back down from the mountain and finish reading *The Velveteen Rabbit*.

"Mommy. When are Daddy and Uncle Henry coming home?"

"Oh, in a couple more weeks. Your father and Uncle Henry will be back down off the mountain, before you know it.

"Mommy. When I get older, I'm going to climb Mt. McKinley too, just like daddy." Bonnie suddenly gave her only son a stern look.

"No, you're not!"

Bonnie hesitated for a second; surprised by the pinprick reaction she has had to her son's innocent statement.

"Not if I have anything to say about it, you're not."

The young boy was wounded by his mother's curt response. His younger sister clasped her stuffed rabbit to her chest.

"What about me, mommy?" The toddler gave Bonnie one of her sad puppy dog looks, which she had learned to perfect so as to weaken her mother's heart.

"Can I climb Mt. KaPinley when I get bigger?"

A tear began to form in one of here eyes, as Bonnie failed to hold her ground. She looked into her young daughter's eyes.

"Oh ... I don't know, sweetie. I don't know. 'Time will tell.' You know that's what Grandpa Reggie always says. 'Time will tell.' We'll just have to cross that bridge when we come to it. Okay?"

The boy frowned and gazed toward his mother with that familiar look of disdain, the very same expression that Johnny, Reggie, Jr. and even Henry had honed over the years, in response to their own mother's short comings. Bonnie was stung helpless by her six-year-old son's judgmental glare.

"Don't you look at me that way, young man? Do you hear me?"

CHAPTER 17

Crevasse

Johnny stood in the middle of a snow bridge, which spanned a five-foot wide crevasse. He, Grace and Henry had managed to push a route up through the jumble of ice blocks, gaping crevasse holes, and cracks of the Lower Icefall. The route behind them had been wanded[108] accordingly, and somewhere below, Gene and Daniel were following in their footsteps pulling heavy loads on their sleds and shouldering large packs, as they alternated this time with Johnny, Henry and Grace taking turns relaying gear up the mountain.

Johnny, Henry, and Grace's loads were lighter, a common practice for the trail blazing team, and so they were moving at a faster pace than their teammates below, yet with obvious caution. Henry was second in line on their rope team, Grace was behind him, for additional back-up in the event of a fall.

Henry looked toward Johnny, who was about thirty feet in front of him; Henry felt a lump form in his throat as he swallowed, a broad chasm of blackness and cold blue ice laid directly below Johnny's feet, a seemingly bottomless pit.

The snow bridge upon which his brother was standing, appeared strong, but as they were soon to find out, it was not. Johnny turned to Henry, as the bright sun shone clearly in the blue sky over their heads.

"Tighten up the rope, Henry. There's still way too much slack between you and me."

Henry began to coil in the excess length of braided Goldline nylon rope that ran diagonally across the crevasse toward Johnny, which also, as Henry hadn't noticed, dropped from sight into the large opening ten feet in front of him. Henry's actions were, as they say, 'a day late, and a penny short.'

---

108 Web link: *Wands*. http://13erworld.com/denaliweb/wands.htm.

The snow bridge collapsed beneath his brother's feet, and Johnny vanished from sight into the crevasse right before Henry's eyes. The coil snapped from Henry's bare hand and zipped across the snow as Johnny plunged into the hole. As the rope quickly tightened between them, Henry felt a tremendous pull, as his face was slammed into the ice.

Grace saw what had happened and braced herself by jamming the shaft of her ice axe into the snow in front of her, but she too was pulled into the snow.

Johnny's 170 pounds of body weight, plus whatever he was carrying on his back began to drag Henry across the glacier toward the edge of open crevasse. Henry had

A climber crosses a precarious 'snow bridge' above The Lower Ice Fall of the Muldrow Glacier.

Photo: Courtesy of Joe Wilcox, author of White Winds. Publisher: Hwong Publishing Co ... 1981.

no time to react, it all happened so fast. All he remembered was zipping across the ice closer and closer to what Henry believed would be his death.

The rope between Grace and Henry tightened. Luckily it caught on a spur of crusted ice that rose above the surface about halfway between them. Had that not occurred the two climbers would have probably been pulled into the hole right behind Johnny.

Just before reaching the edge of the crevasse, Henry's body stopped cold. Henry strained against the pull from Johnny's weight. It felt as though a small automobile was dangling from his sit harness.

"Grace!" Henry gasped for air. "Grace? Have you got me? You got me?"

Grace was lying on her side, the rope pulled tight between her and Henry bending at ninety degrees around that six-inch high ice-crusted chunk, half way between them.

"Yah. I've got chew. I've got chew."

In 1967 members of the MCA team used a tank antenna to probe for crevasses.

Photo: Gayle Nienhueser, the photographer of the author's Mountaineering Club of Alaska team in 1967.

"Hold tight, while I try to put in an anchor." Henry's brain throbbed with a sense of panic; a sudden fear of not being able to remember what he should do. At the McKinley River, it was clear. Jump in and get to Hans. Here, Henry had to piece together the steps of a crevasse rescue, which he had only done a couple of times, at best on the Eklutna Glacier.

Henry struggled to free himself from his backpack, and then he instinctively grabbed hold of the three-foot long aluminum picket that was wedged inside his pack; he thrust the stake into the hard packed snow. The first thing he needed to do was to establish a solid anchor.

After clipping Johnny's rope into the anchor with one of his jumars, Henry breathed a sigh of relief. Next, Henry very carefully slid his body toward the gaping crevasse, shifting Johnny's weight from himself, onto the snow picket anchor. The small pointed teeth of the jumar[109] bit into Johnny's rope and the picket held.

"Okay, Grace." Henry thought of Johnny's last words. "Get me on a tight rope, while I check things out."

Henry was shaking uncontrollably and was probably in a state of shock over what had just happened. Nevertheless, he got to his feet, and very carefully started probing[110] the nearby snow with the shaft of his ice axe. He heard Grace's voice from behind him.

"Henry! Can you see Johnny?"

Henry didn't answer her. "Henry? Henry! Vee've got to do something!"

---

109 Wikipedia web link: http://en.wikipedia.org/wiki/Ascender_(climbing).

110 Web link: StraightChuter.com, *To Probe or Not To Probe*. http://straightchuter.com/2010/12/to-probe-or-not-to-probe/

"I know, Grace. I know." A complete sense of terror continued to consume his being, as Henry made every effort to contain it.

Before they started up the Lower Ice Fall, Johnny had reminded Grace and Henry about the French climber, Jacques Batkin, who became the fourth person to die on Denali, a few months earlier. One calamity after another had befallen that team, and Henry remembered from the *Time Magazine* article how Batkin had fallen into a crevasse unroped, while hiking up the Kahiltna Glacier. Henry was grateful that there was at least a rope between him and his brother.

Johnny was wedged inside the crevasse, his snowshoes jammed awkwardly against the walls of the crevasse below him, and he was beginning to shiver in his newfound cold, cramped, and dark surroundings.

Johnny was wearing only a light wool shirt, when the snow bridge above had collapsed. His wind parka was strapped to the top of his frame pack, which was now wedged tightly between his back and the ice. He looked up at the seemingly small opening about twenty feet above. Like Henry, Johnny too was stunned, possibly even hurt, but he was quick to regain his senses.

"Hey! Henry? Henry! Can you hear me? Henry!"

By now, Grace had re-thrust the shaft of her axe into the snow, and she had put Henry on a firm belay, as he approached the opening of the crevasse. Henry peered over the lip and looked down into the blackness below; he saw Johnny's small face looking up at him from what seemed far below, almost as if he had fallen into a well.

"Johnny. Can you hear me?"

"Yes, I can hear you." Johnny's voice seemed calm, but weak.

"Are you hurt?"

"No, I think I'm okay. Pretty much wedged in, though."

"Hang on. We're going to get you out." Henry spoke with determination, but the quality of his voice lacked confidence.

From inside the hole, Johnny's snow-covered and ice-crusted face, along with his cramped and seemingly disjointed body, appeared almost ghostlike. The bright sunshine from above had been swallowed up in the darkness and dampness, and the shadowy walls of this frozen tomb had already begun to sap the warmth from Johnny's being.

≈

The number one cause of death in situations like this is called hypothermia, which can be divided into three stages of severity.[111]

---

111 Wikipedia link: *Hypothermia*. http://en.wikipedia.org/wiki/Hypothermia.

In stage 1, the core body temperature drops by 1-2 degrees C below normal temperature (35-38 degrees C, 94-100 degrees F). Mild to strong shivering occurs, and the victim soon discovers that he is unable to perform complex tasks with the hands, which quickly become numb. Blood vessels in the outer extremities constrict, lessening heat loss to the outside air. Goose bumps form in an attempt to create an insulating layer of air around the body, and often a person will experience a warm sensation, as if they have recovered, but they are in fact heading into Stage 2.

By now, Johnny had been shivering uncontrollably, and from what little Henry could see, he felt that his brother was very possibly going into the second stage of hypothermia.

"Make it fast. I'm startin' to … To get the shakes … can't stah … I can't stop myself. My snow… snowshoes are wedged in tight…'dah, down below." Henry looked back toward Grace.

"Grace. We're gonna have to hook up a Z-pulley[112] to get him out. He's wedged in real tight."

"I don't know, Henry. Do you think vee can get him out, just dah two of us? It's always taken three or four people to pull someone out before?"

"We don't have much choice. We've got to try."

≈

In Stage 2, body temperature drops by 2-4 degrees C (91-93 degrees F). Shivering becomes more violent. Muscle mis-coordination becomes apparent. Movements are slow and labored, often accompanied by a stumbling pace and mild confusion, although the victim may appear alert. Surface blood vessels contract further as the body focuses its remaining resources on keeping the vital organs warm. The victim becomes pale. Lips, ears, fingers and toes may become blue.

Henry turned away from Grace, and looked back down into the crevasse. "Johnny. Can you hear me? We're going to get you out. Hang in there."

"Yeah, but you'd better hurry. I'm fah … freezing' my butt off … duh, down here."

From high overhead, Grace and Henry looked like two mice on the broad surface of the Muldrow Glacier; Henry scurried back and forth across the ice trying to remember how to attach the pulleys in the correct positions. Grace shouted directions to Henry as best she could, while belaying him at the same time.

Finally, the set-up was intact, so Henry and Grace positioned themselves accordingly and picked up the rope to which Johnny was still attached.

"Okay, Grace. Let's do it."

---

112 Wikipedia link: *Crevasse Rescue*. http://en.wikipedia.org/wiki/Crevasse_rescue.

The two climbers strained against Johnny's 170-pound bulk, along with the backpack that Johnny was unable to take off since it had become wedged in tight against the ice behind him. Henry and Grace pulled with their combined strength as if they were pulling one of their team's fully loaded dog sleds down the tracks near Colorado, but here was no gain.

They loosened their grip on the rope, as Johnny's weight inched back down into the crevasse, as the rope caught against its jumar brake. (A jumar is a climbing device that is used like a prussic knot. When a pull in the opposite direction is applied, a small cam device in the jumar catches and prevents the rope from sliding further).

"'Vee can't do it, Henry. He's too heavy, and vee aren't strong enough." By now, Grace was frantic. Henry too, was praying that Daniel and Gene would arrive on the scene. He glanced down the glacier, but they were nowhere to be seen.

"'Vee've got to go back and get dah udders?"

"There isn't time, Grace. Johnny is fading fast."

≈

It was true. In Stage 3, body temperature drops below approximately 32 degrees C (89.6 degrees F). Shivering usually stops. Difficulty speaking, sluggish thinking, and often amnesia, begins to appear. Cellular metabolic processes shut down. Below 30 degrees C (86 degrees F), the exposed skin becomes blue and puffy, muscle coordination becomes very poor, and the victim exhibits incoherent/irrational behavior including terminal burrowing or even a stupor. Pulse and respiration rates decrease significantly, but fast heart rates can also occur, as was the case with Henry's brother.[113]

In this final stage, Major organs can and will begin to fail, and clinical death eventually occurs. Because of decreased cellular activity in Stage 3 hypothermia, the body will actually take longer to undergo brain death.

≈

"No ... wait!" Come on, Grace. Let's give it one more try. Please." Henry again picked up the rope, and this time he fashioned a figure eight loop in the line, which allowed him to clip into his sit harness. Henry leaned back and placed his full body weight directly upon the rope.

"Come on Grace. We've got to try again. We've got to get him out of that frozen pit, before he starts to lose his core temperature."

---

113 Author's Note: Even today, at age 71, Johnny takes medication for ventricular tachycardia, which he has struggled with for nearly ten years.

A climber at the bottom of this photo is dwarfed by the towering walls of Pioneer Ridge that soar several thousand feet above the Muldrow Glacier.

Photo: Jeff Babcock. Taken from 'The Anderson Pass Expedition' of 1977 photo collection.

*What happened next to Johnny, Grace and Henry in that des-
perate and dire situation remained, in Henry's mind a complete
mystery. Henry has tried over the years to rationalize all possible
explanations, but he has only come up with one plausible scenar-
io, farfetched and perhaps even a tad mystical, as it may seem.*[114]
*(Regard for the plausibility of what you are about to read is com-
pletely left to your own choosing).*

~

Shadows have now crossed the surface of the glacier, as the sun slowly sank behind the walls of Pioneer Ridge. Twenty feet below the surface, wedged in tightly
between the icy walls of a frigid crevasse, Henry's older brother hung still and
helpless. His shaking had subsided, and his consciousness had nearly left him.

Johnny stared blankly into the solid blue ice in front of him, and was very possibly entering into the final stage of hypothermia. A recently discovered process
called terminal burrowing, in which someone near death will use his last few
ounces of strength to bury or burrow himself into a creviced area or even dig
himself into a hole in the ground, or a pile of leaves, may very well have been
taking place in Johnny's mind.

The rope above Johnny tightened like the steel cable used to lift a coffin from
its grave. Grace and Henry leaned hard into the overwhelming weight of their
seemingly insurmountable task.

In the crevasse below, however, beneath Johnny's freezing body, a startling image came into view, something other worldly, or at first something that may have
been perceived to have a sinister intent, appeared from the darkness of the pit
below Johnny's limp and nearly motionless body.

Two pair of frozen limbs with bony white fingers extending upward into a
reaching grasp suddenly appeared from the depths of the glacier below. These
helping hands, it was seen, belonged to what looked like two clearly deceased
climbers from long ago.

As Daniel had jokingly suggested to Henry at Anderson Pass, perhaps the
spirits from the lost corpses of some early pioneer climbers still inhabited
these surroundings.

The clothing on these two men was suggestive of the type that was found on
George Mallory, when his corpse was discovered on the upper slopes of Mt.
Everest in 1999, after he had died seventy years earlier in 1929.

---

114 Author's Note: I will now re-construct this fantasy (for the sake of argument), but I fear you will
think that I, like Dr. Frederick Cook, may have lost a screw or two somewhere along the way.

"Come on Grace. Pull. Pull!"

"I am, Henry. I am."

These ghostly forms, like wisps of crystallized vapor mysteriously passed directly through Johnny's twisted snowshoes, and rose upward alongside Johnny's frozen form. Their ghostlike hands slithered under each of his armpits, as these spirits from the past began to gradually lift Johnny's slumped body toward the fading light above.

The rope between Johnny and his companions above remained tight, as these phantom hands assisted in the rescue, easing gently, just barely allowing Grace and Henry to somehow miraculously bring Johnny to the top.

Johnny opened his glazed eyes and he saw that he was beginning to inch upward. He felt his snowshoes break loose from the crevasse's deathlike grip. Dark blue ice crystals glistened near his face, which was still encrusted in a thin layer of snow. As he exhaled, his breath vaporized in the cold air.

The zigzag system of two pulleys seemed to be working this time with a little help from the unseen spirits below. Johnny's limp and nearly frozen form slowly and steadily inched upwards along the walls of the crevasse.

At last, Grace and Henry grabbed hold of Johnny's arms and dragged him up onto the surface of the glacier. As they did this, Henry saw something his eyes could not believe, a brief glimpse of the apparitions beneath Johnny, for just a split second before they dropped from sight into the darkness below.

"Did you see that Grace?"

"Did I see vhut?"

Johnny lay on the ice still shivering gently as the circulation in his veins slowly began to throb with its life giving warmth.

"Never mind. I thought. I thought I saw something, but I don't know." Henry blinked his eyes a couple of times. Was he starting to imagine things, like he had done at Anderson Pass? "I guess my mind was playing tricks on me."

"Vell, let's get your brudder warmed up. He looks very hypothermic to me."

Together Henry and Grace pulled Johnny up into a sitting position, and Grace held Henry's brother in her arms, while she rocked him back and forth as she tried to warm his frozen flesh.

Henry ran back to his pack to retrieve a thermos of hot tea and an ensolite pad. About a hundred yards below, he spotted Daniel and Gene trudging their way up the glacier. Henry returned to the edge of the crevasse and knelt beside his brother.

"Dan and Gene are coming. I saw them on the trail down below." Henry rolled out the ensolite pad and together Grace and Henry lifted Johnny on one side and shoved the pad underneath him.

Gaping wholes and crevasses like these are encountered while navigating a route through both The Lower Ice Fall and The Great Icefall on the Muldrow Glacier.

Photo: Gayle Nienhueser, the photographer of the author's Mountaineering Club of Alaska team in 1967.

"I'll go and grab dah emergency sleeping bag from my pack. Ve've got to get him varmed up."

Henry unscrewed the cap from his thermos and poured Johnny a cup of hot tea with honey.

"Here, Johnny. Get some hot tea in you."

As Johnny began to take small sips from Henry's cup, he reached and placed his pale hand upon his brother's shoulder.

Grace returned and spread the bag out on top of Johnny, and continued to hold Johnny in her arms, rocking him gently back and forth, as a mother would cradle her injured child. Johnny smiled and looked up into Henry's face.

Henry in turn, looked at Grace.

"Thanks, you two. Thanks for getting me out of there. You've plucked me..." Johnny smiled and looked back down into the crevasse.

"You two have plucked me from the icy jaws of death.

CHAPTER 18

Frozen Stiff

It was the following evening, the day after Johnny's near brush with the Grim Reaper. From high overhead, Johnny and Henry's team was seen situated above a large checkerboard-like mountain of snow, located about half way up the Muldrow Glacier from McGonagall Pass. This strange fairy tale like mound of snow and ice was called The Hill of Cracks. The two MCA orange tents were pitched in a hollow at the crest of the hill, while the five hearty companions sat outside enjoying a meal.

"Well, ole fearless leader. I think my stomach has finally given up the notion that it's gonna get anything more extravagant for dinner than rice and corned beef."

Gene's broad smile and balding scalp reminded Henry somewhat of Grace's sun screened countenance, though not quite as pronounced in its clown-like nature.

"Don't forget about our moose sausage." Henry added.

"Or beef jerky mixed together with a delicious package of Chicken Noodle, Beef Vegetable, or Tomato Lipton Soup," added Grace.

"What about the dried salmon in our lunches? I mix a little of that in with my stew on Fridays." Daniel smiled as he too put in his three cents worth.

"Well, I guess we do have a little bit ah variety, after all. Course, it don't matter all that much, in the long run. It all ends up in the same place." Gene patted his stomach. "We all sure do work up a pretty good appetite, by the time the day's done."

"Well, gentlemen." Johnny looked at Grace. "And lady. It sounds to me like everyone's ready for one of our special occasion delicacies. Since you've all been working so hard lately, I figure the time has finally come."

Johnny pulled out a small can of oysters, and then he unraveled a loaf of banana bread wrapped in wax paper and tin foil. As the climbers relished their well-deserved treats, Grace looked at Johnny.

"Johnny. Aren't doze two mountains across from us dah ones day named after doze two guys who died up here on Denali back in, vhut was it? In dah early thirties?"

"Yeah, that's right Grace. Allen Carpe and Theodore Koven were the first climbers to buy it up here, back in 1932. Carpe lost control and skied into a crevasse while he and Koven were on their way back down to McGonagall."

"Probably like the one you fell in yesterday, right Johnny?" Henry was still having difficulty forgetting about how close he had come to losing his brother. Of course, he would never have said that out loud, but the thought did cross his mind, more than he would care to remember.

"I guess. Carpe pulled Koven in right behind him. Koven was hurt, but he was able to climb back out, even though he was still pretty banged up. Possibly a broken leg, I don't remember. Anyway, he crawled for about a half mile, trying to make it back to their campsite below Karstens, but he died from hypothermia."

Henry suddenly felt one of those Ah-hah moments. His whole body began to tingle, as he thought to himself. "Had the spirits of Allen Carpe and Theodore Koven assisted him and Grace in getting Johnny out of that crevasse?"

"Who found him?" Gene's ears perked up.

"Another team was climbing the mountain, at the same time, the Lindley-Leik Expedition. Kind of like this Wilcox team up ahead of us. Anyway, they came back down on the Muldrow, about a week or so later and found Koven's body, frozen solid in the snow, like a chunk of ice."

"Phew! Lordy … Lordy! What a way to go."

"Jeez, Johnny. That almost happened to you."

"Well, all I can say is, I don't know how you two did it, but I'm sure glad as hell you somehow managed to get me out of that hole."

"He's right ole Henny Penny, Henry." Gene always had a way of coming up with his own version of everyone's name. "You and Gracey did one helluvah job getting our ole fearless leader out of one sticky-picky-poo deelemna!"

Daniel looked Henry in the eyes.

"That's right, Henry. I don't know if we'd of made it in time, if you had had to wait around for us to show up." Daniel's expression remained grim, and Henry could tell that he was quite sincere in his appraisal of incident.

"Thanks, guys." Henry looked at Grace. "I don't know how we did it, either, but we did. Maybe somebody else was watching over us, or maybe giving us a helping hand or two?"

Henry was again thinking about the strange figures he saw beneath his brother, as they dropped from sight back into the blackness of the crevasse, but he would never admit to anyone what he believed he had seen.

FLATIRON
SPUR

11,000' campsite

Koven's body found

PIONEER

Carpé fell in crevasse here

MULDROW

RIDGE

THE
GREAT
ICEFALL

"Could be ole Henny Penny. You never can tell who's lookin' out for whom. Especially up here in the middle of this roly-poly and very holey place. No pun intended." Gene's laughter echoed across the glacier.

"Vell, Johnny, you know vhut day say. Freezing to death is one of dah best vays to go."

Grace smiled grimly, as she polished off her last bite of banana bread. "Dat is, if you have tah choose." She then rose to her feet. Vell, I don't know about dah rest of you guys, but it's getting vay past my bed time."

Grace then winked at Henry.

"I've got to get my beauty sleep. Isn't dat right, Henry?"

Grace Jansen Hoeman died, probably from hypothermia, when she was buried alive in the avalanche below Pitchler's Perch on November 28, 1971.

opposite page top The Hill of Cracks is situated on The Muldrow Glacier just below The Great Ice Fall
Photo: Jeff Babcock. Taken from 'The Anderson Pass Expedition' of 1977 photo collection.

opposite page bottom In 1932 Allen Carpe and Theodore Koven became the first climbers to perish during a crevasse accident on the upper Muldrow Glacier.
Photo: Bradford Washburn, courtesy of the Decaneas Archive, and Betsy Washburn Cabot.

CHAPTER 19

Baptism By Fire

Six tents were pitched on the broad upper basin of The Harper Glacier, at an elevation of roughly 15,100 feet. The sky was reasonably clear and bright, even though it was late in the evening. The twelve man team of the Joseph Wilcox and Howard Snyder (leader of the Colorado group) expedition was experiencing a phenomenon called the midnight sun,[115] which occurs only in latitudes north and nearby to the south of the Arctic Circle, where the sun remains visible even at midnight.

Locations south of the Arctic Circle experienced midnight as twilight instead. Such was the case for the upper slopes of Mt. McKinley in the summer of 1967. Both Henry and Johnny recalled the sun sinking behind the steep slopes of the North Peak, as it sailed across the horizon on the west, when the MCA team reached this very location, the 15,100-foot camp of the Wilcox team, twelve days later. What they discovered then could perhaps be considered just another foreshadow of what would later happen to seven of the Wilcox team's members. This foreboding event was about to take place.[116]

Some of the Wilcox men were seated on pads outside their tents. Others had gone inside, due to a cold brisk wind that was blowing down upon their campsite from Denali Pass, the high point between the North and South Peaks of Denali, roughly two miles above.

After a moment, the remaining three men, the Colorado climbers, slowly crawled into their tent. Laughter and joking was heard from inside another tent,

---

115 Wikipedia link: *Midnight Sun*. http://en.wikipedia.org/wiki/Midnight_sun.

116 Author's Note: This scene is a recreation of an event, which actually took place during the climb, when the Wilcox/Snyder team was camped at the 15,100-foot level. It is not an exact depiction of what happened, but is a simulation based upon various accounts of the event.

as several men talked amongst themselves, as they lounged around inside the larger orange pyramid tent, similar to one of the MCA tents.

Two stoves were blasting away inside this tent, as dinner was being prepared. One man, Dennis Luchterhand, the climber mentioned earlier, who stood at the top of the Coxcomb, was quietly reading a book, Terris Moore's *The Pioneer Climbs*, which had just been released during the winter of that year.

Joe Wilcox, the team's bearded leader was cooking dinner on one stove; a second stove was being used to melt snow for hot drinks. Joe removed the large pot from his stove, and passed it around the tent so each climber in turn could scoop out a cup of Vegetable Beef stew into his bowl.

"Dennis. Put away your book and chow down." Joe spoke in a fatherly manner.

From outside, the Wilcox campsite at 15,100-feet gave the appearance of a well-prepared, well-organized and competent team; not unlike the MCA group below them, nor any of the other four expeditions that were presently on the mountain. The Wilcox group at that time looked as though they knew what they were doing. Yes, there had been some differences of opinion and a few mishaps, not unlike the problems encountered by Johnny's team.

Another group of climbers was ascending Denali via the West Buttress, another via the South Buttress, another making the third ascent of Cassin Ridge, and a final group was making the first ascent via the East Crags of the South Face.

One of the tents at the 15,100 campsite, a smaller blue and orange tent, belonged to the three Colorado men, the climbers who had crawled into their shelter, only moments before. A different voice, not Joe's was heard from inside the larger Pyramid cook tent where the stew was being passed around.

"Damn. This stove's out of fuel." Another voice responded from inside.

"Whoa! Hold on a sec. What are you doing! Don't do that!"

Suddenly, one of the two stoves was tossed through the open door of the pyramid tent; it looked like a small blazing ball of fire, as it bounced across the ice, and nearly ignited the smaller Colorado team's tent across the way.

"Hey! What the hell's going on over there?" An angry voice was heard from inside the Colorado tent.

Then, a strange and terrifying thing happened. A bright flash ignited the twilight sky, almost as if someone had launched a bottle rocket, and a muffled explosion rang across the frozen valley of the lower Harper basin.

The tent, through which the stove had been tossed instantly disintegrated in a puff of smoke; it literally disappeared into thin air, as if some spirit in the sky had waved his magic wand above the campsite and cast an evil spell. The cold air funneling down the glacier from above continued to moan across the ice, as

top The South Summit (on left) and the North Peak (on the right) as seen from the Muldrow Glacier at the base of Tralieka Glacier.

Photo: Jeff Babcock, the leader of 'The Anderson Pass Expedition' of 1977.

bottom Members of the Wilcox Expedition enjoy a meal inside their cook tent shortly before the stove incident, causing the fire. Dennis Luchterhand is the young climber who is smiling and looking toward the photographer. Behind him, John Russell is about to take a bite of stew from his cup.

Photo: Anshel Schiff, Courtesy of Joe Wilcox, author of White Winds. Publisher: Hwong Publishing Co ... 1981.

Members of the Wilcox team scramble to help one another after the tent fire. Anshel Schiff attends to Walt Taylor's injuries.

Photo: Courtesy of Joe Wilcox, author of White Winds. Publisher: Hwong Publishing Co ... 1981

it whisked down from Denali Pass, blowing ice crystals and loose flakes of snow across the 15,100 camp.

The climbers inside the now non-existent Pyramid tent scrambled over one another as they tried to escape the burning nylon material of the tent. Yet, in a matter of seconds the blaze of flames was gone. Only the charred remains of the tent's thicker nylon floor were left smoldering in the snow.

All twelve climbers were now scrambling about on the surface of the glacier, trying to determine what has just happened ... and whether or not anyone had been hurt. John Russell spilled his cup of stew all over his lap, rose to his feet and began to pace around the campsite in what appeared to be a panic attack.

"What's going on? What was that noise? Holy crap man. What happened to our cook tent?"

There was a clamor of arguing and total mayhem, as each of the men tried to make sense out of the terrifying incident.

"Holy smokes! What happened?" Jerry Lewis, a tall bearded man from the Colorado team crawled from his tent.

"I told you not to open that gas can, while Joe's stove was still going!'

"Is everyone okay? What the ...?"

Another man, older than the others, emerged from another tent, with a first aid kit in his hand. His name was Jerry Clarke. Two others sat in the snow, apparently nursing burns received during the brief tent fire.

Dennis Luchterhand, the same young man who watched the ice block tumble down the Harper Ice Fall and roll across the Muldrow Glacier below, stood motionless ... as he held his copy of the *The Pioneer Climbs* in one hand. He stared silently at the bustle of activity surrounding him as a deep and penetrating sense of terror began to emanate from his weary, almost sickly looking pale blue eyes.

CHAPTER 20

Avalanche

Abird's eye view showed that the commotion was fading into the vast expanse of the Harper Glacier Basin. Below the turmoil of the Wilcox team, another nearly as terrifying image came into view. The reasonably smooth surface of the Harper Glacier was now breaking up into the massive jumble of gaping holes and the giant ruptures of an Ice Fall in its most extreme form.

The precarious and totally unfathomable wall of ice called The Harper Icefall was a magnificent yet terrifying sight to behold, one of Mother Nature's living and almost supernatural edifices of terror and wonder.

As before, a huge booming crack, like the sound of a distant canon, ricocheted off the walls below as yet another massive block of ice broke loose from this frozen waterfall of snow and ice. Like Yellowstone's predictable Old Faithful geyser, another avalanche of snow and ice plummeted down into the still, cold valley of the Muldrow Glacier four thousand feet below.

It was an astonishing sight, almost too much for the senses to take in. The tumbling mass of ice crashed down upon a descending wall, kicked off a massive avalanche of snow, ice, and debris from the inner bowels of the Harper Glacier itself, which poured its insides out, down upon the connecting glacier below.

The Wilcox Expedition had been left above with its own worries, and now The Mountaineering Club of Alaska team once again was seen below plodding its way up toward the headwall of the Muldrow and the steep knife-edged ridgeline of Karstens.

Johnny, Gene, and Henry were now slowly making their way across the snow and ice. This time it was Grace and Daniel who trailed behind on another rope.

The upper basin of the Muldrow Glacier was dead ahead. The MCA team was approaching the origin of The Muldrow Glacier, as well as the foot of the

Harper Ice Fall.[117] Gene looked up, and saw the huge avalanche, crashing down from above.

"Holy Moly! Do you see what I see?" Gene was obviously impressed, as were the other five members of his team. "Let's make sure we don't get too close to the likes of that monster, ole fearless leader."

"Don't worry. I have no intention of setting up a campsite too close to the Harper Ice Fall."

The men had been toiling for the past fourteen hours, as they passed through and above the treacherous crevasse fields of The Great Ice Fall. Fortunately there had been no serious mishaps. Once, while Henry was in the lead, he accidentally post-holed into one of the Ice Fall's bottomless crevasses, but he quickly backed away from the small hole he had made, and did not even come close to plunging into the deeper expanse, which lay beneath the bridge of snow that masked the larger pit below. The crevasse incident with Johnny had made each of the climbers extremely cautious, since no one was eager to partake in a similar experience.

The climbers were now moving across a broad flat surface of snow just east of The Flat Iron toward the dark, shadowy canyon basin at the head of the Muldrow, at an elevation of about 10,000 feet. The MCA team was nearing the halfway point in ascending this grand mountain.

Johnny was looking for a place to set up camp. It was late in the day, and everyone was thoroughly exhausted. Ahead of them, the huge four thousand foot high Harper Ice Fall blocked the way to the upper slopes of the mountain. As the spindrift from the avalanche settled in the distance, Henry noticed several other house-sized blocks that had rolled down across the surface of the snow, several hundred yards out from the Ice Fall itself. Henry called to Gene, who was about seventy-five feet ahead.

"Look at those blocks of ice! It seems as though we're approaching some little town, a snowman village out in the middle of nowhere."

The team continued for about another half hour, then Johnny suddenly stopped.

"Okay, Gene. This place looks good enough for me. Come on up to where I am, and switch places with Henry, and then you and I can make a sweep around the area, to check for any holes."

At an elevation of around 11,000 feet, Johnny, Gene and Henry took about a half hour to stake out a safe campsite. Within no time Grace and Daniel had joined them. Once the perimeter had been wanded accordingly, the climbers unhooked from their rope teams and began to set up their two pyramid tents.

---

117 Web link: *The Harper Ice Fall*. http://lamountaineers.org/NAC/browserf/climbs/denalimu/i22.htm.

left The Harper Ice Fall.

Photo: Anshel Schiff, Courtesy of Joe Wilcox, author of White Winds. Publisher: Hwong Publishing Co ... 1981.

right Climbers approach the formidable 'Harper Ice Fall,' which plummets downward nearly 4,000 feet to the head of the Muldrow Glacier.

Photo: Courtesy of Joe Wilcox, author of White Winds. Publisher: Hwong Publishing Co ... 1981.

bottom The MCA camp at the head of the Muldrow Glacier a mile or so out from The Harper Ice Fall.

Photo: Gayle Nienhueser, the photographer of the author's Mountaineering Club of Alaska team in 1967.

"Tomorrow we'll start to move up onto Karstens. There's supposed to be a pretty good cache site at around 11,500 feet according to Washburn. Dan, you, Gene and I will make a carry up to there in the morning."

"Vhut about me and Henry?"

"Grace. You and Henry will go back down to our cache above the The Great Ice Fall and get the rest of that gear moved up to here. If that's okay with you?"

"Yah, yah. I'm okay vith dat. Henry said he vanted to try some of my zinc oxide on his face, to see if it improves his complexion. Dat vould give him a chance tomorrow, if he and I hang out together." Grace smiled.

"Sure Grace. I'd appreciate that. By the way, I've noticed you're skin is starting to look much smoother since you've been using, what's that stuff called? Clown Clinique, by Cover Girl?"

"Dat's correct, Henry. You've got a very good memory."

Three days went by. Johnny and the others had pushed carries up to the 11,500-foot saddle, but no further. The weather had not been cooperative. The MCA team had been dumped on by an ongoing blizzard, and though their foot-steps continued to be covered by a fresh blanket of snow each day, their trail finding bamboo wands remained intact to show them the way back to camp.

Everything by now had been painstakingly moved up from the cache above the Great Ice Fall to their camp below Karstens, and then up to the 11,500-foot saddle on Karstens Ridge. As Henry looked to the upper slopes above The Harper Ice Fall, a prodding question continued to enter his mind.

"Is this something I really want to do?

A horrible, sinister looking cloud cap[118] had settled over the top of the mountain. Strong winds continued to blast snow, ice, along with a sickly looking stream of grayish-yellow clouds several hundred feet out into the dark sky over their heads. It reminded Henry of the clouds he had first seen at Anderson Pass. Henry stopped to catch his breath, as they made a final carry up to the saddle on Karstens, and then he called up to Gene and Johnny.

"I wonder how those Wilcox guys are doing."

Gene looked down at Henry and responded with some trepidation.

"All I know, ole Henny Penny is I'm sure grateful to be hippity skippin' along down here, instead of up there in those winds, right now."

The following day, the MCA team moved camp. Slowly rising up to the snow covered slope on the left, two tents could be seen perched precariously on a small saddle, part way up the three thousand foot high Karstens Ridge.

---

118 Web link: *Lenticular Cloud Cap over Denali*, Photo by Jeff Babcock. http://web.me.com/jmbabcock1/Natures_Edge/Welcome.html.

top A Lenticular Cloud Cap looms threateningly over the two summits of Denali.

Photo: Jeff Babcock. Taken from 'The Anderson Pass Expedition' of 1977 photo collection.

left The 11,500 foot saddle, where the MCA team sat out a terrifying storm that unmercifully pounded the upper slopes of mountain.

Photo: Gayle Nienhueser, the photographer of the author's Mountaineering Club of Alaska team in 1967.

The desired destination on Karstens for setting up a campsite was a small shelf located at 12,100 feet, where most teams established their only campsite on the otherwise dangerous slope. The area was about the same size as Johnny and Bonnie's small backyard porch behind their house in Fairview. The small plateau offered the only relatively level area in which tents could be erected. Yet, the continuous snowfall and blustery conditions for the past several days had forced Johnny and the others to set up a temporary camp at the 11,500-foot saddle. The danger of kicking off an avalanche on the knife-edged ridgeline above of freshly fallen snow presented a very predictable reality. The risk was great.

Johnny was tightening the guy lines[119] on one of the tents, as Gene crossed to the door of the other. Gene looked at Johnny and smiled.

"I think I'm gonna take me a little snooze-a-roo. Droppin' the tents in the middle of that storm last night just about did me in. I don't think I slept a wink. I'm really beat ole Johnny boy."

"Yeah. Those were big winds last night." Johnny replied. "At one point, I thought we were gonna have to drop back down onto the Muldrow."

Grace was once again going through her ritual of applying zinc oxide to her nose, face and lips. Henry was sitting nearby, writing in his journal, when Grace again picked up the running joke they had been playing with ever since their hysterics back at McGonagall Pass. Grace spoke in a feigned, yet seemingly serious tone.

"Now, I don't vant to hear vun snicker out of you."

Daniel picked up a large aluminum grain shovel that was sticking out of the snow pack across from where Henry was sitting.

"Come on, Henry. Let's you and I try to shovel our way up the ridge. That storm last night dumped another two feet on top of our trail from yesterday, but I think if you belay me I can get down to hard ice, if we start shoveling it off. Maybe will be able to get up to the 12,100 shelf.'"

"Sure, Dan. I can do that."

Before joining Daniel, Henry turned his attention back to Grace. "Actually, Grace I think you're starting to take on that movie star look. You're getting a nice suntan. All we need now is a swimming pool."

Grace smiled and looked back with a twinkle in her eye. "'Yah. I tink dare's vun of doze heated svimming pools up dare at the twelve-one campsite."

Johnny interrupted Grace and Henry's banter, and cautioned Daniel. "Go slow, Dan. There's still plenty of avalanche danger."

"Will do, Johnny. Will do."

---

119 Website link: *Tent Guy lines.* http://equipped.outdoors.org/2009/07/tent-tips-guylines.html.

Henry tossed his journal inside his tent and then he tied into the other end of Daniel's rope. They moved carefully to the base of the precarious, near-vertical knife-edged ridge, and then Henry began to pay out the rope as Daniel climbed upward. Daniel slowly moved up the steep flight of small snow-covered steps, which were barely visible beneath the newly crusted wind blown snow pack.

The two climbers moved very slowly, while Daniel painstakingly shoveled off the steps as he moved up the ridge. Daniel finally reached a small shelf, about one hundred feet above their camp, nearly the complete length of the rope between him and Henry. The ridgeline was very narrow and treacherous.

Daniel tossed a large scoop of snow, first to one side of Karstens, then another scoop, toward the other, just as he had been doing all along. As he inched his way up the sharp ridge, his belay trailed down to Henry about fifty feet below; a small loop of slack ran down the slope on Henry's right side for maybe thirty feet. Henry hesitated at first, and then he called up to Daniel.

"Hey, take it easy, Dan! I'm worried about you peeling off. I'm afraid I won't be able to stop you." Daniel turned and looked down at Henry with a broad smile. His teeth seemed to glisten beneath his ice-crusted whiskers.

Each climber now sported a grizzled look; Johnny and Gene actually had beards. Daniel and Henry simply had more of an unkempt look than either of them, unshaven yes but still beardless; Grace's skin had indeed tanned to a dark brown and reminded Henry of the worn, yet smooth complexion that was often seen on many an aging movie star.

"Don't worry, Henry. If I slide off, all yah have to do is jump off the other side of the ridge." Daniel smiled again. "Got it?"

Henry of course remained uncertain as to what he might do, if in fact, the dramatic event actually occurred. He spoke apprehensively, "Oh sure. No problem."

Henry peered down the steep left side of Karstens Ridge, to the Traleika Glacier, about seven thousand feet below. Then he looked back up at Daniel, and casually noticed that one of Daniel's crampons had balled up with snow underneath his left boot, just like in the nightmare he had dreamed that night back in Anchorage about him and Johnny falling to their deaths near the summit.

As Daniel turned to proceed up the slope, he stumbled and he fell hard. A large slab of snow, upon which he was standing, did exactly what Henry had feared; it broke loose from the ridge and began to slide down the near vertical, right side of Karstens. Johnny, who was watching from below, yelled up to Henry with a sense of urgency in his voice.

"Henry! Jump off to the left! Jump off to the left! Do it!"

From a bird's eye view from high above, the unraveling of this dramatic event began to unfold. Daniel was desperately scrambling at the top of an enormous

top The Upper ridgeline of Karstens Ridge. Browne Tower is the massive buttress to the left, named after Belmore Browne.

Photo: Gayle Nienhueser, the photographer of the author's Mountaineering Club of Alaska team in 1967.

bottom left The treacherous knife-edged Karstens Ridge.

Photo: Bradford Washburn, courtesy of the Decaneas Archive, and Betsy Washburn Cabot.

bottom right The knife-edged ridgeline leading up to the 12,100-foot campsite on Karstens Ridge.

Photo: Courtesy of Isabel Browne Driscoll and Belmore Browne, from The Conquest of Mount McKinley, New York, 1913.

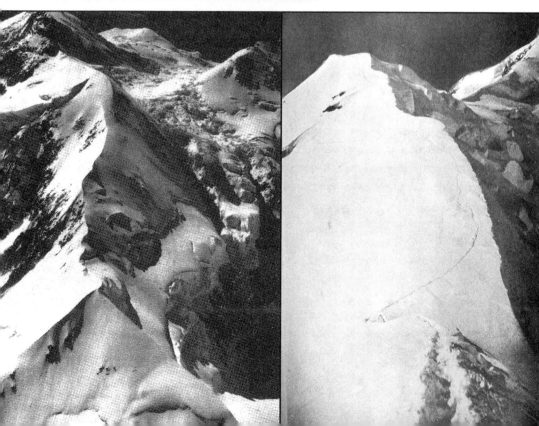

avalanche.[120] He tried, as most climbers and skiers are told, to swim back across the ridge. Instead, Daniel continued to slide quickly down the slope toward the Muldrow Glacier, one thousand feet below.

The others screamed directions toward Henry in a chorus of confusion: "Henry, drop off dah udder side! Go Henry go! Don't think about it, just do it!"

Each of them was helpless to prevent the disaster from unfolding before their eyes, everyone that is except Henry.

At the last moment, just when it seemed as though both Henry and Daniel would be swept to their deaths down the ridge by this monstrous avalanche, Henry leaped into the air off the eastern side of Karstens Ridge.

The pile of rope at his feet zipped down behind him, as his body seemed to free-fall downward through the air. Henry opened his eyes just once, and then he quickly closed them. Henry saw what looked like the bottom of a glacial moraine some six or seven thousand feet below, as if he had just jumped out of an airplane.

Finally, after what seemed an eternity, the rope caught, and both Daniel and Henry pendulumed[121] alongside the ice-crusted walls of Karstens Ridge and eventually slowed to a gradual stop.

The massive avalanche left Daniel dangling high above, as it continued to plummet downward to the floor of the Muldrow Glacier, far below. A huge billowing cloud of snow and spindrift spread out before their eyes and widened across the grand basin. The rumbling, crashing, crescendo of snow and ice echoed against the mountain wall on the far side of the valley.

After several minutes, the huge cloud settled, and Johnny and the others, along with Daniel, who was now regaining his senses could see the run-off far below stretching several hundred yards out and away from the steep western side of Karstens Ridge.

"Holy smokes!" Gene exclaimed with an honest sense of reverence in his voice for what he had just witnessed. "I'll be damned. Look at that. It's gone right across our trail from the other day. We could have been totally wiped out if that had happened while we were making carries up the glacier."

120 Wikipedia link: *Avalanche*. http://en.wikipedia.org/wiki/Avalanche.

121 Wikipedia link: *Pendulum*. http://en.wikipedia.org/wiki/Pendulum.

CHAPTER 21

The Rescue Attempt

From a distance, the two orange MCA pyramid tents were seen on the small snow-covered shelf, which Daniel had been trying to reach the day before, when he kicked off the avalanche. It was the more spacious twelve thousand one hundred foot campsite on Karstens Ridge. Johnny and his four companions were situated around the tents. Daniel and Henry stood beside one tent, while Johnny melted snow in a pressure cooker. Grace and Gene sat nearby on their ensolite pads eating breakfast.

The weather was cloudy, as a light snow fell silently upon the tranquil setting. For the first time in several days, the upper slopes of Karstens Ridge were visible.

Johnny turned off the stove and passed the pot and a small 16 oz. measuring cup around the group, so each climber could begin to seep the tea bag he or she held in one hand. Henry poured the hot water into his cup, and then he plopped in his tea bag.

At the top of the ridge was Browne Tower, a granite buttress that gave the appearance of a large castle turret; below this fortress was a steep rounded slope called The Coxcomb. Visibility above was scattered between swirls of clouds and the lightly falling snow.

Daniel joked with Grace. "How are yah feelin' this mornin' Grace? Gene and I could hear you cough in' up a storm last night." Daniel gazed at the slopes above, then winked at Gene. "But the weather seems as though it's settled down some since last night, at least for the time being.

"That's a good one, ole *Danny Boy!*" Gene chortled. "The pipes are calling. From glen to glen, and down the mountain side."

"It didn't sound like you were havin' much fun, though?"

"Oh, don't vorry about me. I'll be all right. I tink Johnny's cookin' is not settling all that vell with me." Grace looked down into the pressure cooker of hot

top A member of Belmore Browne's 1912 Expedition is seen below at their campsite on the 12,100-foot campsite on Karstens Ridge then called the Northeast Ridge.

Photo: Courtesy of Isabel Browne Driscoll and Belmore H. Browne, from The Conquest of Mount McKinley, New York, 1913.

middle Photo taken by Belmore Browne's 1912 Expedition showing the point at which most teams ascend to Karstens from the Muldrow Glacier. Had the weather been clear when the five Wilcox men descended the Coxcomb, this is the view they would have seen.

Photo: Courtesy of Isabel Browne Driscoll and Belmore Browne, from The Conquest of Mount McKinley, New York, 1913.

bottom The Coxcomb is in the center. Browne Tower is the massive granite buttress in the top left. Right of center is the South Peak Dome, below which is Archdeacon's Tower.

Photo: Bradford Washburn, courtesy of the Decaneas Archive, and Betsy Washburn Cabot.

water and noticed a murky brownish color. Then she filled her cup with the hot liquid and dropped in her tea bag.

"Deeze Locke boys don't do a very good job vhen it comes to cleaning out dah inside of dah pressure cooker." She swallowed the saliva in her throat, "I tink I got a bit of dah indigestion."

Grace coughed a few times, and then she cleared her throat again, this time with a sip of her freshly brewed tea. She looked at Gene and saw him staring up toward the Coxcomb.

"Hey! Lookie up there! Up on the Coxcomb! I see some climbers comin' down! Must be those Wilcox guys."

Johnny reached for his binoculars, stood up, and glassed the slope above.

"Yeah, it's them, all right. But, uh … I only see five?"

Johnny watched them for several seconds without saying a word. The others too were speechless.

"Something's wrong? They're movin' awfully slow. Something doesn't seem quite right?" Johnny looked again, for several seconds.

"I think we'd better fill up our thermoses and get on up there. Find out what's going on. Something's not right."

"Here, let me take a look-see." Johnny handed the binoculars to Gene. He watched the Wilcox climbers as they were slowly making their way down the Coxcomb.

"Yeah, they're really taken' their time, aren't they? Seems like one guy's be-layin' the rest of 'em, 'bout every step of the way?"

"Well, if you ask me…" Daniel spoke in a no nonsense manner. "I think we should get movin'. Wasn't it just below the Coxcomb, Johnny, where Thayer[122] slipped back in '54?"

"Yup. It happened right up there…"

Johnny pointed to a very steep section of the ridge.

"Above that icy pitch. When Thayer peeled off, he took his whole team right along with him. He got hung up on the rope in a bergshrund about a thousand feet below and broke his back. He was the third person to die up here."

Henry grimaced at the thought of a broken back.

"Yah, and Batkin, dat French climber dis past winter, on the Vinter Expedition, dat makes number four. I tink Daniel is vright. Vee had better get moving."

Johnny's team slowly climbed up the dangerous ridge, and stopped just be-low the icy pitch. Johnny cramponed up the steep stretch of blue ice, clearing away the accumulated snow from the steps he had cut the day before. Just as he

---

122 Web link. *Elton Thayer Accident*, http://www.climbing.com/exclusive/features/denali233/index5.html.

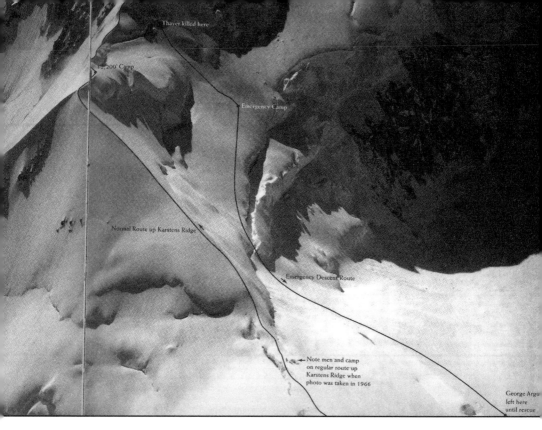

Within the image, the following labels appear:

Thayer killed here

13,200' Camp

Emergency Camp

Normal Route up Karstens Ridge

Emergency Descent Route

Note men and camp
on regular route up
Karstens Ridge when
photo was taken in 1966

George Argus
left here
until rescue

This photo shows the location where Park Ranger Elton Thayer fell to his death when he, Morton Wood, George Argus, and Les Viereck plunged over the narrow 'icy step' at 13,000 feet on Karstens and fell 800 feet, landing luckily on a tiny snow shelf before a final thousand-foot plunge all the way to the Muldrow. Having successfully climbed the South Buttress they reached the summit of the South Dome on May 14, 1954, following almost precisely in the footsteps of Belmore Browne's final 1912 attempt. Thayer and his team had chosen to descend the Muldrow Route thereby completing the first traverse of Denali.

Photo: Bradford Washburn, courtesy of the Decaneas Archive, and Betsy Washburn Cabot.

crested the top of the ice pitch, Johnny met the first of the five Wilcox climbers, Joe Wilcox himself.

"Hey... Everything okay?

"Hard to say... just, uh... tired. Beat. We just want to get down. 'Bout had it."

Joe Wilcox could not think of anything else to say, which as he wrote in his book *White Winds,* he clearly stated; instead he remembered that the MCA Expedition had paid for half of the "fixed line" that was to be used on Karstens. He turned and pointed toward the yellow polypropylene rope that stretched out above them from the base of the Coxcomb.

"That's the fixed line which is now yours."

Johnny replied, "Yes, we know. Here, clip into this. I'll belay each of you guys down this next pitch."

These men were the five survivors of this ill-fated group. Joe Wilcox wore a red wind parka, and the hood on his parka stuck out over his gaunt and slightly bearded face, which seemed almost hidden from view. He was of average height and at the time, exuded a serious, almost solemn attitude. He was clearly upset about something.

Slowly, one by one, Johnny belayed each of the five Wilcox/Snyder climbers down the sixty-foot stretch of small ice steps below. As each man reached the bottom, Henry unclipped his safety rope, so that Johnny could pull the line back up for the next man's turn.

A deathly silence fell over the group. Pulsating gusts of wind scattered the clouds overhead as a light snow fell from the skies around this small band of climbers. Everyone was hoping for a change in the weather, but the odds seemed against it.

Henry observed a look of utter despair in the eyes of each man as he passed by. Like holocaust survivors from WWII, they looked as though they had been through hell.

At last, everyone was huddled together, below the icy pitch. Hot drinks and a quick snack, were doled out, and then the two groups continued their descent down to the twelve-one campsite.

Along the narrow ridgeline, a pair of snow goggles accidentally slid from Joe Wilcox's head. He made a grab for them, but missed, as they bounced down the slope toward the Traleika Glacier basin below. When the men arrived at the 12,100-foot campsite, two tents were set up while Johnny and Wilcox stood talking in a small hollow that gave them some protection from the wind.

"Have you heard anything from the others up top?"

"Nope. Their last radio contact was made from the summit on the 18th, five days ago." Wilcox shrugged his shoulders.

"That can't be good."

"We've been pinned down at fifteen-one. Four of us made it up to the summit, 'bout a week ago. Two days after, five of us came back down to our 15,100-camp to relay more supplies back up to 17,900. But then the weather went sour on us, and we couldn't get back up to the high camp."

"So, you don't really know where the other guys are."

"We figure there's at least one man, Steve Taylor, at the high camp. He was having problems with the altitude, so he finally decided to stay behind, when the other six went for the summit."

"What about those guys? Does anyone have any idea what's going on with them?"

"Not really. We figure they're maybe holed up somewhere in a snow cave? At least that's what we're hoping. Five of them made it to the top. The sixth, probably John Russell, may have tried to get back down to 17,900? Don't know for sure though."

Johnny pondered what Wilcox had just said. "Well, let's hope so. Still, you'd think someone would have heard something by now?"

"Well, let's get the radio set up. We need to check in with Eielson down below. George Hall, the Superintendent and Gordy Haber, the ranger

Anshel Schiff *(left to right)*, Joe Wilcox, and the author's brother at the 12,100-foot camp on Karstens Ridge.

Photo: Gayle Nienhueser, the photographer of the author's Mountaineering Club of Alaska team in 1967.

at Eielson Station, are the two we've been talking with ever since this storm kicked in. Wayne Merry, from Wonder Lake has been in on the transmissions, too. Maybe one of them has heard something by now. We told 'em we'd give 'em a call when we got down to Karstens."

Grace made eye contact with Jerry Lewis, the tall, bearded giant of a man, and one of the three Colorado climbers. Jerry averted his gaze as he slowly crawled through the entrance into his tent.

Henry stood outside his tent as large snow flakes continued to fall from the clouded skies over their camp. Grace had already crawled inside. Her coughing had gotten worse during the team's mid-morning climb to meet up with the others. Henry wondered if she was struggling with something more serious than mere indigestion.

"Daniel? Where are the other guys? There's supposed to be twelve?"

Daniel shrugged his shoulders. "Just have tah wait. Let Johnny find out what's going on? These guys are hurtin."

Anshel Schiff and Paul Schlichter set up a dipole antenna[123] using two wires, which were extended out from the radio Joe Wilcox held in his hand. The dipole was then pointed toward Eielson Ranger Station about thirty miles slightly NE of the 12,100 foot camp, where park personnel had been monitoring radio communications with the Wilcox Party.

Johnny, Joe Wilcox, and Howard Snyder, the leader of the Colorado team huddled together around the radio. They listened to Gordy Haber's questions and responses, as did the others from a distance.

---

123 Wikipedia link. *Dipole Antenna*, http://en.wikipedia.org/wiki/Dipole_antenna.

top Climbers from the Wilcox team set up their tents at the 12,100-foot campsite.

Photo: Gayle Nienhueser, the photographer of the author's Mountaineering Club of Alaska team in 1967.

bottom Joe Wilcox, the gaunt looking bearded leader of the Wilcox Expedition looks toward the camera with a forlorn look of desperation on his face.

Photo: Gayle Nienhueser, the photographer of the author's Mountaineering Club of Alaska team in 1967.

"Roger... you would like … uh... an all out rescue initiated, uh... as soon as weather permits … Roger, we copy that."

Joe Wilcox did the talking. Listening from a short distance, Henry could hear bits and pieces, but for the most part, he didn't have any idea what was going on. Finally, Wilcox signed off, and then he talked briefly with Johnny and Howard, before returning to his tent.

Snow was by now falling heavily from an angry looking sky … so Henry too, decided to go inside his tent. Shortly thereafter Johnny entered the tunnel entrance to their tent. As he crawled inside, Grace and Henry sat cross-legged; anxiously waiting to hear what Johnny had to say.

"'Vell, Johnny. Vhut's dah story?"

Johnny began to explain the situation to Grace and Henry, as the winds continued to gust heavily outside.

The tunnel entrance of their tent was seen from outside. Johnny reached and tied the door to their tent shut, as the winds continued to gust and slam against the walls of the four small tents, situated on the small icy shelf. Higher on the mountain along the narrow knife-edged ridgeline of Karstens, the wind, intermittent clouds, and snow continued to block the slopes above. An eerie looking cloud cap slowly descended over the upper slopes of Denali.

Inside their tent Johnny had been relaying the information he had gleaned from Wilcox and Howard Snyder to Henry and Grace.

"Vhut do you mean? Dee udders ver taking a day off? You never vaste time, ven you're high on dah mountain. Specially if you've got dah good veather."

Grace had another coughing attack, and then she cleared her throat.

"Well, that's what they did. Some of them were having problems with the altitude, so Wilcox felt it wouldn't hurt. Anyway, the Colorado guys and Wilcox came back down from the summit."

"If they ver havin' problems with the altitude, somebody should have made them go down."

"Well, they all stayed put the next day as a violent storm swept the upper slopes, and then on the following morning on July 17, the men who had successfully reached the summit decided to descend to fifteen-one in order to conserve on food and fuel at the high camp. They offered to take with them anyone who was still feeling bad. The plan was for them to act as a back-up team. They would take any sick climbers down to help them acclimatize, then they would also make additional carries of food and supplies back up to the high camp."

"Both leaders vent down? Vhy did they do that? Dat doesn't make any sense?

Grace had another coughing fit, which lasted several seconds. Johnny looked at her with some concern.

top A lenticular cloud cap slowly descends over the upper slopes of Denali.

Photo: Jeff Babcock, the leader of 'The Anderson Pass Expedition' of 1977.

bottom Joe Wilcox gathers rope for their summit climb several days earlier on July 15. He, Howard Snyder, Paul Schlichter, and Jerry Lewis made the 49th ascent of the South Summit without mishap.

Photo: Howard Snyder, Courtesy of Joe Wilcox, author of White Winds. Publisher: Hwong Publishing Co ... 1981.

"Grace, are you gonna be all right?"

"'Yah, Johnny. I'll be okay. I tink I might be coming down vith a cold."

Henry offered Grace his water bottle, but she declined. Henry noticed a look of anxiety in Grace's eyes that reminded him of both Bonnie, as well as Katherine. Grace, as Henry's own mother had done many times in the past, gave Henry the impression that she had been caught in the act of doing something she didn't want anyone else to know about?

"Well, anyway, Wilcox appointed a deputy leader. Someone he trusted. I think the guy's name was Clark. Another fellow decided to go down to 15,100 with Wilcox and the Colorado guys; Anshel Schiff is number five in their group.

"Dee udder sick climbers should also have come down, too. Somebody should have made dem!"

Again, Grace coughed several times, almost choking on her own saliva. She motioned to Henry for his water bottle, so he passed it to her. As she took a couple of swigs of the grape flavored water from Henry's bottle, Grace's lips turned a purplish color, as did her tongue.

There was something very sad yet poignant about the way Grace appeared and at the time it was very puzzling to Henry.

"Apparently, the others all felt they wanted to give the summit a go. Except for some young guy from Chicago named Steve Taylor. He apparently ended up staying at the high camp all by himself while the others went for the summit."

Grace coughed up pinkish-purplish colored sputum into a Kleenex tissue she held in her right hand. After witnessing this, Henry too began to feel a bit queasy. He also saw how quickly Grace attempted to hide the tissue, but Johnny too took notice.

"Anyway, the storm hit, the same one that's kept us pinned downed this past week. It kept Wilcox and the others holed up at fifteen-one, too. When it cleared this morning, they figured it was time to come down."

"Johnny! Doze udder guys haven't been heard from for five days?"

What Grace said next took Henry completely by surprise?

"Day could all be dead by now."

"Dead? You think they're all dead." Henry was clearly shocked.

Grace all of a sudden had another violent coughing attack. She hacked away for nearly a full minute, as Johnny summed up the situation.

"I don't know what to think. But as of now, we're smack in middle of this mess, whether we like it, or not. The park wants us to get up to the top, as fast as we can. You know, make a beeline for their high camp. Find out what's going on? We're supposed to be the lead search and rescue team, now?"

Grace's coughing fit finally subsided.

"Also, one of the Colorado guys may have frostbite, Grace? Snyder asked if you'd take a look at his feet."

Grace cleared her throat. "Sure, Johnny." Grace coughed again. "Vhy don't vee get him here, in our tent tonight. Henry, you can svitch places with him. Is dat okay vith you?"

"Uh ... yeah. Sure, Grace. That's fine with me."

Henry moved to the Colorado tent about fifteen minutes later, after Jerry Lewis arrived at their tent entrance with his sleeping bag and pad. Jerry was a large man, more than six feet tall, and though it was clear he was not feeling all that well, he still maintained his sense of humor.

"You sure you folks are okay having me for a tent mate? Howard and Paul say I take up more than my third when it comes to sleeping arrangements?" Jerry smiled, as he stuck his head inside Johnny and Grace's tent entrance.

"No, come on in Jerry. I'm very used to cramped quarters by now. Dees Locke boys take up more den dare share, too. I tink I am down to about a quarter of dah space in dis tent, so it vill feel just like home."

Jerry and Henry exchanged tent positions. Henry took his sleeping bag and pad to the Colorado tent.

He looked up and noticed a light snow was continuing to fall from the clouded skies overhead, and a deadly looking cloud cap still hung threateningly over the mountain above.

Back inside their tent, Grace examined Jerry Lewis's frostbitten toes. She gave him a couple of pills, as Johnny prepared dinner. Shortly, the loud Optimus 111B stove was turned off and the tent became silent, except for the blustery sound of the winds gusting against the walls of their tent. Johnny doled out dinner to Grace and Jerry.

"You know, Grace. It'd probably be a good idea to keep Jerry's toes frozen, at least until he gets down off the mountain.

"I beg your pardon, Johnny." Grace coughed then cleared her throat. "But, I'm dah doctor, here. His feet aren't going to thaw out." Grace handed Jerry a small bottle of pills (Roniacol tablets[124]).

"Here Jerry, take two of deez pills in dah morning with your breakfast. This vill help to improve dah circulation ... and also, she coughed, again ... help to clear dah fluid build up in your lungs."

"Grace. What about you?"

"'Vhut do you mean, Johnny?"

---

124 Web link: Nicotinyl alcohol (Roniacol). http://www.drugs.com/mmx/roniacol.html.

Clouds and a light snowfall cover the slopes overhead.

Photo: Gayle Nienhueser, the photographer of the author's Mountaineering Club of Alaska team in 1967.

"I think you should go out with these guys tomorrow." Johnny let his suggestion sink in for a few seconds before speaking again. "I really do."

Grace was taken back, by Johnny's request. She looked at him with an angry glare.

"Nonsense, Johnny. Jerry vill be fine! If he takes deez pills, and goes slow, he'll have no trouble getting back out to Vunder Lake."

"I'm not talking about Jerry, Grace. I'm talking about you.

"Vhut do you mean, me? There's nothing vrong with me?"

Johnny had lost his patience. The desperate situation into which his team had accidentally fallen had finally gotten the best of him. Grace now became the target of his pent up rage.

"You know damn well as I do it's not my cooking that's been giving you trouble; persistent coughing, migraines, spitting up blood-streaked phlegm? You're coming down with altitude problems, Grace! There's no doubt in my mind!"

"No, Johnny. You're mistaken. I'll be fine. Give me anudder day or so. Don't make me go down!"

Grace became frantic—by now, she was almost talking to herself. "Vin is counting on me. I don't vant to let him down. I vant to be among dat handful of vomen who get to the top of dis mountain, right behind Barbara Vashburn. It's my turn for a little recognition. No, Johnny! No!"

"I'm sorry, Grace. But that's all there is to it. I'm sending you down, tomorrow. We simply can't risk having a sick person with us at this stage of the game."

A Lenticular Cloud Cap dominates the upper slopes of Denali completely covering both the South and North Peaks.

Photo: Jeff Babcock, the leader of 'The Anderson Pass Expedition' of 1977.

Johnny began to put on his mukluks. "I'm going next door to tell the others." He got up on his knees, then crawled through the tunnel entrance and went outside.

A sad expression fell across Grace's face, as she looked at her dinner. Grace was silent, as she stirred the rice concoction in her large plastic cup. Johnny got up on his knees, as he crawled through the tunnel entrance and went outside. Grace looked at Jerry with watery eyes.

"Johnny's right. I know dat. But, I vanted so much to climb to dah top of dis mountain."

There was a tear running down Grace's cheek.

"Look at me. Dis may be my last chance." A sad clown's smile crossed Grace's face. "I'm no spring chicken."

Jerry Lewis stared at Grace with a similar expression on his face. They both sat there for a few seconds in silence; the circus giant and the sad clown. Then, Jerry coughed a few times, and then he cleared his throat.

"You know, Grace. A couple of the guys up top should have come down with us, when we dropped back down to fifteen-one, but they were too stubborn."

Jerry paused before he spoke again. For him, the cold harsh reality of people dying had finally set in. Like Grace, Jerry's eyes began to moisten.

"You know what I think."

Grace looked at Jerry, and she nodded her head up and down, knowing all too well what Jerry was about to say.

"I'll bet it's too late now, for those guys, if you ask me."

CHAPTER 22

A Visit from Elton Thayer

Henry sat inside the tent with the other two Colorado men, Howard Snyder and Paul Schlichter. Howard busied himself preparing their dinner meal, a portion of which he now offered to Henry. Paul sat at the far end of the tent, near the inter-connected tunnel entrance to Wilcox and Schiff's tent. Paul was warming his bare toes with the palms of his hands. Howard took the pot off the stove and scooped a portion of the stew into two cups that were on the tent floor in front of him. He then filled a small plastic cup, and handed it to Henry.

"Here Henry. Try a little bit of our chow."

Henry decided to be cordial and not refuse Howard's thoughtful gesture.

"Thanks. It looks good. I'm getting pretty tired of what we've been eating. Our main course has been rice and corned beef, with a Lipton Soup thrown in for variety."

Howard nodded thoughtfully and smiled.

"Paul, here." Howard handed the pot to his tent mate. "Pass the rest of this through to those two."

Henry detected a slight tone of disgust in Howard's voice.

Paul passed the pot through the connecting tunnel entrance to Joe and Anshel's tent. Howard turned off their camp stove and then he began to poke at the Turkey Tetrazzini in his own cup; Henry noticed the dinner's name on the foil package, which lay crumpled beside him.

Yet, Howard had apparently lost his appetite; something else was eating away at him instead. He looked toward Henry with moistened eyes, and then he tried to hide his feelings by wiping away the tears from his own cheeks.

"Pretty sorry state of affairs, huh? This whole thing is a nightmare, one hellish nightmare!"

Howard looked toward the entrance to the other tent and pointed an accusing finger in Joe Wilcox's direction.

"And it's all because of that ass…"

Johnny's voice suddenly interrupted Howard's inflammatory remarks. From outside the tent, the voice of Henry's brother rang loud and clear, in spite of the incessant drone of the wind. He was talking to Joe and Anshel, probably leaning partway through the far tunnel entrance to their tent.

Minutes later, Johnny's voice was heard again from outside Howard and Paul's tent.

"Howard?"

Again, Howard wiped the tears from his face, as he fumbled to untie the drawstring to the tunnel entrance of their tent.

"Yeah, Johnny. What's up?"

Johnny's head appeared inside their tent. He smiled at Henry and then turned his attention toward Howard.

"I've been talking with Grace and Jerry… Joe, too. How would you feel about Grace going down with you guys tomorrow? She's, uh … she'd like to be of assistance to you, Joe and the rest of your crew, on the way down. She could keep an eye on Jerry's feet. Help out, in whatever way she can. That sound okay, with you?"

"Yeah, sure Johnny. Okay with me."

"Good." Johnny nodded his head, and then he looked toward Henry. "This guy causing you any trouble?"

"No, Johnny. Henry's doing fine. We've even given him a taste of our dinner meal. Says he's getting kind of tired of the corned beef and rice meals you guys have been eating."

Howard smiled, for the first time, since Henry entered their tent, in an joking boastful manner; the implication being that his team's choice of meals was perhaps superior to those of the MCA team.

"Well, don't give him too much luxury, I don't want him to get spoiled."

After Johnny left, Howard tied the tent entrance tight and then he settled down into his sleeping bag. He still appeared restless to Henry, and after a few minutes of silence, Howard began to go into a litany of various incidents that had occurred during their climb, and in each case, according to Howard, Joe Wilcox carried the brunt of one poor decision after another.

Clearly Howard was upset, and for whatever reason, he had chosen to use Henry as his sounding board. Laying all blame aside, however, from what Henry could piece together, Howard Snyder had pretty much held things together up until this point in time. Now it was his turn to let loose.

Unfortunately for Henry, Howard's release of emotions did little to help quell Henry's feelings of fear and anxiety, over what would soon become their team's problem. The fact remained; there were still seven missing climbers above, and the odds of finding them alive seemed to be slipping away with each passing hour.

The nightmare of Henry's life was slowly revealing itself in small doses. Had he known what was in store for him above, Henry would have probably chosen to descend the mountain, then and there. Grace Jensen Hoeman would not have been the only MCA climber hiking back out to Wonder Lake with these five survivors. Henry Locke, their leader's younger brother, would have been number

Climbers are seen descending from the 12,100-foot plateau campsite on Karstens Ridge.

Photo: Willy VanHemert, a member of 'The Anderson Pass Expedition' of 1977.

seven—the very same number of Wilcox men that would never again be coming down from the icy slopes of Denali. These poor souls, it seemed to Henry were now doomed to remain forever on the mountain.

At noon the following day, Grace and the five Wilcox/Colorado men began their descent from the twelve-one shelf. As she went down the ridge, Grace glanced back toward Johnny with a look of disgust, disappointment and sadness. Johnny silently raised his right hand as a final gesture of good will and goodbye. Grace's sadness broke into a fleeting smile, and she too returned the gesture. Johnny saw her silently mouth two words.

"Good luck." Then Grace turned and proceeded down the ridge.

Johnny, Daniel, Gene and Henry stacked a small cache of food, their two tents, and some other miscellaneous gear behind a snow wall at the twelve-one camp. The park assured them that they could rely on Don Sheldon[125] for airdrops, as they proceeded up the mountain.

---

125 Web link: *Don Sheldon—A bush pilot's pilot!* http://www.avsim.com/pages/1102/bush_adventures/pipercub/don_sheldon_story.html.

The winds had died down some, yet the MCA team began their rescue attempt in the midst of cloud cover and a light snow.

Photo: Gayle Nienhueser, the photographer of the author's Mountaineering Club of Alaska team in 1967.

Afterward, the MCA climbers began their slow, steep climb up the knife-edged ridge that led to the upper slopes of Denali. As Henry moved up the frozen steps of the sixty-foot ice-pitch, a light snow began to fall. A steady wind blew across the crest of Karstens Ridge, as Johnny's voice broke the icy silence.

"Henry, pick up the pace! The weather is startin' to take a turn. Let's move out. We've got to get up to Browne Tower, and dig in before we get socked in again."

"I know, Johnny. I know. I'm going as fast as I can."

Henry looked up at Johnny with fear in his eyes.

"I'm scared, Johnny. I'm really scared."

"Don't worry. It'll be okay. We're gonna be fine." Johnny's reply was meant to instill assurance, but it did not. Johnny too, was in doubt over what he had gotten his team into.

The four men moved slowly up the steep sixty-degree slope. Finally, they reached a small outcropping of rock, next to which they had established a small cache two days earlier. Johnny decided to stop there in order to throw another two gallons of fuel on top of his already heavy pack.

Daniel and Gene moved past the Locke brothers on a separate rope as they moved ahead of Johnny and Henry. From high overhead, the four men could be seen plodding up to a second cache at the bottom of the huge Coxcomb, the near vertical upper slope that led to the top of Karstens. Johnny stopped briefly, and retrieved another gallon can of fuel, which he stuffed into the top of Henry's pack. "As long as we've got snow saws, shovels and lots of fuel we'll be okay. Food, fuel, and some way to dig in will keep us all alive." Johnny smiled.

A blustery wind and falling snow still obscured the slope above.

Gene and Daniel continued to climb above Johnny and Henry about thirty feet ahead.

"By golly. We can't see anything up above. It's like we're climbing up a stairway to heaven."

top Members of the MCA team take a break at the base of the dangerous and very steep section of Karstens Ridge called 'The Coxcomb.' Note the beginning of the fixed lines placed by the Wilcox Expedition.

bottom Climbers approach the snow crusted granite buttress called Browne Tower, located at the top of Karstens Ridge.

Photo: Jack Duggan, a member of 'The Anderson Pass Expedition' of 1977.

Daniel called down to Gene with a grim expression on his face. "Let's just hope we're not headed in the other direction."

Daniel and Gene finally reached the upper crest of Karstens Ridge, a good distance ahead of Johnny and Henry. They slowly made their way to the granite walls of Browne Tower, now barely visible in the swirling snow above.

By the time Johnny and Henry had plodded to the same rock outcroppings below Browne Tower, Gene and Daniel were already on their hands and knees digging into the slope.

"Damn. It was kind of dumb for us to leave our tents down below, don't yah think? It's gonna take us forever to dig out a cave, let alone build an igloo."

Gene chiseled away at the snow and ice with his axe.

"It wasn't Johnny's idea. The park told him to go light. They're gonna airdrop supplies to us, up on the Harper."

"Oh yeah. Sure we'll get lots of airdrops in this weather! What are we suppose' to do between now and then? Bury our heads in the snow? Damn, this snow pack's as hard as concrete!"

Three hours or so later, an overhead view showed their hollowed out bivouac camp at 14,600 feet, nearly hidden amongst the boulders below Browne Tower.

The MCA climbers were now perched precariously on the top of Karstens Ridge and at the base of Browne Tower. The Harper Ice Fall loomed directly below them to the west, while 4,000 feet below, the Muldrow Glacier spread out for six miles toward McGonagall Pass beneath an eerie looking blanket of clouds.

During the course of the night the men shook restlessly in the open snow pits they had burrowed into the slope. Henry tossed and turned unmercifully as grizzly images raced across his mind. His thoughts were plagued with the nightmarish images of finding frozen corpses along the way as they moved up the mountain.

Then, drifting in and out of a restless sleep, Henry found himself suddenly stirred awake by the repetitive

Hudson Stuck's 1913 team sets up a campsite below Browne Tower at the Parker Pass at 14,600 feet.

Photo: Hudson Stuck, from 'The Ascent of Denali,' Publisher: New York Charles Scribner's sons, 1914.

sound of boots kicking into the ice, and the distinct sound of the shaft of an ice axe periodically being thrust into the snow. Henry gradually opened his eyes and witnessed an eerie vision slowly emerging through the mist on the steep ridgeline below their makeshift camp.

The 1932 campsite of Allen Carpe and Theodore Koven. In the background *(left of center)* are Karstens Ridge, The Coxcomb, and Browne Tower.

Photo: Courtesy of the Rasmuson Archives, University of Fairbanks.

Off in the distance Henry saw a climber cresting the ridgeline below. It was more of a shadowy apparition of a climber, slowly approaching the base of Browne Tower. Henry was startled when suddenly he recognized what he believed to be his crazy Aunt Sophie's face staring toward him through the fog.

Then the thought slowly crept into Henry's mind, perhaps this was the ghostly spirit of Park Ranger, Elton Thayer.

Twenty feet from where he lay, this ghostly vision stopped dead in his or her tracks. This climber seemed thin and hunched over, and terribly worn, almost ghost-like. Henry heard a raspy, crackling voice, as though one of this person's lungs had been punctured. It was a horrific sight.

The only thing Henry could imagine was this was the ghost of Park Ranger, Elton Thayer. Then the wheezing voice of this strange apparition spoke.

"Turn back ... now."

His voice was hollow sounding, as air seemed to wheeze, almost crackle from his damaged lungs.

"Don't go on. The others are waiting for you. If you find them, you will become just like them," Thayer turned and looked down the slope below him. "And, just like the rest of us."

Henry saw three more ghostly apparitions standing on the steep slope below. Then Thayer's shadowy form toppled into the snow, as if his spine had suddenly snapped at the waist.

Henry's eyes were still closed, when at last he startled himself awake from the terror of his nightmarish state of mind.

Henry gasped in terror. "What? What did you say? Who's waiting for us? What are you talking about? Grace? Sophie? Is that you?"

Johnny was lying right next to Henry, and he too was awakened by his brother's furtive ramblings.

Belmore Browne's team descends 'the crest of Karstens Ridge (The Coxcomb) in 1912. Below is the basin of the Traleika Glacier almost a vertical mile below.

Photo: Courtesy of Isabel Browne Driscoll and Belmore H Browne, from The Conquest of Mount McKinley, New York, 1913.

"What? What the hell's the matter? Henry?" Johnny grabbed hold of Henry's shoulder and shook him awake.

"Wake up! Henry? Wake up. You're talking in your sleep."

"What? Huh?" Henry finally came to life and looked into Johnny's eyes. "What? What did you say?"

"I said you've been talking in your sleep. What's going on?"

"Oh. My …!"

Henry was at last conscious and staring directly into his brother eyes. He looked around at their camp's dismal surroundings, as the wind blew snow and ice crystals across their sleeping bags.

"Nothing, Johnny. Nothing. I was just having a nightmare."

Images of his crazy Aunt Sophie and even Aunt Hazel flashed before his eyes. Henry saw Aunt Sophie's strange bizarre smile. A chill ran down Henry's spine.

"It was a nightmare. That's all." Henry gasped again and looked back down the frozen shoulder of the upper Coxcomb ridge.

"Oh, Johnny… what a hellish nightmare!" Henry took in several deep breaths, before finally calming down.

He looked around at their camp's dismal surroundings, as the wind blew snow and ice crystals across their exposed sleeping bags. "What do you mean?"

"You're shaking like a leaf." Johnny looked into his little brother's eyes. "You gonna be all right?"

"Yeah … yeah. I'm all right."

Henry sat up and looked down the ice-crusted slope. A cold wind moaned eerily, as wisps of snow and ice danced across the ridgeline below Browne Tower. After finally getting a hold on himself, Henry turned back to Johnny.

"Go back to sleep. I'm okay. Really, I'll be all right."

"Yeah, right. Sure."

Johnny smiled, and chuckled to himself as he rolled on his side. "We're all fine. Right? Nothing wrong, here."

Henry laid flat on his back and gazed up into the blustery cloud-filled sky over-head; he felt so alone. The wind moaned on and chilled him to his core with a deep fear that he would never forget, along with the nightmarish vision of Elton Thayer's foreboding premonition, and his Aunt Sophie's creepy smile.

CHAPTER 23

The Ice Axe

After a sleepless night below Browne Tower, the MCA team thankfully awoke to clear skies and sunshine. As they rounded the shoulder of the Northeast Ridgeline, the broad expanse of the Harper Glacier glistened in the sun giving them a fantastic view of the upper slopes of this grand mountain. The North Peak rose dramatically on the opposite side of the Harper, and stood out majestically in the blue cloudless sky. To the left The South Peak Dome seemed much nearer to them than it was in reality, still at least three days away. In between the two peaks lay Archdeacon's Tower, the shark finned pinnacle named after the leader of the first team to reach the top, Archdeacon Hudson Stuck himself.

Ahead of them their route followed Parker Pass, named after Hershel Parker[126] the good friend and climbing companion of Belmore Browne, whose 1912 team had braved the same hazards that Johnny's team now faced, only fifty-five years earlier. This steep side-hill traverse had given the descending Wilcox survivors several tense moments as weak and weary Jerry Lewis stumbled along its ice-crusted flanks. Now, the four MCA men crossed the sixty-degree slope, peering down into the cracks and crevasses below them, which broke off into the Harper Ice Fall.

"Let's get onto the Harper, before we crank up the stoves for breakfast," Johnny suggested.

"Who knows? With the weather as nice as it appears, maybe we'll luck out and see someone coming down from up above."

Johnny looked across the vast Harper Glacier, which was now clearly visible for the first time. The massive ridgeline of the North Peak cut into a clear blue sky. On the horizon to the left they could see clearly the two prominent features of the South Peak: Archdeacon's Tower and the South Peak dome.

---

126 Web link. *Hershel Parker*, http://www.pulist.net/mount-mckinley-the-conquest-of-denali.html.

A climbing party skirts the treacherous side slope of Parker Pass, which leads from Browne Tower to the upper Harper Glacier. Denali's ice-clad summit is still a vertical mile above; although here at 14,600 feet the men are at a point about equal in height to the Matterhorn.

Photo: Bradford Washburn, courtesy of the Decaneas Archive, and Betsy Washburn Cabot.

"Shouldn't take us that long, now that we can finally see where we're going. Everyone okay with waiting, until we get across Parker Pass?"

"Okey-dokey with me," Gene responded with a smile on his face.

"Yup. Let's do it," replied Daniel.

Henry simply nodded and before he knew it, they were underway traveling as before, in rope teams of two. At one point, Gene lost his balance, slipped and began to slide down the ice-crusted slope below him and Johnny. Henry felt his heart skip a beat, as he watched Johnny instinctively thrust the shaft of his axe into the slope, and saw Gene take a short pendulum across the ice below. Within seconds Gene came to a stop, regained his balance, then slowly climbed back up toward Johnny, as if it were no big deal.

Within less than forty-five minutes, they were safely across Parker Pass, and the men soon trekked across a more level section of the Harper toward the scattered remains, including the charred ground cloth from the tent fire, at the Wilcox 15,100—foot campsite.

"Okay, guys. We need to get some kind of permanent shelter put up here, in case we run into anybody comin' down."

Johnny's suggestion was taken to heart by each of the men, since they remembered all too well the graveyard bivouac of the previous night with too little rest and too much apprehension.

"Yeah. That's good thinkin' ole fearless leader," Gene coughed and then surprisingly hacked up a small ball of phlegm into the snow. Johnny took note. Gene coughed again, as he stepped upon the yellowish chunk in the snow.

"Yesirree, I need to get some food into my tummy. I don't know about the rest of you turkeys, but I'm famished, and the day's only just begun."

Daniel pulled out a snow saw,[127] a wooden handled aluminum machete like sword, with a serrated edge.

"I'll start cutting blocks for an igloo."

---

127 Web link. *Snow Saw*, http://www.blackdiamondequipment.com/en-us/shop/ski/snow-saftey/ flicklock-snow-saw.

Johnny cranked up one of the stoves; then he set the large pressure cooker on top after filling it to the brim with hard chunks of snow and ice. Gene and Henry joined Daniel with the task of constructing a good-sized igloo.

Henry turned sharply and looked upward into the sky, as he and everyone else heard the grating sound of a small plane engine cut across the horizon below. A bright yellow Piper Super Cub suddenly appeared out of nowhere, and then passed over their heads. It flew directly toward the MCA group, flipped its wings from one side to the other, and then passed over their heads.

"Hey. Lookie, lookie! That must be Sheldon. Maybe he's gonna drop us some tents?"

Like the rest of Johnny's team, Gene too was exuberant at the prospects of outside assistance, as the park had promised.

"Maybe we really aren't totally on our own, after all?" Henry looked toward his brother.

"I doubt it," Johnny interjected. "My guess is he's lookin' for any signs of those missing men."

Don Sheldon, Talkeetna's most famous mountain pilot, flew directly over the 15,100-foot camp, and then he circled around the broad expanse of the Harper Glacier basin. Sheldon did drop something from his plane, but everyone saw the bundle fall down onto the far side of the glacier onto a slope at least a mile or so across, and far above their igloo campsite location.

"Wonder why he made a drop all the way over there? That seems kinda screwy?" Gene was puzzled, as were the others.

"We'll just have to wait and search for it tomorrow. We need to get a secure camp put in here by tonight, get a couple of good meals in our bellies, and then get an early start tomorrow morning. None of us got much sleep last night, and the last thing we need now is for one of us to come down with altitude problems." Gene gave Johnny an anxious look.

Johnny was playing it safe. He would later be criticized for not pushing on up the mountain more quickly; particularly by Grace's husband Vin, who would lead his own humanitarian climb on August 19, nearly three weeks after the MCA team got down.

Vin, Ray Genet,[128] (a member of the '67 winter assault team, and the first entrepreneur of guiding concerns on Denali) and two other men would climb the West Buttress to look for answers to questions he felt remained unanswered, surrounding the unfortunate tragedy. Yet, by then most of what Johnny's team was about to discover would be buried under the ice.

---

128 Wikipedia link. *Ray Genet*, http://en.wikipedia.org/wiki/Ray_Genet.

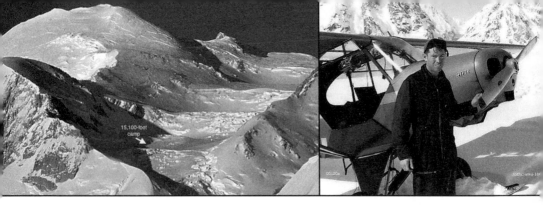

left Crossing (left to right) through the shadowed area from Browne Tower; the 15,100-foot campsite is located at the point where the shadow meets the sun on the Harper Glacier.

Photo: Jeff Babcock, the leader of 'The Anderson Pass Expedition' of 1977.

right Bush pilot Don Sheldon and his Piper airplane at Mount McKinley in Alaska, Taken 1955.

Courtesy of the Anchorage Museum at the Rasmuson Center.

Ray would go on to guide expeditions on Denali for the next twelve years of his life, and then like Vin Hoeman, he would die in the Himalayas, alongside one of his clients, from hypothermia and altitude sickness while descending Mt. Everest on October 2, 1979.

The next day Johnny's team plodded across the Harper Glacier and climbed alongside the base of the North Peak. By sheer luck, they located the white pillowcase Don Sheldon had dropped the day before, on the far side of the basin. Daniel discovered the small bundle and inside he found three radios and a note written to Sheldon. Daniel read the hastily scrawled message, which was pinned under several strands of surveyor's tape wound tightly around the radios.

"Listen to this, Johnny. It says, 'Don. Keep one of these radios with you in your plane, drop one to the MCA group, and the other to the Western States group on the south side of the mountain.'"

"So, we get all three? That sure is kinda screwy, ain't it?"

Gene was breathing heavily, and coughed a few times before he spoke. "I wonder what he was thinkin'?

"Who knows? Let's keep moving. This whole nightmare just keeps getting worse, the higher we go. Something's not right!"

≈

Johnny's confidence in the park's ability to offer air support was beginning to dwindle, and rightly so. Communications at Park Headquarters[129] in

---

129 James Tabor, *Forever on the Mountain*, New York: W.W Norton & Company, July 17, 2007.

the summer of 1967 were indeed primitive to say the least. Only one phone (at Park Headquarters) was available for outside communications, and crank battery operated systems were used for communications within the park itself. So when someone wanted to talk to Wayne Merry at Wonder Lake, or Gordy Haber at Eielson Ranger Lookout, a crank would be turned to generate a ringing current, to gain someone's attention at the desired location.

These Magneto systems were in use in one American small town, Bryant Pond, Woodstock, Maine as late as 1983. In general, this type of system had a poorer call quality when compared to common-battery systems.

Furthermore, radio communications on the mountain itself were often limited to one way verbal questions from the Park, (as was the case with transmissions at the 12,100-foot camp with Wilcox and Johnny), followed by yes or no click responses from the climbers on the mountain. Today's rapid transfer of voice communications throughout the world, via cell phones, was of course nonexistent in the summer of 1967.

Some have laid blame on Park Headquarters for miscommunications during the rescue effort.[130] Yet the author, now more than forty years later, has since come to believe that each of the people involved in this horrific tragedy were all caught up in a bizarre circumstance of events well beyond anyone's control.

No matter what resources were available at the time for the rescue mission at hand to have been successful, it really wouldn't have mattered one way or another. When a climber found himself stuck at 19,000 feet in the middle of one of Denali's severe storms, with little food and fuel, regardless of whatever shelter may or may not have been available, it is simply a question of time. The chances of his survival are close to non-existent, and that person will probably die, as has been the case, ever since.

This was true in 1967, as it is most assuredly true today.

Many believed that the seven ill-fated climbers from the Wilcox tragedy were in the wrong place, at the wrong time, and the odds, as is often stated in stories like this one, were extraordinarily against them.[131]

~

"Yeah, I shudder to think what's waitin' for us up above." Gene once again leaned over at the waist and took in several deep breaths.

---

130 James Tabor, *Forever on the Mountain*, New York: W.W Norton & Company, July 17, 2007.

131 Website link: Kurt Repanshek, *National Parks Traveler*, http://www.nationalparkstraveler.com/review/2008/forever-mountain.

It was clear to Johnny that fears about the higher elevations and the onset of acute mountain sickness were beginning to have an impact on Gene, let alone the rest of the MCA team. If Johnny didn't make the right choices the next few days, Gene's fate could very easily have turned into that of Ray Genet's on Mt. Everest, or any of the other scores of climbers who have perished at high altitudes under similar conditions.

Johnny decided to stay with Gene for the remainder of the MCA climb, while Daniel and Henry led the way, pushing on up ahead about a half mile or so above them. The four men soon found themselves crossing below the famous Sourdough Gully as they pushed on up the Harper Glacier.

"So, that's Sourdough Gully?" Henry stopped and leaned over, as Gene had done, and he too took in several deep breaths.

"I can't imagine climbing from the base of Karstens…"

Henry gasped desperately to fill his lungs with the oxygen-starved air.

"Up that shoot, to the top of the North Peak, and back, in what… eighteen hours?"

Daniel too, was bending over at the waist and like Henry, he too breathed in deeply. "That's what those guys did, on a sack of dough-nuts and a thermos of hot chocolate."

Also known as acute mountain sickness (AMS),[138] altitude sickness is a pathological condition that is caused by acute exposure to low air pressure (usually outdoors at high altitudes, generally beginning around 10,000 feet). The cause of altitude sickness is still not understood. It occurs at low atmospheric pressure conditions but not necessarily in low oxygen conditions at sea level pressure.

Although treatable to some extent by the administration of oxygen most of the symptoms do not appear to be caused by low oxygen, but rather by the low CO_2 levels causing a rise in blood pH, alkalosis. Acute mountain sickness can progress to high altitude pulmonary edema (HAPE) or high altitude cerebral edema (HACE).

Edema refers to fluid accumulation in the tissues of the body; caused by local vasodilatation of cerebral blood vessels, or by vasoconstriction in the pulmonary circulation, both conditions leading to increases in capillary pressures. The rate of ascent, altitude attained, amount of physical activity at high altitude, as well as individual susceptibility, are all contributing factors to the onset and severity of high altitude illness.

Symptoms may include severe dyspnea at rest, a dry cough (which may progress to produce pink, frothy sputum), headache, visual impairment, bladder or bowel dysfunction, loss of coordination, paralysis on one side of the body, and confusion. The only remedy for such afflictions is descent to lower elevations.

---

132 Wikipedia link: *Altitude sickness*, http://en.wikipedia.org/wiki/Acute_Mountain_Sickness.

Sourdough Gully is the first couloir on the right side of Brad Washburn's outstanding aerial photograph, which shows the route the Sourdough Expedition took in on April 5, 1910. Pete Anderson and Billy Taylor went all the way to the top (19,470 feet). Charlie McGonagall remained about 500 feet below the summit and secured the 14-foot spruce pole there at the last rock outcroppings along Pioneer Ridge.

Photo: Bradford Washburn, courtesy of the Decaneas Archive, and Betsy Washburn Cabot.

Henry and Daniel continued to move very slowly up the glacier, leaving the base of Sourdough Gully behind them. Henry looked down and could see Johnny and Gene far below, inching their way up the ice maybe a hundred yards or so behind. Clearly the altitude was beginning to take its toll on each one of the MCA climbers.

Interestingly enough the dangers of too rapid an ascent seemed not to be taken into consideration by Park Headquarters and those on the ground, except perhaps by Park Ranger Wayne Merry. Whether it was Vin Hoeman's condemnation that Johnny and his team moved too slowly, or Park Headquarters request that they get up to the Wilcox high camp as quickly as possible now seems a moot point.

To fall back on second guesses of what the MCA climbers should, or should not have done, falls only into the category of biased hindsight. Upon reflection, it was poignantly clear that Johnny and his team were stepping way over the edge of whatever minimal safety net may have been in place for their own protection at the time. Henry's brother was well aware of this, even though others have criticized him, in retrospect.

≈

The first unsolved mystery was about to occur as Daniel and Henry reached an elevation of around 17,200 feet adjacent to the second icefall on the Harper Glacier. As Daniel slowly ascended the ice slope ahead, the rope Henry had been hypnotically following for the past several hours came to a stop. Henry turned his eyes upward and saw Daniel bending and picking something up from the ice at his feet.

"Henry, I've found an axe! There's an ice axe up here."

Henry turned and looked behind him to see Johnny and Gene, maybe fifty yards below. Daniel and Henry had been breaking trail through a section of deep snow, so the gap between their two rope teams had shortened in the past hour or so.

"Johnny!" Henry shouted. "Daniel's found something up above!"

Henry saw Gene collapse to the ground as Johnny continued to press on past him. Henry could hear the shallow crackly, raspy sound of Gene's breathing coming from his lungs, even though Henry still stood a good distance from where Gene sat.

Johnny looked troubled, but he continued to inch his way up the slope toward Henry. He called past Henry to Daniel.

"What is it, Dan? What did you find?"

Within a few minutes, Johnny was passing Henry, his breathing sounded nearly as labored as Gene's, though without the crackly wheezing sound that emanated from Gene's lungs. Johnny stopped beside Henry, and they switched rope positions.

"Here."

Johnny unclipped from the rope, which led down to Gene.

"You hook in with Gene, and I'll take your place. Get Gene up and movin' as soon as you can, though. We've got to get up to their high camp, and dig in."

"It's an axe, Johnny. There's an axe up here, just lying on the ground?" Johnny turned and looked up toward Daniel.

"Hold on!" he shouted. "I'll be up to you in a sec."

Johnny labored on. As soon as he reached Daniel, he stopped, leaned at the waist, and panted in and out, taking in the now customary exchange of air before having enough strength to speak.

"Where did you find it?" Johnny looked at the axe, which Daniel held in his hand.

The unmarked Stubai ice axe found near the upper Harper icefall by the MCA team on July 28, 1967.

Photo: John Ireton, the other photographer of the author's Mountaineering Club of Alaska team in 1967.

"It was just lyin' here, right on the ice. I've been looking off all around, but I don't see signs of anyone. You think maybe it was blown down from above."

"Who knows? Here, put me on a tight rope, and let's scout around a bit, see if we can see any trace of footprints, or anything else?"

Johnny took in several more deep breaths, before moving out across the small expanse of the glacier between the sloping rock walls of the North Peak and the nearby, crusted upper slopes of the Harper's second ice fall. Henry watched from below as Johnny and Daniel slowly checked out the area above. Henry shouted back down to Gene.

"Gene. You ready? Let's move out. We've got to get up to Johnny and Daniel." Henry noticed little movement in Gene, but then he slowly rose to his feet and made a weak reply.

"Okey dokey, Henny Penny. I'm with yah. Let's do it."

By the time Gene and Henry had reached the location of the mysterious ice axe, Johnny and Daniel were coming back across the ice having done a wide sweep of the nearby area adjacent to where Daniel had discovered the axe. Both men were extremely winded, but there was no time for rest.

The MCA climbers slowly make their way up the Harper Glacier. The 15,100-foot camp can be seen on the far right behind the large ice block. The trail beyond the camp leads across Parker Pass to Browne Tower.

Photo: John Ireton, the other photographer of the author's Mountaineering Club of Alaska team in 1967.

"We gottah keep movin'. I don't want any of us to get caught in another storm, without some sort of shelter. We're gonna have to dig caves, yah know. That's gonna take some time."

"Do you think somebody got down to here?"

Gene had collapsed in the snow, reluctant to rise again to his feet. The wheezing, crackling sound continued to echo across the ice as he gasped for air.

"Hell. Who knows? We gottah keep movin' though, and get up to their high camp."

Despite the seriousness of the present situation, Johnny smiled and even cracked a joke.

"As fast as we can." No one smiled.

CHAPTER 24

Keep Digging

The sound of a lightly blowing breeze was heard, in what appeared to be a dream-like state of grayness. As if waking from a deep sleep, the surrounding grayness brightened to the strange sight of a climber, sitting upright on the ice ten feet away. Only his backside was visible. It was a strange sight. The climber was encased in an orange nylon tent material, which was draped around his shoulders like a shawl. All around him, everything was crystal clear in the blue sky and bright sun overhead.

It was as if we were looking through the eyes of this man sitting in the snow, similar to when the Wilcox survivors descended the Coxcomb through Johnny's binoculars. From the climber's point of view, the wind blown remains of a campsite were seen a few feet below him; the tops of snowshoes stuck out from the surface of the snow, while two tents, one orange, another red, appeared torn to shreds. The climber turned, and his view showed what was behind him. Above camp, slowly rotating in a 360 degree pivot, Denali Pass came into view, followed by the ridge line leading to Archdeacon's Tower. Beyond the shark fin rock pinnacle of Archdeacon's Tower, the South Peak dome glistened in the blue-sky overhead.

The only sound was the gently blowing wind flapping against a small section of tent material, which tapped lightly against the climber's back. From the summit began a slow descent down the NE ridge, the very same slope upon which Belmore Browne and Hershel Parker were forced to retreat because of the fierce winds blasting down over them from the South Summit only half a century before.

Finally our lonely climber focused his attention down upon the broad expanse of the Harper Glacier basin below. The granite walls of Browne Tower could be seen far below and to the right. Continuing across the Harper basin, the ridgeline leading down from the North Peak was seen. The upper section of Sourdough

NORTH
PEAK
19,470'

18,700'
The Sourdough's flagpole
was set up in these rocks

18,200'

DENALI
PASS
18,200'

MCA route
to the
17,900' Camp

17,500'
Stuck's Final Camp
1913

16,600'
Stuck
1913

1910

18,200'

SOURDOUGH GULLY

UPPER
ICEFALL

HARPER

17,400'
1912

GLACIER

1912 & 1913

16,600'
Parker-Browne Final Camp
1912

LOWER
ICEFALL

TO
BROWNE
TOWER

top The North Peak (19,470 feet) seen from the air looking across the Great Basin of Harper Glacier; the 1910, 1912, 1913, and the 1967 MCA routes are shown.

Photo: Bradford Washburn, courtesy of the Decaneas Archive, and Betsy Washburn Cabot.

bottom This is what the MCA team saw as they slowly approached the remains of the 17,900-foot high camp of the Wilcox Expedition.

Photo: John Ireton, the other photographer of the author's Mountaineering Club of Alaska team in 1967.

Gully was also visible, just above the bulging cracks of the smaller Upper Icefall on the Harper.

Then, not far below, four climbers came into view slowly moving up the glacier. They were approaching what appeared to be a bamboo pole stuck in the ground about a hundred feet below. It was Johnny and Henry's team. All four climbers were moving at a snail's pace, headed in the direction of this climber wrapped in the orange tent material. Daniel, Henry, Johnny and Gene were now traveling together on one rope team.

The four men crested a small mound of snow, and then they could see it, the wind blown remains of the Wilcox/Colorado seventeen thousand, nine hundred foot camp.

"There it is. That's gottah be their high camp." Johnny was the first to speak.

"What's that stickin' out of the ground down below?" Daniel noticed what looked like a pole stuck in the ice about a hundred feet below the camp. It was taller than the standard sized wand, which is generally 3-4 feet in length. The pole was decorated with streamers and what appeared to be a small flag.

"I don't know. Let's get up there and find out."

If a bald eagle could have soared over their heads at this elevation, the four climbers below would have been seen slowly plodding their way footstep by footstep, painstakingly breathing in and out, as they moved at a snail's pace up toward the scattered remains of the 17,900-foot campsite.

Again the men looked like a tiny column of ants that had lost its way from the rest of the colony on this huge white mound of snow, rock, and ice. Inching its way toward their unknown destination, the small band finally reached what appeared to be a slanting half-inch thick bamboo pole, which was adorned with brightly colored surveyor's tape and a small flag.

At the base of the pole they found a sleeping bag, encased in a red outer shell. Apparently someone had decided to wrap the bag around the pole, or miraculously it had blown down from above and magically caught on the pole. Shortly, all four climbers were rallying around this pole. Again, Johnny was the first to speak.

"Looks like some kind of marker?"

Gene's breathing was very loud now, and piercing. Its raspy, hollow sounding crackle reminded Henry of his nightmare vision of Elton Thayer. As Gene lay on his side in the snow, still gasping for air, he offered his opinion.

"Or maybe, somebody got too tired." Gene made several more wheezy attempts to take in more air, and then he collapsed on his back next to the pole.

"Maybe they got too tired, to carry it up to the camp." Gene smiled, but was dead serious.

left The frozen corpse which the MCA team discovered at the 17,900-foot camp.

Photo: Gayle Nienhueser, one of the two photographers of the author's Mountaineering Club of Alaska team in 1967.

right About a hundred feet below the 17,900-foot camp, the MCA climbers found this pole stuck in the snow with a sleeping bag wrapped around it.

Photo: John Ireton, the other photographer of the author's Mountaineering Club of Alaska team in 1967.

"Matter a fact, that sounds like a good idea to me. Think I'll maybe drop my pack right here, too, alongside this pole."

"No, come on Gene. We gottah keep movin'… We've got to get up to the high camp. That's all there is to it. Up and at 'em." Johnny reached down, grabbed hold of Gene's arm and pulled him to his feet.

Daniel led off, while Henry fed out the rope, and soon he was following in Daniel's footsteps, while Johnny and Gene trailed slowly behind. Within a half hour Daniel reached the high camp, and with each passing breath and step, he slowly made his way up into the scattered debris above, and became the first to discover what they had all feared most.

When Daniel turned to coil in the rope between him and Henry, Henry could see the sad expression on his face, a look of utter despair and hopeless fatigue. Henry approached the final few yards, one slow step after the other, between one inhalation and exhalation and then another step. Henry stopped and looked at Daniel. Then came his grim reply.

"There's a dead man in camp."

At first Henry stood motionless; then, bending slightly at the waist, as if some-one had punched him in the stomach, he began to hyperventilate, one deep breath after another. Henry had lost control. Then came Johnny's voice yelling up to him from below.

"Henry! Pull in the rope! Damn it, Henry! Pull up the rope!"

Slowly Henry pulled in the rope between Johnny and himself, as his eyes turned in the direction of the fallen climber. His nightmare from their bivouac camp above Karstens had come true. The grizzly form of a man wrapped in a nylon tent shawl stared vacantly toward Henry, his frozen features a ghastly re-minder of the severe consequences of their immediate surroundings.

Everything was still and quiet, except for the gentle breeze that blew steadily across the ice. Finally, Johnny stood next to Henry in this forlorn and desolate camp. As Henry had done a few minutes before, Johnny leaned over at the waist and took in several deeps breaths. Daniel looked at Johnny and spoke.

"He's dead. Frozen solid."

"Yeah … I figured." Johnny continued to breathe deeply, trying desperately to fill his lungs, as he pulled in Gene's rope. As Gene approached their new camp, his raspy breathing crackled more loudly than before with each step, nearly drowning out the sound of the gentle breeze.

Henry looked down the glacier and saw a dark shadow slowly cross the basin below, as the sun slowly dipped behind the granite walls of the North Peak.

"Okay you guys! Let's get with it." Johnny began barking orders. "Come on. Come on! Everyone! We've got to dig in. Let's get the show on the road. We don't want to end up like this guy."

Johnny motioned briefly in the direction of the frozen man, and then he threw a shovel toward Henry's feet. "Let's go Henry!"

Despite the fact that each man was nearly spent, the MCA climbers hastily dug into the frozen ground of the wind blown glacier. Minutes turned into hours. Though it was already late in the day, there was no other choice. They needed to fabricate a secure shelter from Mother Nature's worst potential.

Johnny dug away, until finally he had fashioned a grave like hole, large enough for Henry to crawl into. Johnny gazed briefly toward the vacant shell of the fro-zen corpse, and then he turned his focus on Henry.

"Henry, crawl down inside with your ice ax, and start chipping away at the ice. I'll shovel it out, from up here."

As Henry positioned himself in the hole, Johnny stopped digging for a second. Henry turned and looked up at his older brother. As Johnny stood there above Henry, his dark silhouette made Henry begin to shudder. For a second, Henry felt as though Katherine or possibly Aunt Sophie was gazing

The author and his brother undertake the laborious task of digging out a snow cave shelter in the frozen snow and ice.

Photo: Gayle Nienhueser, one of the two photographers of the author's Mountaineering Club of Alaska team in 1967.

down upon him, with that mysterious "fog apple" gaze of a drunken stupor, a phrase Skipper had coined one day, which Henry had always remembered from his childhood.

Henry imagined some evil spirit had suddenly cast a dark spell over his brother. Given the gloomy prospects of their current situation, and the utter fatigue each man felt, perhaps Johnny's mind was beginning to play tricks on him.

It was true. Johnny's imagination had begun to take over his mind, which was now clearly out of control; the image of two naked bodies appeared before Johnny's eyes. Together as if they had bedded down in this frozen grave like hole, Johnny saw Henry lying on top of Bonnie in the act of making love.

Johnny shook his head but was unable to erase the startling image from his mind. With a bizarre twisted tonality in his voice, Johnny spoke.

"Henry. Henry! Listen up! I've … I've got something on my mind. Something I've been meaning to ask you ever since you boarded the train back in Anchorage."

Johnny breathed in deeply, dizzy from the diminished amount of oxygen in the air. Like Gene, and the others, Johnny too, had reached his breaking point.

His utter frustration and seething pent up anger had now become focused, and it was clearly leveled toward Henry.

"There's something I want to ask you about. Do you hear me? And I want the truth!"

Daniel and Gene were now below the surface of the ice, about ten yards away, so Johnny's and Henry's conversation remained private. Henry slowly turned and looked up.

"Yeah, what?"

Johnny squatted down and looked Henry in the eye. Henry could tell that his older brother was angry about something. He had the same look the day he tossed Henry to the ground at the train depot, like two red hot daggers that were ready to burn a hole through Henry's forehead.

"When I was up in Fairbanks, the week before we came up to the park. Do you remember?"

Henry stopped chipping away at the ice. He could see where Johnny was going with this line of questioning.

"Yeah, what... uh, what about it?"

"Did anything happen between you and Bonnie?"

"What, huh?" Henry's heart started beating faster.

"What do you mean?"

Johnny jumped down into the hole and grabbed hold of Henry's parka by the neck. Johnny tightened his grip, as he pulled the parka's material tightly around Henry's neck, so that Henry could barely breathe.

Henry grimaced and started to panic at the closeness of his brother's rage and this seemingly uncontrollable and sudden attack.

"Don't mess around with me! You know damn well what I'm talking about."

"Johnny. No, no! Bonnie and I … uh, didn't do anything … like that. We... uh, we sat around, and talked... uh... about you and the kids... and then I went to bed. I went to bed out in the garage."

≈

Bonnie was on the ground beneath the steps of their backyard screened-in porch. She had just tripped and was now sprawled out in the mud. Henry was kneeling beside her. He began to help Bonnie to her feet.

"Ouch. I think I might have sprained it."

"Here, let me help you up."

Bonnie put her left arm around Henry's neck, while Henry wrapped his right arm around her waist. Together they hobbled toward Henry's bedroom in the garage, and they entered together closing the door behind them. Once inside Henry helped Bonnie to his small bed. Bonnie sat on the edge, while Henry stood beside her. Henry appeared nervous.

"My leg's okay." Bonnie confessed. "I just wanted to come in here, and be with you for a while longer. Is that okay?"

"Sure. Yeah, that's okay."

Bonnie took Henry's hand and pulled him gently down. Henry sat beside her on the bed. Then Bonnie slowly leaned forward, pushed Henry back onto the bed, and began to lay down, slowly and gently on top of Henry, similar to what Johnny had imagined, only Bonnie was on top.

Henry was scared and confused, yet the warmth of Bonnie's body was intoxicating, almost irresistible. Henry was torn between the pleasure of making love with the sister-in-law he had always fancied, and the guilt-ridden pain of cheating on his older brother, Johnny, by sleeping with Bonnie.

"Wait a minute. Wait a minute. What am I doing?"

"Come on Henry, its all right."

This did feel good, almost too good, but in the shadows of his mind Henry knew there was something very wrong about what he and Bonnie were about to do.

Henry looked into his sister-in-law's eyes, and he saw something he had not expected. There was not an impassioned look of love and desire in Bonnie's eyes; no, it was the face of a woman lost in the angst of betraying her husband and accepting the inevitable demise of their marriage.

Henry however sensed he was looking not only into the eyes of Bonnie, but also into the eyes of his mother, his crazy Aunts Sophie and Hazel, and all the other scorned women from his family's past. For Henry, that night in the garage in the back of his brother's house turned out to be one of the saddest moments of his life; yet it was also a key to his future hope for happiness. Something clicked inside his brain, and even though Henry didn't understand it at the time, he would never be the same.

Bonnie suddenly caught herself, and she stopped her attempt to seduce Henry. Tears began to trickle down her cheeks, and a deep heart felt sadness began to pour out of her being from the utter depths of her soul. She was crying not just for herself, she was crying for Katherine, and for her own mother, Shirley and for all the other lost and forgotten women of the world.

Henry's defenses and feelings of arousal were gone. He put his arms around Bonnie and embraced her with a shared awareness and a genuine sense of love. Neither of them spoke. They stayed like this for perhaps a minute or so, as they just held each other, without saying a word.

As the sun sank below the North Peak; a dark shadow crossed the upper basin of the Harper Glacier. The MCA climbers had nearly completed their snow caves as the shadow crept across their tomb-like shelters.

Photo: Gayle Nienhueser, one of the two photographers of the author's Mountaineering Club of Alaska team in 1967.

Then, Bonnie regained her composure and slowly rose from the bed. She picked up Henry's blue kerchief from the table beside his bed and dried her tears. Bonnie smiled at Henry, rustled the crop of tangled brown hair on the top of Henry's head, and then she crossed to the door. Before leaving, she turned again and looked at Henry one more time.

That deep sense of sadness still permeated her expression; the same look Henry had seen in his mother's eyes, and in her sisters, Henry's Aunt Sophie and Hazel. Bonnie turned and went out the door without saying a word.

From the ice-crusted hole in the Harper Glacier, Henry looked up into his brother's eyes. Like Bonnie, Johnny stared back at him and said nothing. By now his face was completely silhouetted by the sun. As the North Peak's shadow slowly crossed Johnny's face, it also cut into Henry's like the jagged blade of a knife.

Never had Henry felt so cold and alone. Johnny's dark glare locked into his eyes, as if he were staring into the eyes of the Grim Reaper, himself, or possibly Joe Wilcox's dark hooded face.

"You better be telling me the truth, little brother." Johnny held his stare for a few seconds longer.

"I am, Johnny. I am."

"All right … Never mind. Forget about it. Keep digging."

CHAPTER 25

To the Top of the Continent

A brisk wind was blowing small plumes of snow across the surface of the ice. Archdeacon's Tower and the South Peak Dome could be seen behind and high above the scattered remains of the Wilcox, now the MCA campsite. Not much had changed from before, aside from the fact that there were now four living men situated within the 17,900-foot camp.

Johnny was standing and talking on a hand held radio, the very same radio Joe Wilcox had used with his team and had been gracious enough to let the MCA team make use of. Daniel and Henry were seated nearby on their pads eating their McKinley Stew from large plastic cups. Gene too was chomping away, but was only half visible since he was standing in the dug out entrance to his and Daniel's snow cave. It was 8 PM, the agreed upon contact time, and the MCA team's first radio contact with Park Headquarters from the high camp.

"Eielson Ranger Station? This is the Mountaineering Club of Alaska. We are at the 17,900-foot Wilcox camp. Over."

Through the static driven sound of the radio, a faint voice could be heard. "We read you faintly on that. Are any members of the seven … are any of the seven members alive?"

"We found one body … one body, over."

"Have you seen anything of the other six?"

Gene staggered from his cave entrance like someone who had one too many drinks … up to the surface of the ice, and stood next to Johnny.

"Negative … negative, over."

"Do … is the … is the body Dennis Luchterhand?"

"Do not know, over. Do not know, over. We'll try for the summit tomorrow, over."

"Try for the summit tomorrow…"

"Roger, roger. We will search on the way. We will search on the way, over."

"If you can possibly make identification of body at high camp, ah, please do."

Johnny paused, looked toward the frozen climber, a few yards away ... then turned, noticed Gene next to him ... who seemed to sway from side to side ... and then he spoke into the radio.

"We cannot look at him. He's decomposed, greatly ... over."

"Okay. One additional thing, ah, look for messages ... that the individual you have found may have left."

The sad truth about looking for messages was the fact that what was once a living human being was now a solid block of frozen flesh. Imagine trying to cut into a rigid block of ice in an attempt to retrieve a pocket journal or note pad that may have been placed on the inside pocket of this man's frozen parka, one that was now wrapped inside the frozen orange tent material that encased his rigid body.

Now imagine that you tried to do this at an elevation of 17,900 feet at sub zero temperatures, while a brisk cold wind was further freezing the bare skin on your face, and your gloveless hands.

If you thought about the conditions under which such a search was to be performed, you would perhaps get an idea of how difficult such a request was for Henry's brother, let alone for anyone else who was asked to peel apart and cut into the frozen layers of the man who sat staring at him with vacant deathlike eyes.

At sea level, forensic experts often find such a task distasteful, even under laboratory conditions. Imagine the MCA climbers' dismay, if you will, at 17,900 feet; each of them suffering to a greater or lesser extent from the effects of too rapid an ascent to the frozen and solitary upper slopes of the Harper Glacier, and to the tattered remains of the high altitude camp of the Wilcox/Snyder Expedition.

"Roger, roger." Replied Johnny, choosing in his own mind to avoid the request, in spite of the intentions of those concerned at sea level with their desire that he follow through.

"That is all at this time, ah KHD6990 Eielson clear."

"Unit two, clear."

From a distance, the four men were seen standing together quietly in silence with little to say to one another, as the wind blew across the glacier.

"Well guys, let's call it a night. We've all got a big day ahead of us tomorrow."

Then one by one, each man disappeared beneath the ice, as if he were climbing down into some ancient Egyptian Catacomb on the sands of the Sahara.

It was the next morning. Henry's eyes opened as he felt the cold and stared at

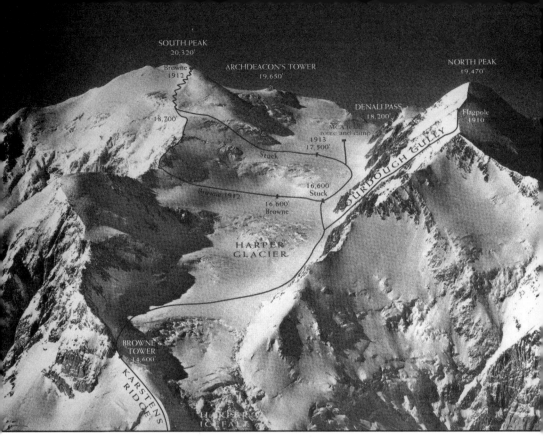

The Upper slopes of Denali, showing the early Pioneer Routes of 1910, 1912, 1913, and the 17,900-foot high camp of both the Wilcox and MCA teams.

Photo: Bradford Washburn, courtesy of the Decaneas Archive, and Betsy Washburn Cabot.

the ice ceiling above his head. Johnny had already crawled from his sleeping bag and was moving his pack away from the cave entrance, when he turned to Henry.

"Let's get a move on Henry. We've got to get an early start."

"What time is it?"

"2 AM. I'll crank up the stove and start melting snow. But we've got to be underway in another hour or so. Start getting your stuff together. It's probably 20-30 below, so bring everything you've got for warmth. It's going to be a cold one."

It was later, nearly 4:30 AM before the MCA team got underway. From high overhead, the four climbers slowly moved across the upper portion of the Harper glacier, headed in the direction of Denali Pass, about a quarter mile above their camp. The scattered remains of the Wilcox high camp were barely visible from high overhead, as the men slowly plodded their way over the ice. Two deep breaths to each step punctuated the team's tawdry pace. Progress was steady, but painstakingly slow. After an hour of slow drudgery, the men finally reached Denali Pass.

As Johnny, Gene, Daniel, and Henry turned to climb up the South Peak ridge-line above the pass, a loud deafening roar was heard in the sky overhead.

The four men stopped in their tracks. Henry turned and looked up into the clear blue sky over his head. The sun shone brightly in his eyes.

Above them the climbers saw a strange and impressive sight. A huge cargo Air Force plane (C130) made several passes back and forth over the top of the mountain, as it dropped one billowing parachute after another to the floor of the Harper Glacier from directly above Denali Pass.

Several of the shoots landed at the base of some large rocks to the left of the Pass. However, a few missed the mark entirely, and dropped over the pass land-ing on the steep cliffs below. Two men pushed the bundles from an open side door of the plane. One of the men was Grace's husband, Vin Hoeman.

From inside the plane Vin looked down upon his friends on the mountain below. Using a Nikon 35mm single lens reflex camera, Vin snapped three or four shots as his friends slowly plodded up the South Peak ridgeline from Denali Pass. Grace had chosen to wait back in Anchorage, rather than accompany her husband on this last fleeting attempt by the Park, Alaska Rescue Group, and The US Air Force to finally do something tangible to help resolve this otherwise cata-strophic event. The man next to Vin pushed another large green bundle out the door, and its bright orange parachute suddenly sprung open in the sky below.

As Johnny, Gene, Henry and Daniel trudged up the ridgeline, a large rock out-cropping came into view above the pass. Henry looked up toward Gene. By now Henry had nearly become accustomed to the raspy echo of Gene's breathing and his hacking cough. It almost seemed natural, not life threatening.

Gene stood wheezing a short distance above Henry, and called down with his frail weathered voice.

"Well, ole Henny Penny ... I guess our air drop, uh ... our air drop ... has finally arrived."

"I don't know Gene." Henry felt cold and lost, almost abandoned—like a child left alone by his parents—so far from the comfort and safety of the civilized world.

"If I had my way, I wish ... I wish I could be in that plane right now. I wish I was headed back to Talkeetna, or Anchorage, or wherever that plane is headed for."

"Me, too." Gene bent over at his waist. His voice had a strange, slightly gurgling quality to it.

"Me, too ... ole Henny ... Penny." The raspy crackling noise turned to a cough, as Gene hung over at the waist, and spit another chunk of phlegm into the snow at his feet. For a few seconds Henry watched him stumble from side to side, al-most delirious. Gene looked down at Henry.

"Holy Moly, Henry. I don't know if I'm gonna be able to keep this up all day?"

Johnny had overheard Henry and Gene's exchange and he called down to them from above.

"Okay, you guys. Let's keep moving. We don't have all day."

"Johnny...! Gene's not good. I think we need to stop."

"Gene! Keep coming. I'm bringing you up to me. Don't give up. Come on up here, and we'll take a break."

When Henry reached the spot where Gene had been standing, he noticed specks of blood-streaked sputum in the snow. Henry turned and looked up into the bright sun, as the plane made another pass.

~~

It was nighttime, and the light on a lamppost was seen outside an apartment dwelling in Branford, Connecticut. Through a recognizable outside window, Katherine and her twenty-three year old son Reg, Jr. (Skipper) were sitting inside their apartment, as were Henry and Katherine several months earlier over Spring break. Their eyes were fixed on the screen of Katherine's black and white television set. However, they were not watching an episode of Star Trek. Instead, Walter Cronkite was delivering the evening news.

"Good Evening. Seven mountain climbers remain missing on the upper slopes of Alaska's Mt. McKinley. Separated from the rest of their group by a severe storm, the climbers have not been heard from for more than a week. An all-out search and rescue operation is currently under way to locate the missing climbers from the Joseph Wilcox Expedition. Five men came down safely on July 23rd and met up with another team climbing the same route—from The Mountaineering Club of Alaska."

Katherine broke down into tears.

"I knew something like this would happen. I could feel it in my bones."

Behind her Cronkite continued his newscast.

"Yesterday the frozen body of one man was discovered at the team's high camp, at an elevation of 17,900 feet."

Reginald, Jr. stared blankly at the screen as Katherine quietly sat on the couch with tears welling up in her eyes.

"Today an US Air Force C-130 completed a scheduled air drop of supplies to the rescue team climbing near the summit, making one of the highest air rescue attempts in the history of the United States Air Force."

Katherine's voice cracked, as she tried to hold back her tears. She got up and headed into the kitchen to again refill her empty bourbon glass. She was

South Summit
(20,320 feet)

Archdeacon's Tower
(19,650 feet)

An aerial view of what the men inside the HC-130 probably saw as the MCA climbers slowly plodded their way up toward the South Summit from Denali Pass.

Photo: Bradford Washburn, courtesy of the Decaneas Archive, and Betsy Washburn Cabot.

clearly distraught over the terrible tragedy in which her two sons had become enmeshed. Reg, Jr. attempted to console his grieving mother.

'Come on, mom. Don't worry. They're gonna be all right. It's not Johnny and Henry who're in trouble. It's that other Wilcox group."

Katherine turned and looked toward her middle son.

≈

The four MCA climbers now sat behind a rock, along the ridgeline leading to the summit. Gene's raspy, crackling breathing appeared to have lessened in severity. The men were just finishing up a short ten-minute break.

"Gene! Gene! You ready? Let's go. We've gottah keep moving! We can't leave you here. We need to stay together. We can't chance you wandering off and getting lost. Okay?"

Johnny made a tough call.

Gene slowly stumbled to his feet. Henry looked back over his shoulder, as the sun shone brightly into his eyes, blinding his view, and triggering in his mind a fond memory.

Henry's mother Katherine was smiling at him from inside her apartment. She was much younger and happier, the mother Henry chose to remember in later life, free from the sorrow and sadness of her own family's strife. Katherine would always struggle with alcohol until she died from a brain aneurism, which burst one day when she became dizzy and fell to the ground. Henry and his three-year old son Gunnar were taking a walk with her on a dirt road near the apartment dwelling in which she and Captain Reggie lived after moving to be with Henry and his family in Wasilla. Katherine was hospitalized in Anchorage, and died three weeks later.

"Shall we watch some TV tonight, after dinner? If we both tackle the dishes together, we'll still have time to catch the *Honeymooners*. What do you say?"

"Sounds good to me, mom. It's a deal."

"I'll put on some tea."

"Don't forget the chocolate chip cookies." Henry smiled.

Henry remembered wrapping the string around his tea bag, as Katherine and he would later spend the evening watching not only the *Honeymooners*, but also an episode of a new science fiction outer space show called Star-Trek. Henry smiled as he thought about Captain James Kirk being magically transported up through space to the Starship Enterprise.

"If only I could be transported to that plane,"—Henry's positive reflection of Katherine disappeared in the bright sun, as the plane roared overhead, making its final pass.

The last parachute drifted slowly over the icy cliffs below Denali Pass, having missed its mark. The plane continued south and soon drifted from sight on its way back to Elmendorf Air Force Base in Anchorage. The engine's dying drone was replaced by the wind's lonely and desolate moan.

Three more hours slowly ticked by before the small band of brothers reached a broad plateau named The Football Field, located between the South Summit and Archdeacon's Tower. Yet, still, there were no signs of the six missing men. The Wilcox climbers had vanished. In Henry's mind it seemed as though they were playing a deadly game of hide and seek.

At 19,650 feet Johnny found refuge beneath the rocky shark's fin of Archdeacon's Tower. They stopped again to rest, struggling in vain to fill their already inflated lungs with more air. Henry inhaled deeply until he thought his lungs would burst, yet this ongoing repetitive cycle of breathing in and exhaling out never satisfied his need for more oxygen.

Johnny pointed toward the summit dome.

"That's it. That's the top. Let's keep moving. We're close now."

~

These were nearly the same words Jerry Clark had probably spoken on July 18, as he and four others saw the clouds clear over the summit, after spending a frigid night below the icy slopes of Archdeacon's Tower. Uncertain which way to go, in the white winds, their exhausted group made the fatal mistake to bivouac overnight on what they believed to be the summit ridge.

Instead they had begun an ascent up Archdeacon's Tower. A brief glimpse of the summit dome the following morning gave them their bearings, as they lay most likely in open pits, as the MCA climbers had done below Browne Tower four days earlier.

Not unlike Clark and his team, Johnny, Gene, Henry and Daniel struggled to their feet, and moved in slow motion, like zombies, across the broad plane, roughly the same size of a football field, hence the name.

Henry watched Branford High's Jumpin' Johnny Locke plod his way out onto the snow-covered field, as he led his team toward the goal line before them and toward the touchdown of his life.

Johnny soon crossed the fifty-yard line, and shortly the men found themselves moving up the steep five hundred foot slope to the final ridgeline that would take them to the South Summit.

"This is just like the 500-foot slope below Pitchler's Perch, on Eklutna," Henry thought to himself. "Except this one's at 20,000 feet."

Another aerial view, this time of Archdeacon's Tower. On the left are the granite slopes rising to the North Peak, to the right is the broad expanse of "The Football Field."

Photo: Chuck Kime, Writphotec, Inc. 'Archdeacon's Tower' viewed from a southerly direction.

Each step now became a slow, mechanical movement of feet, while the rope dragged slowly between each man: One step up... inhale, exhale... inhale, exhale... Take another step... inhale, exhale ... and, so forth.

The golden braids of nylon snaked across the ice steps at Henry's feet. Like robots from outer space, their movements were mechanical and heavy-footed, as if they were walking on the moon. At last the four men crested the final ridgeline that led to the summit, still another fifty yards away.

As Joe Wilcox and the three Colorado climbers had done eleven days before them, the Mountaineering Club of Alaska team slowly made its way toward the South Peak.

Henry looked at Johnny's feet and noticed one of his crampons beginning to ball up with snow. He flashed to the nightmare of Johnny plummeting down the steep slope to their right, as Daniel and Henry had done on Karstens. However, the problem was easily remedied when Henry saw his brother whack the side of his crampon with the shaft of his axe. The ball of snow dropped harmlessly from his boot, then rolled down the gully to the right and vanished from sight.

Johnny turned and looked back. "Henry? How's Gene doing?"

Henry glanced back at Gene. The weather was clear, but Henry noticed clouds were beginning to accumulate in the lowlands below. Behind Gene, Henry saw

The author follows his older brother up the steep ridgeline of the South Summit.

Photo: Gayle Nienhueser, one of the two photographers of the author's Mountaineering Club of Alaska team in 1967.

Clouds are beginning to form in the lowlands. The peak left of the climber is Denali's Wife, otherwise called Mt. Foraker (17,400 feet), the fourth highest peak in the United States.

Photo: Gayle Nienhueser, one of the two photographers of the author's Mountaineering Club of Alaska team in 1967.

The author (left) and his older brother (right) standing on the summit of Denali, North America's highest land mark at 20,320 feet.

Photo: Gayle Nienhueser, one of the two photographers of the author's Mountaineering Club of Alaska team in 1967.

another massive snow-covered mountain almost as high as Denali. Henry called down to Gene.

"Gene... How yah doing? You going to be able to make it?"

"I haven't come this far." Gene coughed, bent over and breathed in deeply.

"I haven't come this far, just to stop here, and turn around." He coughed again. "Keep ah truckin'. I'll make it. Ole Henny Penny."

Henry turned and called up to Johnny.

"I think he's okay. He says to keep going."

Johnny looked back down at Henry, and he too saw the massive peak towering below. "That's Mt. Foraker. Denali's Wife."

Henry turned around and looked again, as Johnny pointed off to the left. "Over there is Mt. Hunter." Johnny smiled. "That one's supposed to be the child. You know, the little baby... like you."

Henry laughed at Johnny's joke. "Right."

"Too bad Hans isn't here to see you set foot on the summit."

Then it happened. A cool brisk breeze blew across a cloudless sky overhead, as Johnny, Henry, Gene, and Daniel slowly trekked across the final twenty feet to the top of North America.

Johnny pulled in the rope, as Henry joyfully joined him on the summit. Johnny's eyes beamed with pride, as Henry slowly stumbled his way to his brother.

"Well, you made it, big guy. Nice going, little brother, you're now standing on the top of North America."

Johnny threw his tired arms around Henry, and this time their embrace was a gesture of true love and compassion for what they had just accomplished together.

Henry looked into his brother's eyes.

"Oh, man Johnny. You should see your face. Your lips are all cracked and bleeding."

Johnny's lower lip had a distinct crack right in the center. A bright red trail of frozen blood ran down into Johnny's ice-encrusted beard. Henry smiled.

"Here, put some zinc oxide on it. Grace gave it to me, before she went down."

Johnny removed his mitt and took the tube from his brother, as Henry slowly pulled in the rope between Gene and himself. Gene stumbled across the final few feet and collapsed to the ground at the summit.

"I made it... I made it!" As Gene gasped deeply, Henry noticed the crackly wheezing sound could be heard again, penetrating into his lungs. Johnny and he squatted down next to Gene, as a steady breeze chilled their faces. Johnny poured a cup of hot tea from his thermos and handed it to Gene.

Between sips of tea, and labored breaths, Gene looked appreciatively into Johnny and Henry's eyes.

"I really didn't think I was gonna make it. You know?"

top The summit of Mt. Foraker is seen below and to the left, behind the climber who is slowly making his way toward the summit of Denali.

Photo: Jack Duggan, a member of 'The Anderson Pass Expedition' of 1977.

bottom This photo was taken by the MCA team in 1967 looking north-northeast from the summit of the South Peak (20,320 feet) on July 29, 1967. The North Peak (19,470 feet) is at left, two miles away and 850 feet lower. "Farthing Horn" (the northeast shoulder) right of center is where Belmore Browne gave up the ascent in 1912 only a 200-yard stroll to the summit in good weather. He wrote in his book, "I was struck with the full fury of the storm. The breath was driven from my body and I held my axe with stooped shoulders to stand against the gale.... As I brushed the frost from my glasses and squinted upward through the stinging snow, I saw a sight that will haunt me to my dying day. The slope above me was no longer steep!"

Photo: Gayle Nienhueser, one of the two photographers of the author's Mountaineering Club of Alaska team in 1967.

Brad Washburn took this photograph looking north-northeast from the summit of the South Peak (20,320 feet) at 5:15 PM of July 23, 1942. The North Peak (19,470 feet) is at left, two miles away and 850 feet lower than the camera. Bob Bates and Terris Moore are standing precisely where Belmore Browne gave up the ascent in 1912.

Photo: Brad Washburn, courtesy of the Decaneas Archive, and Betsy Washburn Cabot.

Tears began to run down Gene's cheeks, but quickly froze in the chilly wind. "Thanks for getting me up here, guys. Thanks a million. I did it … didn't I? I'm here. I made it. I'm on top, right?"

Johnny smiled. "You made it, Gene. You're on top."

Henry grabbed Gene's rope and began to pull in the slack between him and Daniel. Johnny looked at Daniel, as he too slowly approached the summit.

"Daniel. This is it! You're finally here! You've made it! The first Native Eskimo to set foot on top, right up there with Walter Harper."

Daniel smiled, but said nothing. Henry thought of the old Native woman he had met on the plane. Had she been there, Henry thought to himself, even she would have shared in their team's moment of pride, especially on Daniel's behalf. The four men joyously embraced each other at the top of North America.

From high above the South Peak Summit, Johnny, Gene, Daniel and Henry were seen taking turns, shooting photos of each other on top. They drank hot cocoa and tea from thermoses, just like the Sourdoughs had done on the North Peak in 1910,

On the left side of this photo stands the author (right) and his brother (left) on the summit. Behind them to the far right is the North Peak. Note the cloud build-up in the lowlands and the high cirrus clouds in the sky overhead, signaling an approaching storm front.

Photo: Gayle Nienhueser, one of the two photographers of the author's Mountaineering Club of Alaska team in 1967.

which could be seen directly across from the summit, about two miles away. The men ate a lunch of gorp, moose sausage, dried salmon, and frozen cheese.

Despite their numb fingers and a blustery wind blowing across the summit, each man's heart and mind was filled with warmth and gratitude for having achieved their goal. Gene took a final photo of Johnny and Henry, which was later used in a book about Don Sheldon.[133]

Shortly after this photo was snapped, Henry noticed Johnny gazing down into the sea of clouds below that was beginning to encircle the mountain. He could see the worried expression on his brother's face. It was at that moment that the grating noise of a lone plane engine cut across the cold crisp sky; behind Archdeacon's Tower Henry saw a small plane making its way up and across the Harper Glacier basin. It was Don Sheldon.

The team quickly shouldered their packs, and within seconds they were descending from the summit to the football field below. The small yellow Super Cub was the same one they had seen down at the 15,100 foot igloo camp earlier in the week. This time the plane climbed higher and higher toward the upper slopes of Denali and Archdeacon's Tower, and by the time Johnny's team had reached the plateau below, they could see Sheldon circling overhead. It appeared as though he might have spotted something.

---

133 James Greiner, *Wager with the Wind: The Don Sheldon Story*, Rand McNally & Company: San Francisco, pp. 204-205, First Printing 1974.

CHAPTER 26

The Storm

From inside the cockpit of his small plane Don Sheldon looked down upon the upper slopes of Denali. He banked his Super Cub to the right, and slowly made a huge arch crossing above Denali Pass as the Air Force plane had done five hours earlier. But by now, low-lying clouds had formed a sea of grayness in the valleys below, and the twin peaks of Denali appeared as an islands in the stream.

Mild gusts of jet stream winds, called Mare's Tails, were beginning to funnel through Denali Pass, as they buffeted against the wings of Sheldon's plane. He completed his second circle of the upper slopes of the Harper and was now gazing down toward the steep, icy slopes below Archdeacon's Tower. This time he was much closer to the frozen wall of snow and ice, and this time the bright colors he had spotted earlier were more apparent. Below him he saw two frozen corpses, two more victims from the missing Wilcox seven, perhaps thirty yards or so apart, slumped in the snow; one of them, according to Sheldon, appeared to be clutching the head of an ice axe.[134]

Sheldon banked to the left and glided over Archdeacon's as his plane headed directly for the South Summit. Below he spotted the four MCA climbers as they were making their way across the football field. Sheldon hastily scrawled a note describing what he had discovered, attached it to a red, delicious apple with rubber bands and surveyor tape streamers, and then dropped closer to the MCA men below.

As Johnny, Gene, Daniel and Henry peered up into the sky over their heads, Sheldon tossed the message from his cockpit window as his plane roared by. With streamers flickering across the sky, the apple dropped from Sheldon's plane

---

134 James Greiner, *Wager with the Wind: The Don Sheldon Story*, Rand McNally & Company: San Francisco, pp. 219-220, First Printing 1974.

down onto the football field near the base of Archdeacon's Tower. Johnny and Daniel crossed the snowfield to retrieve it, while Gene and Henry sat and waited below the jagged shark fin of Archdeacon's Tower. The two men moved slowly to where the apple had landed. Johnny picked it up, and removed the rubber bands and tape with his frozen fingers, then silently read the note.

Daniel too was curious to discover what Sheldon had seen.

"What does it say?"

Johnny looked at the note in his hands. Instead of reading it aloud, Johnny paraphrased the message.

"Sheldon's spotted something on the other side of Archdeacon's. Bright colors. He thinks its two more climbers, probably both dead."

From high overhead, the four men below again appeared like ants, as Daniel and Johnny moved across the snowfield toward Gene and Henry.

Gene remained collapsed on the ground, his breathing hampered as before. Henry rose to his feet to greet them. Sheldon's message was relayed to his brother and Gene, then Johnny opened his Swiss Army knife, and divided up the frozen but succulent fruit, which the four men savored like the delicacy it was.

Daniel made a bold suggestion regarding this new dilemma.

"Johnny, Henry and I can drop down the other side of Archdeacon's and go check it out. What do yah think?

"I don't know, Dan?"

"Come on, Johnny." Henry spoke hesitantly. "It's not that far out of the way?"

Johnny looked to the clouds moving up the mountain from below.

"You guys noticed the weather's starting to sock in on us again, right? Check out those high cirrus clouds, overhead. That's not good."

Daniel's reply went against his usual support of Johnny's input.

"I don't know Johnny? I think we'll pretty much be able to see each other, the whole time. Shouldn't take us that long to check it out."

The four men were now standing at the base of Archdeacon's Tower[135] at an elevation of slightly above 19,000 feet. Daniel's clarity of reason and good judgment, like Henry's and even Johnny's, was now being clouded by the urgency of the situation, as well as the probable side effects of hypoxia (reduced supply of oxygen) upon the brain. Gene, of course was suffering the most from extreme shortness of breath and he was still coughing up a pinkish frothy fluid; sure signs of high altitude pulmonary edema (HAPE). Getting Gene down to a lower elevation was imperative to his survival.

---

135 Web Link photo: *Archdeacon's Tower*. http://www.flickr.com/photos/30652603@ N07/2884322280/

The Party at McGonagall Pass from the 1942 Army Mt. McKinley Test Expedition, which was led by Bradford Washburn, seated last on the right in the back row.

Photo: Unknown, Courtesy of Alaska and Polar Regions Collections, Elmer E. Rasmuson Library, UAF; July 7, 1942.

When Bradford Washburn conducted experiments during his 1942 and 1947 expeditions[136] in which his team stayed at high altitudes for extended periods, he discovered that most participants in the controlled study group were found to be functioning at around fifty percent of the mental capacity. The ability to make plausible decisions and to think clearly has often proven less than desirable with climbers living at high altitudes.

Such was probably the case, with the six men from the Wilcox team who chose to bivouac below Archdeacon's Tower. Many critics of this particular decision believed they should have made the decision to go down. Here, the MCA team was confronted with a similar choice. Should they take the time to investigate Don Sheldon's discovery of two corpses on the far side of Archdeacon's Tower, or should they have all descended the mountain when it appeared the weather was taking a turn for the worse?

"Come on, Johnny. We'll be okay. The Park is counting on us! You get Gene back down, and Daniel and I will check it out. We'll be back in no time."

Johnny begrudgingly gave in to Daniel and Henry's pleas of responsibility and following through with the Park's request.

"If we start to lose visibility, I want you two to head back toward us. Dan, you understand?"

"I understand, Johnny."

As Daniel and Henry crossed below the slanting ice crusted slopes of Archdeacon's Tower, Henry waved goodbye to his brother. Johnny and Gene began their descent down the standard ridgeline route toward Denali Pass.

---

136 Brad Washburn and David Roberts. *Mount McKinley-The Conquest of Denali*. Abradale Press, Harry N. Abrams. Inc., Publishers: New York, 1991. First Edition. 206 pp, 120 photos, 41 color, 77 duotone.

Within fifteen minutes Daniel and Henry had descended about fifty yards down a particularly steep, ice crusted slope below Archdeacon's Tower. It was slow going because Daniel had to kick steps in the hard-packed and wind chiseled surface of the snow. The slope was layered with small cracks and a few bergshrunds (larger cracks) that riddled the slanting slope, caused by the gradually shifting downward flow of the snow pack on the Harper Glacier.

As the winds picked up, the clouds scattered across the slope and the basin of Harper Glacier below. Just ahead, through the windblown mist, both men spotted what Sheldon had seen.

"There they are."

"Any chance of one of them being alive."

"Nope. It's been too long and let's face it, they're out in the open."

Soon Henry and Daniel could clearly see the two frozen men, who were still roped together and lay half-buried, encased in the seemingly cement based snow below their waists.

Heavy snowfall and thick clouds, however, had now begun to move in and around Daniel and Henry, so by the time they got to within a few yards of the first man, Daniel (like Henry) had become less enthusiastic about their venture.

"I don't know Henry. I think maybe Johnny was right. We probably should've stayed with them, and gone down the standard route."

The winds continued to pick up speed and by now, Daniel and Henry were barely able to stand up; it was a situation similar to what Browne and his two companions had faced in 1912. As they turned around and started back up the slope, the fury of the storm continued to build. Soon the two climbers could barely make out the slopes above, which led downward from Archdeacon's Tower toward the summit ridgeline and the route back down to Denali Pass.

Henry had reversed positions with Daniel as he plodded his way back up the steep slope as spindrift began to fill in their trail. Both men were beginning to think that things could not possibly get any worse, when without warning they did.

Henry suddenly vanished from sight into a crevasse, and Daniel slammed, face first into the snow.

≈

Around this time, Johnny and Gene had reached the large outcroppings of granite, adjacent to Denali Pass, the same rock formations they had been climbing toward when Vin Hoeman snapped their photo from the Air Force C-180 that was making the airdrops earlier in the day.

Once they reached the pass, Johnny poked through a few of the scattered parachute bundles, but soon decided to head down the glacier. The incessant winds at this point had become unbearable. Gene had again collapsed behind a rock, but Johnny knew it was imperative to get him up and moving.

"Come on Gene. We've got to get the hell down to our caves!"

The winds were now approaching gale force (40-50 mph) and visibility was about zero. Johnny took out his compass, and after a slow and somewhat doubtful descent, he was finally successful in locating their snow cave campsite at 17,900 feet amidst the howling wind.

"Gene. I'm going to wait outside for Daniel and Henry to show. You get down below and crank up a stove. Try and get some snow melted, if you can."

At this point, Gene was barely able to crawl into his cave. Johnny grabbed a handful of wands (the bamboo markers with red surveyors tape) and painstakingly he made his way back up into the blinding snow, to better mark the route from Denali Pass down to their snow caves. Johnny was deeply worried about the safety of his younger brother, as well as his good friend Daniel. However, at this point, there was little else he could think of to do.

As he went along, Johnny placed each wand at, more or less ten-foot intervals. Fourteen years later Joe Wilcox would entitle his 499-page account of his tragic climb with two words; he would call it *White Winds*, and that was exactly what Johnny, Daniel and Henry were confronted with at that very moment. With only three wands left in his hand, Johnny arrived at the boulders near the pass and waited impatiently, but since the winds had become so extreme, Johnny begrudgingly decided to return to camp. Like Daniel and Henry, he too was afraid he would not be able to find his way back.

As Johnny was nearly blown down the slope from Denali Pass, he saw a climber's head appearing slightly above the surface of one of the two cave entrances. It was Gene.

Like Steven Taylor ten days earlier, Gene waited alone trying to comprehend the potential severity of their situation, wondering whether or not he would ever see his teammates again as the storm continued to rage on around him. Finally, Gene's spirits were lifted as he saw Johnny arrive safely in their camp. Gene screamed above the wind.

"Any signs of Henry and Daniel?"

Johnny simply shook his head back and forth.

"Nope, nothing."

Johnny crawled down into Gene's cave entrance to get out of wind.

Before going inside the cave, Johnny turned and slowly raised his head above the surface of the ice. His face was blasted by the fury of the wind, as he lifted his snow-covered goggles to get a better view. Johnny squinted his eyes against the force of the wind, as he gazed directly into raging blizzard of whiteness.

≈

The fronds of a coconut palm blew in the wind, at the top of the tree's curved trunk, blocking the sun's glare. Several large coconuts hung beneath the spreading green fingers that swayed in the warm breeze above. A man was walking beneath the tree.

It was Yacht Captain Reggie Locke, Johnny and Henry's sea faring father. He crossed a street and approached a concrete dock at the Bahia Mar Marina[137] in Ft. Lauderdale, Florida. Reg, Sr. was a balding man of fifty-five, yet he appeared to be in good shape. He wore a tan Captain's uniform and cap. Hundreds of expensive yachts, the playtime toys of the wealthy and affluent, were seen all about as Captain Reggie passed by a series of docks.

Across from where Reg stood, a large swimming pool could be seen. Lounging around the pool were several young and beautiful women, basking in the bright sun.

The lips and nose of one middle-aged, yet attractive, bikini-clad, blond-haired beauty were coated heavily with a white colored sun cream, similar to Grace's zinc oxide. She waved to Reggie and smiled.

"Hi, Reggie. You having a good day?"

Reg waved back, in turn with a devilish look in his eye.

"Hi dee there, young ladies." Reggie spoke in jest. "Now don't any of you young ladies get yourselves all sun burnt."

Two or three of the women chimed in together. "Oh, come on Reggie. We wouldn't do that. You don't have to worry about us, Captain. Everything's all covered up."

The bikini-clad middle-aged women looked at her friend beside her and smiled. "We're also using protection. You know, Reggie, just like you do, whenever I come for a visit."

There was a burst of gleeful laughter, as the young woman continued to smile and wave in Reggie's direction.

"Take care Reggie. Be good."

"Oh, you devils, you." Captain Reggie appeared slightly embarrassed. Generally a modest man, Captain Reggie looked from side to side to see if any of his Captain buddies were in the vicinity.

Reg continued down the paved sidewalk, and then he stopped at a metal

---

137 Web link: Bahia Mar Marine. http://www.brandymarine.com/BahiaMarMarina.htm.

newspaper box at the beginning of a concrete dock. Captain Locke inserted a coin, and then he removed a copy of *The Miami Herald*.[138] As Reg continued to walk down the dock toward his boat, he gazed down at the front page of the newspaper in his hands.

A close-up of the date revealed July 31, 1967. Visibly shaken, Reg suddenly stopped; he took in several deep breaths, then he collapsed on a nearby storage box. Tears began to well up in his eyes. A poor reader, Captain Reggie slowly began to mouth the words of the news article on the front page. Another Captain friend, who was passing by noticed Reggie sitting on the box.

"Captain? Hey? Reggie? What's wrong? Reg? What's going on?" The two men gazed down at the front page of the paper. Both men noticed a close-up shot of the headline: *White-Out Cuts Off Search For 4 Mt. McKinley Climbers*. Vin Hoeman's 35mm photo of Johnny, Henry, and Gene approaching the granite rocks above Denali Pass was seen above the Headline.

⁓

Henry had fallen into a crevasse and fell about fifteen feet, landing on a small shelf, below the snow-crusted surface of the slope. Yet, Henry's fall was not without injury. He had cracked the backside of his head against the ice wall, and now he lay unconscious after landing hard upon the frozen shelf. Henry was stunned by the fall and lay motionless.

Quickly, Daniel rose to his feet once he realized he was not holding on to a tight rope. He moved cautiously toward the opening in the slope into which Henry had fallen, as all the while the wind wailed on, pounding into his face and body with increasing force. The ground surrounding the hole seemed solid so Daniel peered down into the blackness below.

"Henry. Henry? Are you all right?"

There came no reply.

Daniel pulled in the slack on his rope, and soon found that the limp body weight on the other end of the rope would not budge. Realizing that it would be impossible to pull Henry up, even with a Z-pulley set up, Daniel felt utterly helpless. At best he could rappel down into the crevasse, to at least check on his friend, but what if he couldn't get back out. Thoughts raced across his mind along with the possible consequences. Finally, he made up his mind.

"Henry! Henry!" Daniel yelled against the sound of the raging wind. "I'm going for

---

138 Website: The Miami Herald, *White-Out Cuts Off Search For 4 Mt. McKinley Climbers*.
     Published: July 31, 1967.

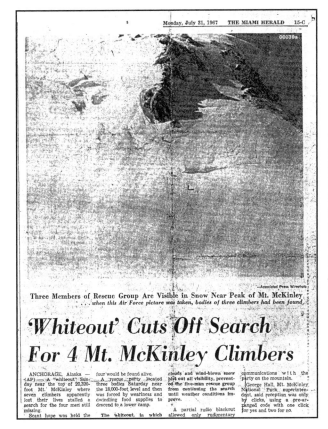

The newspaper clipping from The Miami Herald documenting the Associated Press Photograph taken from the HC-130 as it flew above Denali Pass on July 28, 1967.

Photo: Vin Hoeman, Associated Press Photo, Miami Herald, July 31, 1967.

help. I'm gonna get help. Johnny and Gene aren't that far away. A half hour, maybe, forty-five minutes top."

Like Johnny before him, Daniel was now faced with the unnerving decision of choosing what was the right thing to do.

"We'll come back for you, and we'll get you out!"

Daniel thrust his axe into the hard packed snow, untied himself from his sit harness, then he refastened the end of the rope firmly around the head of his ice axe. He then grabbed two bamboo wands from the side of his pack and marked the location of the crevasse.

"We'll be back for you Henry. Hang in there. We'll be back as soon as we can."

With a desperate look of anxiety on his face, Daniel turned into the wind, and slowly plodded across the steep snow slope below Archdeacon's Tower, hopefully traversing toward what he believed would be the ridgeline that would take him back down to their high camp and to the safety of their two snow cave shelters.

Daniel hoped that the storm would soon subside so that he and Johnny could return to discover the condition of Henry, who now remained unconscious upon the small ice shelf where he had landed.

≈

Henry's eyes slowly began to open. He still felt dizzy and the backside of his head ached, as if someone had struck him with the wooden shaft of his ice axe. Henry reached up and felt a small lump on the side of his head. He pulled off his Kelty pack and unzipped the pocket on the top left side. He placed a small headlamp[139] around his forehead, attached the battery pack to his sit harness belt, and clicked on the switch.

A broad faint light flashed across the walls of the crevasse into which Henry had fallen. The pale white light cast a ghostly aura on the eerie cave like opening in the ice. Henry stood up and looked about him as he tried to size up his present predicament.

This event did not occur during the climb of 1967. It is simulation of an actual event, which the author experienced during his Anderson Pass Expedition ten years later, when the author's team was actually caught in a terrible five-day storm while descending Denali and camping at the 17,200-foot shelf on the West Buttress side of the mountain.

Six of the author's eight-person team awoke to the blasting turmoil of Joe Wilcox's 'White Winds' when three of their team's two-person tents (Gerry Himalayan) were destroyed in the early morning 'Witching hours' during this horrific event. The author tied into a climbing rope and crawled on his hands and knees for about fifty yards in search of a small igloo that had been left at the 17,200 plateau by another three-man expedition a week or so earlier led by (the author believes) Gary Bogard of Mountain Trip expeditions. The author dragged the rope behind him, which allowed the five remaining members of his team to pull themselves safely up to the small igloo, in which two of the author's team had already chosen to sleep that night, rather than set up their own tent. The author's eight-person team, which included two women, then spent the next five days waiting out the terrific storm with little food, but thankfully enough fuel to keep its members hydrated.

The author discovered the igloo, after an agonizing search—and just when he thought he was about to experience a déjà vu demise comparable to the Wilcox tragedy of ten years past—the clouds parted and there, twenty feet from where he felt he was about to die, the author saw the igloo which allowed his team to survive. The author wanted to include this experience in *Should I Not Return* as the climatic scene of his novel, and so chose to depict this experience in the scene as told in the context of his story.

---

139 REI Website: *headlamps*. Author's Note: Headlamps have changed considerably since 1967. http://www.rei.com/gear/feature/search/MSN/headlamps?&cm_mmc=ps_msn_CH-_-Category%20-%20Camp_Gear-_-Camp_Gear_Headlamps_General-_-headlamps&s_kwcid=TC-13018-5056090481-p-711656063.

Turning to his left he saw, at the far end of the crevasse, something that froze him to the core. He was not alone. Henry stood there and gazed upon a grizzly sight no more than ten feet from where he stood.

Three more frozen corpses, the remaining members of the missing Wilcox men lay sprawled upon their backs, partially buried in the snow and spin-drift that had blown down into this small opening beneath the ice-crusted slopes of Archdeacon's Tower. Was it by accident that Henry had fallen into the final resting place of these men, thereby resolving the sad story of his team's rescue attempt?

No one would ever know, but deep down inside Henry felt that this was no mistake. As the wind continued to rage overhead, Henry could think of nothing else but to get out of this god forsken place as quickly as he could. Henry looked up and saw the rope leading to the surface above, which Daniel had secured to his ice axe. Henry could think of only one thing to do.

"I've got to get out of here. If I stay here, I'll go crazy."

Henry had made up his mind. His only choice was to get out of this deathlike tomb, and somehow find his way back down to camp. Henry was struck with the absolute terror of the situation. He threw on his pack and started to pull himself up the icy walls of the crevasse, kicking the sharp points of his crampons into the icy wall with each foot as he pulled himself up to the top. Adrenalin raced throughout his worn and exhausted body, but there was no turning back now. Thoughts raced cross his mind.

"Go for it! You can do it. Get the hell out of this grave, and find your way back down to camp!"

As he reached the surface above, the sheer turmoil of the winds blasted into his face. Carefully Henry inched his way upward and back onto the slope above. Part of him somehow hoped that Daniel would still be at the other end of the rope, but when he saw his ice ax thrust into the snow, Henry knew he was alone.

Yes, Henry was alone now, and it would be up to him to find his was back across the slope toward the ridgeline below Archdeacon's Tower. The wind was unmerciful and now made it impossible for Henry to stand.

Henry unfastened the rope from the head of Daniel's axe, then repositioned his snow goggles over his eyes to protect them from the blistering sting of the fierce winds. Slowly, Henry began to snake his way across the slope heading in the direction of what he hoped was Johnny and Gene's route, and more recently Daniel's trail down to Denali Pass. By now, however, any signs of Daniel's footsteps had been covered with spindrift. Meanwhile, the deafening roar of the storm had increased twofold and Henry's journey to safety was quickly becoming overwhelming.

Behind Henry, a whiteness of snow and ice crystals disappeared into the blasting fury of the unceasing winds. The rope behind him flailed aimlessly into a frigid and harsh whiteness; Joe Wilcox's White Winds.

A distinct feeling of panic slowly crept into Henry's frozen flesh, as he crawled blindly along into the raging blizzard; it was the same feeling he had felt the night he sat on the couch in his mother's apartment staring at Captain Kirk on Katherine's old black and white television set.

"What if I can't find the way back down?" Henry thought to himself.

The arctic winds slammed into Henry's hooded face, protected now only by his ski goggles and ice encrusted balaclava. The surging and pulsating blasts funneled over his body. Henry's Kelty pack frame and bag flailed wildly over his head, pulling Henry's body in the opposite direction, almost raising him off the ground like a small parachute. Henry scanned the slope below, searching in vain for the trail leading down to the pass. There seemed to be no hope as the light on his headlamp began to fade. Henry tore off the headlamp and tossed it aimlessly into the storm.

"This is it Locke."

Desperate thoughts began to race across Henry's mind.

"You've finally done it this time. There's no way you're getting out of this one. It looks as though mom's premonition is going to come true."

Then, as Henry's movements slowed to a gradual halt, largely due to the severe cold and the progressive onset of hypothermia, Henry peered off into the frigid inferno of blasting snow and ice. By now Henry had unwittingly found the ridgeline leading to Denali Pass and he was crawling down the slope, when below him a bizarre sight began to unfold.

As with his nightmare below Browne Tower, it seemed to Henry as if he was again entering into another dreamlike state. In the middle of this horrendous storm, this living nightmare, Henry saw below what he thought was the form of a man, what he believed to be another climber.

Henry was overjoyed at first as he screamed into the howling winds.

"Johnny! Johnny! Is that you?"

Henry believed it was his older brother, who had once again arrived just in the nick of time, as he had done on other occasions in their childhood to show him the way out of a spooky cave in the woods of Killiams Point, or the way back to their Brocketts Point home after trick or treating on many a dark Halloween night.

Johnny had obviously braved the storm, had come back up with Daniel to get him out of the crevasse, and safely back down to camp. Yet, to Henry's surprise, Johnny did not seem to be getting any closer. In fact, he seemed to be walking away from Henry.

"Johnny wait! Johnny it's me! Don't leave me here. Wait! Please wait for me. I'm right here!"

In his befuddled state of mind, Henry followed this distant shadow. Yet there was something particularly odd about this climber beyond. Was the high altitude and extreme fatigue playing tricks with his mind? This climber ahead of him was actually 'standing up' in these jet stream winds, surely an impossible feat under these intolerable conditions?

Never the less, Henry decided to follow this mysterious form; he could see no other choice, and continued to literally pull himself down the frozen slope, thrusting the pick of his ice axe into the ice, as he dragged his body downward toward what he hoped to be the direction of Denali Pass.

Then Henry noticed the climber below had stopped, almost as if he was waiting for Henry to catch up. Finally, Henry was but a few feet from what he believed and hoped could only be his brother Johnny. Yet Henry was in for a startling surprise.

There before him stood another climber, with an ice axe that appeared much longer

Belmore Browne stands upon the NE Ridge of Mount McKinley in 1912. The handwritten caption by the photographer is on the back of the photo.

Photo taken by Merle LaVoy. (Courtesy of Isabel Driscoll and her brother Belmore H. Browne, grandchildren of Belmore Browne)

than his own; the man stood there holding his axe in his right gloved hand, the point of which touched the icy ground at his feet, while the head of the axe rose to slightly above his waist. A coil of hemp rope dangled over his left shoulder and crossed down his chest; as one loop of the rope fell loose below his waist. This 'old school climber' wore wool knickers, and a belt was wrapped tightly around his waist from which Henry spotted what appeared to be some kind of a flask attached on the man's left side. A parka hood was drawn over the man's head, and above the his brow Henry noticed a old pair of dark snow goggles. Henry had remembered seeing this image before in a book he had checked out from his college library back east, but he couldn't remember the man's name?

Gazing ahead into the wind blown snow, ice, and mysterious fog, Henry had come upon yet another ghostly image; it was not his brother who had come to rescue him—it was the spirit of some other pioneer from Denali's past.

When he got closer, Henry could clearly see that it was not a person at all, but the transparent apparition of a man standing about six inches above the frozen ground; Henry stared in utter disbelief!

Then the apparition removed the glove from his left hand and Henry saw him point a bony forefinger downward toward the storm blasted slopes below. Henry gasped in horror and looked off into the direction where the man pointed. After wiping a thin layer of snow from his own snow goggles to get a better look, Henry turned back toward the climber, but the haunting and mysterious spirit was gone.

Henry felt he had finally snapped and he was clearly headed for that great castle in the clouds, to join the other pioneer spirits, who had been assisting him and the other members of his team during this perilous journey up this great mountain of his fears.

Yet, Henry was wrong. Just when he thought all hope was lost, a small section of clouds parted in the sky overhead. Then, like a miracle from above, Henry saw below him, for a brief few seconds, a bright shaft of light, which shone down upon Denali Pass.

A small open area was suddenly revealed, scattered with several colorful parachutes being blasted back and forth by the howling winds. Henry could also see the beginning row of the closely placed wands that Johnny had earlier set in place, to better mark the route back down to their snow cave camp at the 17,900 feet.

Henry thrust the pick of his axe into the frozen slope, and dragged himself to the nearby boulders, which marked the beginning of Johnny's route down the glacier, the very same place where Gene had collapsed but an hour or so earlier. As the winds poured over Henry's frozen flesh, he pulled in the rope from behind.

Henry turned his face into the jet stream winds, which were now funneling their way through Denali Pass. Joe Wilcox described this narrowing increase in the wind's velocity in his book, as the venturi effect—the primary reason behind many of the fierce winds experienced by climbers on high altitude mountains with more than one peak.[140] The jet stream air-flow above the mountain is forced to travel through a smaller constricted area, and in so doing the actual speed of the wind flow increases dramatically.

Henry thrust the shaft of his axe into the snow, looped the rope around the axe's head, and began to lower himself down the Harper, in an attempt to keep from being blown away.

Henry slowly released the full 150-foot length of the rope, which wound its way around the head of his axe. Carefully Henry followed Johnny's trail of wands, which led the way down to their camp.

Johnny scanned the upper wind blasted slopes above their snow cave camp. Nearly two hours had passed now since he had last seen his younger brother's face. His anxiety over having let Henry and Daniel talk him into descending the slopes below Archdeacon's to look for the corpses Sheldon had spotted below, was eating away at the core of his being. What if Henry was hurt, or worse yet—freezing to death jammed tightly between the icy walls of the crevasse he had fallen into?

Then Johnny could hardly believe his eyes. He saw something slowly emerge through the white turmoil of the storm above their camp. About twenty feet in front of him, Johnny saw the shadowy figure of a man crawling over the ice, headed in the direction of their snow cave shelters. It was Henry!

Johnny jumped up from his protective barrier, bracing himself against the sheer force of the winds. "Henry! Henry? Is that you?

When Henry arrived at camp, he saw Johnny's head raised just above their snow cave entrance, peering up the glacier into the jet stream winds, scanning the ice for any signs of his little brother's escape from the jaws of death. Then Daniel's head appeared from beneath the entrance to his and Gene's cave.

The noise of the wind was so overwhelming that their screams of joy were barely heard.

"Thank God, you're back." Johnny was ecstatic, as he sprung to his feet and somehow, it seemed to Henry, raced across the ice to greet him. Johnny grabbed hold of Henry, as did Daniel shortly thereafter, and the three men stumbled from side to side in the strong winds.

"Good thing you put in those wands, or I'd never have found camp." Even Daniel's normal reticence had disappeared in the sheer joy of their reunion with Henry.

---

140 Joe Wilcox, *White Winds*, Los Alamitos, California: Hwong Publishing Company ... 1981.

"Holy smokes, Johnny! When I came to after falling into that crevasse, I thought it was all over." Henry paused for a few seconds.

"You're not going to believe me, but those other guys were down there with me. Of course, they were gone too, just like the other two Daniel and I found."

Henry paused for a second, and took in a deep breath, slightly embarrassed by what he had just so nonchalantly expressed.

"Well, when Daniel showed up and told me what happened, we packed up and tried our best to get back up to you. But we had to bag it up at the pass, the winds were just too strong."

The wind continued to howl as Johnny tried to make sense of the excitement and scattered ramblings of Henry's bleak adventure.

Daniel put his hand on Henry's shoulder. "So you hit a solid shelf and were able to climb back out using the rope I left."

Daniel too caught himself, and then slowly released a deep sigh of relief.

"That's what happened. I'm so glad I'm back here now."

By now, even Gene had popped his head up above the ice into the turmoil of the storm and the joy of their reunion with Henry.

"Well lookey, lookey." Gene yelled up to Johnny and Daniel with a big smile on his face. "I guess we've got more company! Welcome back ole Henny Penny. It's good to see your smiling face again."

Soon the three men had crawled back down into their tomb-like holes on the frozen surface of the ice.

CHAPTER 27

The American Dream

O nce they were down inside their snow cave, Johnny moved a large snow block back in front of the cave entrance. An occasional burst of spindrift managed to push in and around the sealed entrance, but soon the wind itself had filled in the cracks.

Afterward, Johnny positioned their two Kelty pack frames against the snow block. The raging storm outside had been silenced for the time being. Johnny then re-poked a tubular tent center pole through the roof of their cave for ventilation. For the most part their refuge below ground appeared not only safe, but also secure. Henry lit a small candle and instantly the rounded white walls of the snow cave magnified the light like a frozen mirror. Henry remembered his mother telling him how the doctors had used a similar method when they had operated on President McKinley.

Henry watched Johnny pump the shiny gold metal stopper on their stove's tank to build up pressure, and then he dampened the stove's overlapping burners with white gas from a small plastic bottle. Finally he struck a dry wooden match on the corrugated metal cap of the stove's tank, and the burners on the stove burst into a roaring blue flame.

Johnny dumped a few cups of snow into the pot and prepared to simmer the McKinley stew leftovers he had made earlier while waiting for his brother's return. After awhile, Johnny lowered the stove to a simmer and their cozy shelter once again became reasonably quiet, as the storm over their heads raged on in silent tyranny.

"Well, you got back here just in the nick of time. If things had gotten much worse?" Johnny frowned, shook his head, but said nothing.

"Yeah. When I stepped out of the clouds and spindrift, it must have seemed as though I had been beamed down from Archdeacon's to the *Starship Enterprise*?'

Johnny smiled. "Yeah, right. You and Captain Kirk."

"I've never been in winds like that before, Johnny. I could hardly breathe, let alone stand up. It was terrifying. I thought I was going to die."

"Yeah. It's really bad out there. Probably pretty close to what those guys got ten days ago." Johnny scooped up another cup of snow and plopped it into the pot. "So, you think you found the other four guys? I did hear you say that, didn't I, when we were outside?"

"Yeah, I did. It seemed liked there were only three, though. Maybe I didn't see the fourth? They probably rappelled down into that crevasse, to get out of the storm. Hard to believe it would turn out to be the same one that I would fall into? What are the odds of that happening?"

Johnny shrugged his shoulders and once again shook his head.

Henry was still having a hard time comprehending everything that he had just been through. "They were gone, though, frozen stiff, like the other two we found out in the open. They must have run out of fuel. Maybe that's what those guys below Archdeacon's were trying to do, you know, get back down to camp for more fuel."

"Who knows? It was a hell of a storm! That's for sure. No one could have lasted more than a few days up here, without food and fuel. That's a fact."

Henry was hesitant, but he had to tell Johnny about what he thought he had seen on his way down from Archdeacon's Tower. Henry just hoped his brother wouldn't think he'd gone off the deep end, as their Aunts Sophie and Hazel had done.

"You're not gonna believe this Johnny, but I thought I saw you out there, when I was headed back down from Archdeacon's. Did you come looking for me up there?"

"Well yeah, but Daniel and I only made it up to the pass. The winds kept us from going on. We also ran out of wands. So I just prayed to God you would make it down to the pass, on your own, or at least maybe stay put until we could get back up to you."

Johnny plopped another cup of snow into the pot, then he too spoke with some hesitation. "Why? Did you see somebody else up there?"

"I don't know Johnny. You're not gonna believe me, but I thought I saw another ghost."

Henry looked into his brother's eyes, which showed signs of doubt.

"Remember that crazy nightmare I had when we were bivouacked down below Browne Tower?"

Johnny nodded his head. "Yeah, you were pretty shaken up."

"Well if I was shaken up then, I went completely over the edge this time. I mean it was so bizarre. It seemed as though I was actually following someone, or some thing most of the way down from Archdeacon's." Henry paused for a few seconds. "My mind must have been playing tricks on me; it gives me the creeps."

By now, their reheated stew was ready to eat. Johnny passed Henry a cup.

"Here, get some food in your stomach. You'll feel better."

Johnny filled his own cup with broth, having eaten his share of stew earlier; then he gave the rest to Henry. Afterward, Johnny laid back on his sleeping bag.

"The snow and the wind can play tricks on you, sometimes, especially when it's as bad as it is out there now. Stuff like that happened to me a few times, down in South America. Though I can't say I've ever run across any ghosts. I did see a couple of frozen corpses, though once, when I was climbing Chimboraza in Ecuador." Johnny breathed a sigh of relief. "Anyway, at least you guys found your way back down to camp."

"Yeah, thank God we did."

There was a long pause before either Johnny or Henry said anything; they simply sat there in silence, Henry chomping down on his dinner meal, while Johnny sipped his hot broth.

Finally Henry decided to broach another topic that had been weighing heavily upon his mind, ever since Johnny's angry confrontation from the previous day. In fact, this particular dilemma had been slowly eating away at him from the day Katherine had become so adamant about him not coming up to Alaska. After all, she was the one who had first planted the seed in his mind that things don't always appear as they seem.

Henry didn't really know how to explain it to his brother, but somehow it seemed to him that he was on the verge of a break-through, one of those mystical revelations, which were so popular back in the sixties. Like in one they sang about in the Broadway musical *Hair*.

Henry's trip to Alaska, and his climb up Denali had somehow triggered something inside him, which Henry felt was going to be a key to his future peace of mind. Yet he couldn't quite put his finger on it, at least not yet.

Henry didn't know why he felt this way, he only knew that there was something brewing deep down inside and it all had to do with Bonnie and Johnny, as well as his mother and father; and even his crazy aunts, Hazel and Sophie.

"Yah know, Johnny, I've been thinking about what you asked me yesterday, about Bonnie. You know, when we were digging out our snow cave?"

A stern look came into his brother's eyes. "Yeah? What about it?"

"You know, it's weird. I mean it's kind of crazy."

Johnny's facial expression went dark. "What? What's crazy? Or maybe I should say who?"

Henry spoke quickly, trying to explain himself more clearly, even though he didn't have the slightest idea where this discussion was going to end.

"Well, you know. What I'm trying to say is—all this time, I've always felt like you and Bonnie had the perfect life. You know, four beautiful children," Henry smiled. "A fancy log cabin home in Alaska."

Henry's heart began to beat faster; he sat up cross-legged on his sleeping bag. He even felt the urge to take a pee, but he chose to hold it in.

"I really thought you and Bonnie had it made, you know, somehow I figured you had escaped our…? Our what? Our own little brand of, what would you call it? Our own little brand of family insanity, you know, back east? Mom and Poppa, Aunt Hazel and Sophie, and, of course, Pop Spaulding; that whole sad scary story. You know what I mean?"

Johnny's frown turned into a sardonic smile, a sign, Henry felt that perhaps Johnny was beginning to understand what had been ticking away inside Henry's brain, not only with Bonnie, but more importantly with Henry's newly perceived Ah-Hah revelation surrounding their family's complicated, yet common dysfunctional nature.

"I mean I actually thought someone in our family had finally figured it out. You know? How to be happy?"

"Yeah, right? You mean the good old American dream. Right?"

"Well yeah, something like that. You know, I read a play last year in college, by Edward Albee, but I really didn't understand what it was all about. Something about some grandmother, and some son that had been killed, and then all of a sudden, his twin shows up? It was all too abstract for me? I even got to play a part in his other play, that one called *The Zoo Story*. Did you ever read that?" Henry's mind was buzzing.

Johnny looked at Henry with a puzzled expression. "No, can't say I have?"

"Well, anyway. Being up here with you and Bonnie, this summer has really gotten me thinking. When you come right down to it, it's all a big lie, isn't it?

"What do you mean? Slow down will you. You're giving me a head-ache."

"I mean life, or what we all hope to get out of it."

Johnny again looked at Henry with a puzzled expression. Johnny was clearly exhausted, and the last thing he wanted to do was to get into one of his little brother's philosophical bull sessions.

"Well, for one thing. Bonnie told me I needed to take off my rose-colored glasses. Since I've been here in Alaska, with you guys, those glasses have been totally shattered; and, well, its sort of funny. Believe it or not, things are starting to seem a lot clearer to me, now."

Henry finally paused and took in several deep breaths.

"Nobody's got a perfect life, do they?" Henry looked at his older brother and smiled. "Not even you."

"So. You mean to tell me you haven't figured that out yet?" Again, Johnny appeared confused, but he waited to hear Henry out.

"You two aren't all that different from mom and dad? Are you? You and Bonnie, I mean?

Johnny took another sip of hot broth. "Nope, we're not."

Johnny reached down and turned off the stove. The cave grew silent. "What'd you expect?"

"I don't know? I think I'm still hung up on happy endings." Henry smiled. "Too many Walt Disney movies, I guess."

Johnny looked at Henry, and he too smiled. Henry laid back on his sleeping bag and looked up at the icy ceiling of their snow cave. Then he turned and looked back at Johnny.

"Does anyone ever get to live a happy life?"

"I kind of thought climbing up here was part of the answer?"

"Yeah, I guess so."

"Well, that's how I see it. Being up here makes me feel alive. Back in Anchorage, it sometimes feels like, like I'm dying a slow death. I certainly felt that way back on the east coast."

"Yeah. I feel that way back east, too."

"Join the club, little Henry."

Johnny reflected on the popular Beatle's song. "You know, *Sgt. Pepper's Lonely Heart's Club Band*.'

Henry smiled, and then he slid gratefully into the warmth of his Auckland New Zealand down sleeping bag. Johnny was right. There were no quick fixes. Henry thought about the *The Velveteen Rabbit*.

"You become. It takes a long time. That's why it doesn't happen often to people who break easily, or have sharp edges, or who have to be carefully kept."

Henry also reflected upon what a professor had once told his Philosophy class back at New England College.

"You know children, there are no quick trips to Nirvana. If someone told you that is the case, then you are being deceived."

"Well, I don't know about you big brother, but I think I'm going to crash. Right now, I'm pretty much dead to the world, myself."

Johnny rolled on his side and looked at Henry and smiled.

"No, little brother. You're not dead. You're alive. If you had given up, you'd be dead. Instead, you hung in there and lucked out. Ghost, or no ghost, you came back down alive."

"Yeah, we're alive, aren't we? We're all still alive. I guess that's what it's all about, huh? Just staying alive."

Henry tightened the drawstring around his head and rolled over on his side and faced Johnny. The silence in their cave was interrupted only by the sounds of their breathing, as it echoed quietly against walls of ice. The candle Henry had lit earlier began to flicker. Henry rolled over again onto his back and looked up at the icy ceiling of the snow cave.

"I love you, Johnny."

"Get some sleep, Henry. It's a tough world out there. It's time you figured that out. By the way, I love you, too."

Children begin by loving their parents;

After a time they judge them;

Rarely, if ever, do they forgive them.

Oscar Wilde, 1854-1900

CHAPTER 28

What Is Real?

Gliding gently down through the clouds, the sky opened to the small Alaska town of Wasilla, Alaska, twenty years later. It was nighttime and the city lights below were reminiscent of Henry's hometown of Branford, Connecticut. The main street of Wasilla was adorned with Christmas lights, as were the streets of Henry's teenage hometown in December of 1967, during the festive holiday season he shared with his mother Katherine, and his father Captain Reggie, who always got a week off for vacation from the *Franny B* over Christmas. Reggie Jr. was there, too, but within a year he would marry and start a family of his own. It was three months later, after that Christmas when Henry would fly to Alaska to climb Mt. McKinley with his older brother Johnny.

Now, twenty years after their fateful climb up Denali, the main street of Wasilla looked similar, but Teeland's Country store and the Wasilla train depot suggested a locale far more Alaskan, than New England in nature, as did the distant snow covered mountain peaks of the beautiful Matanuska Valley.

By now, Johnny and Bonnie had divorced, yet they had remained friends, as their children had grown into adulthood. In fact, two of their children now had families of their own. Henry too had married, and divorced, and now he lived with his newly blended family on Firth, not First Drive, on the outskirts of this small Alaska town. Both Claire and he had been together now for two years.

It was nighttime and the lights from the homes in the nearby Scottwood subdivision on the outskirts of town flickered in the cold darkness like the stars overhead in the sky, where Claire and Henry lived with their family of four children. The bright stars overhead were accentuated even more so by a dazzling display of the Northern Lights, which danced across the arctic night.

A Ford pick-up truck came into view with a small camper on back. The rugged Alaska vehicle was traveling through Henry and Claire's Scottwood

The author's home on Firth Drive in Wasilla, Alaska.

Photo: Jeff Babcock, taken in the early spring of 2011.

neighborhood. The truck slowed down at the corner of their street, where a green *Firth Road* metal sign sat atop a single metal pole. The camper truck veered down Firth, which ended in a cul-de-sac a short distance ahead.

A light snow was gently falling from the cold clear Alaska sky and settled in the backyard of one of Firth Road's fancier wilderness homes, a two story high cedar-sided house with a red metal roof. It wasn't a log cabin, but this was the home of Claire and Henry Locke's blended family, now going on three years of renewed family togetherness.

Through the back porch window and glass door, a middle-aged man was seen seated in a large cushiony chair, with four small children surrounding him. Henry, an older looking and now possibly wiser man, was reading a familiar story to his children. A gaily decorated and very tall Christmas tree reached to the top of the stairs in their high, vaulted-ceiling living room. Claire sat on a nearby sofa and listened to Henry, as he read from yes, Margery William's Christmas/Easter classic, *The Velveteen Rabbit*.[141]

"Autumn passed and Winter, and in the Spring, when the days grew warm and sunny, the Boy went out to play in the wood behind the house. And while he was playing, two rabbits crept out from the bracken and peeped at him. One of them was brown all over, but the other had strange markings under his fur, as though long ago he had been spotted, and the spots still showed through. And about his little soft nose and his round black eyes there was something familiar, so that

---

141 Margery Williams, *The Velveteen Rabbit*. Finely bound by The Chelsea Bindery, New York: George H. Doran Company, 1922.

the Boy thought to himself: "Why, he looks just like my old Bunny that was lost when I had scarlet fever!"

Henry's voice suddenly cracked, as tears began to well up in his eyes.

"But he never knew that it really was his own Bunny, come back to look at the child who had first helped him to be Real."

Laura, Henry and Claire's youngest three-year old daughter was snuggled close to her very own Velveteen Rabbit, which she held in her arms. Laura looked up at Henry.

"Daddy, you're crying. You've got a tee ah in your eye."

"I know Sweetie, I know."

Whenever Henry read this story, even as he would do for Laura's own daughter Alexia, many years in the future, Henry would always get choked up at the end.

Henry could still remember when his own mother Katherine had read him the story when they were all kids in Brockett's Point, and Henry even remembered when he read the poignant tale to Johnny and Bonnie's children in the summer of 1967.

Laura looked up at her father with concern.

"Are you okay, daddy?"

Henry smiled at Claire, who gazed back at him with a glint of love and admiration in her eyes. Henry looked down at his youngest daughter.

"I'm fine, Sweetie. I'm fine. I'm just—happy. That's all, I'm just happy."

The front doorbell rang and the children jumped with glee, knowing full well who was coming for a visit. Claire got up, and then she went to the front door and opened it.

A cool breeze blew fresh snowflakes inside onto the hardwood floor from the darkness outside. Standing at the entrance to Henry and Claire's home was his older brother Johnny and his new wife, June. The children sprang from their chair and ran to greet their Uncle Johnny Bird.

"Uncle Johnny Bird! Yea! It's Uncle Johnny Bird! And Auntie June!"

Gunnar, Brooke, Laura and Leif raced across the room toward the front door. It was a truly joyous moment.

From the front yard, Johnny and June were seen silhouetted in the doorway to Henry and Claire's Alaska home, with their Christmas tree lights flickering in the large paned window at the left. Their children were laughing and jumping up and down, as Johnny gathered Laura and Brooke up into his arms. Leif and Gunnar bounced with enthusiasm alongside the four adults.

As the front door closed, the stars overhead filled the sky, and the majestic Northern Lights became crystal clear high above a misty circling mass of snow and clouds.

For Connie. (Katherine)

Sleep sleep happy child,

All creation slept and smil'd!

Sleep sleep, happy sleep.

While o'er thee thy mother weep.

By William Blake, from Cradle Song 1789

Epilogue

As I sit here at my desk on the morning of October 10th, 2011, the clock on the wall next to Belmore Browne's painting reads 4:15. Frances Chamberlin Carter, I believe is still alive at this sad time, my very own witching hour.

Freddie is in the intensive care unit of the Kino Branch of the University of Arizona Hospital on East Ayo Avenue in Tucson. She was admitted there two days ago after having suffered a major heart attack, brought on by what appeared to be some form of blood poisoning along with a severe case of dehydration. I received the phone call Sunday afternoon on October 9, 2011 from one of her close friends (actually two sisters who now live together), companions with whom Freddie often hiked on the nearby trails of Madera Canyon over the past several years.

Freddie confessed to me however, that of late she would generally sit on a park bench near the road's end, where the trails leading to the summit of Old Baldy would begin, and she would be quite satisfied just sitting there in the beautiful park watching the birds and breathing in the fresh mountain air. Sally and Kayri, women several years her junior, would take Raggs along with them on their short jaunts over the lower trails of Madera, while Frances would either wait for their return, or sometimes hop back in her car and meet them at a lower parking lot while Raggs and her friends hiked down to the entrance of the canyon.

Over the past few years, Freddie had pretty much given up hiking since both of her legs bothered her greatly, and since her breathing had become too hampered to continue a regimen of even casual hikes. Madera Canyon, which is one of Arizona's most popular southern wilderness parks, is a twenty-minute drive from Green Valley where Freddie had chosen to spend the latter part of her life.

My wife and I were watching our ten-month-old granddaughter Alexia at our home in Green Valley, when I received the phone call from Sally and Kayri.

Alexia had spent the night with us, since her parents and our daughter Brooke, who was presently visiting us from North Carolina, had chosen to take in the Halloween extravaganza called *Night Fall* at the nearby Old Tucson wild west Amusement Park. Old Tucson is also located on Ayo Avenue, only west of Highway I-10, which is in the opposite direction from where Freddie now rested in the ICU.

Our children had spent the better part of Sunday sleeping in, since they hadn't returned from their haunting adventure until the wee hours of dawn, having partied further with friends in Tucson.

Nevertheless, I gave them a call and we rendezvoused with baby Alexia at the hospital on East Ayo. We took turns in pairs, on Freddie's behalf, visiting her in the ICU, while she lay there hooked up to the usual paraphernalia associated with dire situations such as the one Freddie now found herself in. Upon departing, I bid Freddie farewell.

"Look Freddie, I will be seeing you sometime tomorrow morning, after I finish up my physical therapy. Just remember, you and I will be taking a drive up to Madera Canyon, as soon as you get out of here and back up on your feet."

"Well, that sounds like a good plan, Jeff. Seeing you and everybody else here tonight makes me want to keep on going. So I'll plan on it."

"I've also got a copy of that Walt Disney movie, *Third Man on the Mountain*, the one I told you I had requested from Netflix. Well let's plan on getting together and watching it maybe next week. It has all those peaks in it that you climbed, along with the Matterhorn, of course. So that's one more thing you can look forward to."

"Well that sounds wonderful, Jeff. You bet, we'll do that together, too … ole Jeff. Oh, it's so good to see you here. I'll look forward to seeing you tomorrow."

≈

I looked at the picture above my desk in what used to be my father-in-law's study. In Belmore Browne's painting, a man on horseback is crossing a riverbed not unlike that of the West Fork of the Chulitna. Behind him the snow covered peaks of some majestic mountain range, comparable to Mt. Tatum, Mt. Carpe, and Mt. Koven, seem to be beckoning him onward to still loftier heights, like those of the upper slopes of Denali. Browne's painting reminds me of those youthful days when I, like Freddie was more able, more physically fit, and a tad more fool hearty than either of us are today, the necessary prerequisites required by anyone seeking to be lured into climbing to such heights.

Two months have gone by since my knee surgery on August 8, 2011. It is still very difficult for me to get a full night's sleep. The toothache in my right knee wakes me up routinely after four or five hours. Ice packs placed above and below the knee joint sometimes allow me another hour's worth of sleep, depending upon the level of activity pulsating through my brain, which sometimes decides it is time for me to wake up. Such is the case this morning.

I have finally weaned myself off of the Vicodine 5/500 pain tablets, to which I had nearly become addicted, ever since the distal end of my femur and the proximal end of my tibia were sawed off and replaced, along with the articular surface of my patella, with the metal and plastic components of my new knee. My orthopedic surgeon, Dr. Felix Jabczenski, Jr., performed the task admirably with all the skill and dexterity of an accomplished furniture maker. Nevertheless, recovery from my knee surgery has been a slow process.

In any event I have completed my novel, as I said I would do. An email copy in Microsoft Word has been sent off accordingly to my publisher in Anchorage, Alaska. Now, it is my hope that it will be simply a matter of time, along with the necessary assistance from a good editor, before *Should I Not Return* will at last be published. As commentary radio journalist Paul Harvey[142] would recite in the middle of each of his broadcasts, "And now, for the rest of the story."

Three days went by before our team descended from the storm blasted upper slopes of Denali. When we reached the 12,100-foot shelf, the oxygen-starved air had become replenished with the elixir of life, and with each downward step it seemed as though a new lease on life had been granted each of us for what we had somehow survived.

Passage through the Wall Street glacier went quickly, yet when we reached the lower end of the Muldrow it was overcast in a sea of fog. Thankfully my brother brought us safely into port at the shores of McGonagall Pass, the gateway that would take us back into the lush tundra, with its pesky hoards of mosquitoes, its glacial stream river crossings, and finally the now fairly well-populated campground at Wonder Lake. Somehow, with or without the assistance of phantom spirits from the past, each of us had survived the nightmare of our lives.

Wayne Merry and his wife arrived at the trail head in one of the Park's Ford pick-up Ranger trucks, and we were whisked away from a hoard of questioning campers to a supply shed beside Wayne's Ranger Station cabin. Once there we were afforded the luxury of hot outdoor showers, and a surprise lunch of cold meat and cheese sandwiches with fresh lettuce and tomatoes, potato salad, and all the lemonade we could drink.

The following day we were transported back to Park Headquarters eighty miles to the northeastern end of Mt. McKinley National Park, and there we had

---

142 Wikipedia link: *Paul Harvey*, http://en.wikipedia.org/wiki/Paul_Harvey.

Dennis Luchterhand's sister, Pete Sanchez, Judy (Steve Taylor's sister), Mr. & Mrs. Luchterhand, George Perkins, Perry & Beth Taylor (Steve's parents), Joe Wilcox, Park Superintendent George Hall, Jim Goodfellow.

Photo: Unknown, Courtesy of Joe Wilcox, author of White Winds. Publisher: Hwong Publishing Co ... 1981.

the sad yet poignant experience of meeting and visiting with some of the family members who had flown up to Alaska with the hopes of seeing their loved ones rescued from the terrible disaster of which they had become part.

It was my final confrontation with death on Denali. I remember how the teen-aged sister of Dennis Luchterhand sat with me outside on Park Superintendent George Hall's rustic looking front porch.

I remember to this day how she looked at me with those sad eyes, which I had become accustomed to seeing that summer with Bonnie, little Portia, and back east with my own mother and her younger sisters. Her parting words struck a chord with me which is as heartfelt for me today as it was then, and I will never forget what she said.

"You know. I really think that Dennis would have preferred it this way, I mean being left up there on the mountain, instead of having his body brought back down here."

Her eyes moistened, as did mine. I felt a lump forming in my throat as she continued to tell me about her older brother.

"He once said to me jokingly, '*Should I not return*, what better place could there